Journalism in a Small Place

Latin American and Caribbean Series
Hendrik Kraay, General Editor
ISSN 1498-2366 (PRINT), ISSN 1925-9638 (ONLINE)

This series sheds light on historical and cultural topics in Latin America and the Caribbean by publishing works that challenge the canon in history, literature, and postcolonial studies. It seeks to print cutting-edge studies and research that redefine our understanding of historical and current issues in Latin America and the Caribbean.

No. 1 · **Waking the Dictator: Veracruz, the Struggle for Federalism and the Mexican Revolution** Karl B. Koth

No. 2 · **The Spirit of Hidalgo: The Mexican Revolution in Coahuila** Suzanne B. Pasztor · Copublished with Michigan State University Press

No. 3 · **Clerical Ideology in a Revolutionary Age: The Guadalajara Church and the Idea of the Mexican Nation, 1788–1853** Brian F. Connaughton, translated by Mark Allan Healey · Copublished with University Press of Colorado

No. 4 · **Monuments of Progress: Modernization and Public Health in Mexico City, 1876–1910** Claudia Agostoni · Copublished with University Press of Colorado

No. 5 · **Madness in Buenos Aires: Patients, Psychiatrists and the Argentine State, 1880–1983** Jonathan Ablard · Copublished with Ohio University Press

No. 6 · **Patrons, Partisans, and Palace Intrigues: The Court Society of Colonial Mexico, 1702–1710** Christoph Rosenmüller

No. 7 · **From Many, One: Indians, Peasants, Borders, and Education in Callista Mexico, 1924–1935** Andrae Marak

No. 8 · **Violence in Argentine Literature and Film (1989–2005)** Edited by Carolina Rocha and Elizabeth Montes Garcés

No. 9 · **Latin American Cinemas: Local Views and Transnational Connections** Edited by Nayibe Bermúdez Barrios

No. 10 · **Creativity and Science in Contemporary Argentine Literature: Between Romanticism and Formalism** Joanna Page

No. 11 · **Textual Exposures: Photography in Twentieth Century Spanish American Narrative Fiction** Dan Russek

No. 12 · **Whose Man in Havana? Adventures from the Far Side of Diplomacy** John W. Graham

No. 13 · **Journalism in a Small Place: Making Caribbean News Relevant, Comprehensive, and Independent** Juliette Storr

Latin American and
Caribbean Series
ISSN 1498-2366 (Print)
ISSN 1925-9638 (Online)

UNIVERSITY OF CALGARY
FACULTY OF ARTS
Latin American Research Centre

© 2016 Juliette Storr

University of Calgary Press
2500 University Drive NW
Calgary, Alberta
Canada T2N 1N4
press.ucalgary.ca

This book is available as an ebook which is licensed under a Creative Commons license. The publisher should be contacted for any commercial use which falls outside the terms of that license.

LIBRARY AND ARCHIVES CANADA CATALOGUING IN PUBLICATION

Storr, Juliette, author
    Journalism in a small place : making Caribbean news relevant, comprehensive, and independent / Juliette Storr.

(Latin American & Caribbean studies ; 13)
Includes bibliographical references and index.
Issued in print and electronic formats.
ISBN 978-1-55238-849-5 (paperback).—ISBN 978-1-55238-851-8 (pdf).—
ISBN 978-1-55238-850-1 (open access pdf).—ISBN 978-1-55238-852-5 (epub).—
ISBN 978-1-55238-853-2 (mobi)

    1. Journalism—Caribbean Area. 2. Press—Caribbean Area. I. Title.
II. Series: Latin American and Caribbean series ; no. 13

PN4930.5.S76 2016   079'.72   C2016-905246-X
                                                   C2016-905247-8

The University of Calgary Press acknowledges the support of the Government of Alberta through the Alberta Media Fund for our publications. We acknowledge the financial support of the Government of Canada through the Canada Book Fund for our publishing activities. We acknowledge the financial support of the Canada Council for the Arts for our publishing program.

  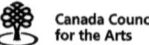

Cover image: #4613384 and #3978273 (Colourbox.com)
Cover design, page design, and typesetting by Melina Cusano
Copy editing by Ryan Perks

For Gladys, James, Val, and Nick

*Caribbean journalists, who speak truth to power,
enrich democracy, and comfort the afflicted.*

Contents

Acronyms	*ix*
Acknowledgments	*xiii*
Preface	*xv*
PART I	*1*
1. Journalism and Media in the Caribbean	*3*
2. Practicing Journalism in Small Places: National and Regional Implications	*31*
3. Caribbean Journalism's Media Economy: Advancing Democracy and the Common Good?	*59*
PART II	*91*
4. Caribbean Journalism: Comprehensive and Proportionate	*93*
5. Caribbean Journalism: Relevant and Engaging	*123*
6. Caribbean Journalism: Maintaining Independence	*153*
7. The Future of Caribbean Journalism	*183*
Notes	*207*
Bibliography	*237*
Index	*255*

Acronyms

ABC	American Broadcasting Corporation
ACHPR	African Commission on Human and Peoples' Rights
ACM	Association of Caribbean Media Workers
AD	Anno Domini
ALBA	Alianza Bolivariana para los Pueblos de Nuestra América
AOL	America Online
ATI	Access to information
BBC	British Broadcasting Corporation
BC	Before Christ
BCJ	Broadcasting Commission of Jamaica
BNA CO	Bahamas National Archives Colonial Papers
CANA	Caribbean News Agency
CARICOM	Caribbean Community
CARIFTA	Caribbean Free Trade Agreement
CARIMAC	Caribbean Institute of Media and Communication
CBA	Commonwealth Broadcasting Association
CBC	Caribbean Broadcasting Corporation
CBS	Columbia Broadcasting System
CBU	Caribbean Broadcasting Union
CCN	Caribbean Communications Network
CEO	Chief Executive Officer
CIA	Central Intelligence Agency
CMC	Caribbean Media Corporation
CNN	Cable News Network
COSTAATT	College of Science, Technology, and Applied Arts of Trinidad and Tobago

CSME	CARICOM Single Market and Economy
EPA	Economic Partnership Agreement
EU	European Union
FES	Friedrich Ebert Stiftung Foundation
FOI	Freedom of information
FOIA	Freedom of Information Act
FOX	Fox News Corporation
FTAA	Free Trade Area of the Americas
GBN	Grenada Broadcasting Network
IMF	International Monetary Fund
IPI	International Press Institute
JOA	Joint operating agreement
MAJ	Media Association of Jamaica
MIT	Massachusetts Institute of Technology
MSNBC	Microsoft and National Broadcasting Company
NBC	National Broadcasting Company
NGO	Non-governmental organization
NUJ	National Union of Journalists
NWICO	New World Information and Communication Order
OAS	Organization of American States
OGNR	On the Ground News Report
OJR	Online Journalism Review
PAJ	Press Association of Jamaica
PLP	Progressive Liberal Party
PPP	People's Progressive Party
PRG	People's Revolutionary Government
PUP	People's United Party
RJR	Radio Jamaica Communications Group
SMS	Short message service
SPJ	Society of Professional Journalists
UBAD	United Black Association for Development
UK	United Kingdom
UNESCO	United Nations Economic, Scientific and Cultural Organization
UNICEF	United Nations Children's Education Fund

US	United States of America
UWI	University of the West Indies
VIBAX	First private radio station in the Caribbean
WAN	World Association of Newspapers
WAN-IFRA	World Association of Newspapers and News Publishers
WSIS	World Summit on Information Society
WTO	World Trade Organization

Acknowledgments

I started thinking about this project more than fifteen years ago, first as a graduate student and then as a media scholar. I found it troubling that there were very few voices from Caribbean journalists and media practitioners telling their stories about their daily, lived experience in the profession. In a time of rapid change brought on by the advent of new communication technologies and market-led reforms, it is perplexing that a region located so close to the United States, home to some of the world's largest media powerhouses, has spent very little time reflecting on its use of communication and media to understand and resolve its complex problems and advance the democratic principles enshrined in its national constitutions. Some economic and political scholars have argued that the region, home to some of the world's youngest democracies, has spent most of its resources building postcolonial economic and political structures that are highly centralized and exclusionary. Because of their narrow focus, areas such as journalism and communication were overlooked in favour of more economically palatable activities such as tourism, banking, and oil. This book is my attempt to provide a theoretical understanding of the use and purpose of journalism, media, and communication in the societies of the English-speaking Caribbean.

This book could not have been completed without the stories of the Caribbean journalists, editors, talk show hosts, columnists, media owners, media scholars, community leaders, and social critics who were willing to talk to me. You gave me an opportunity to hear about both the triumphs and the defeats that you experience as you go about the daily task of bringing truth to citizens. The list is too long to mention you each by name, so I thank you collectively here for your time, your stories, and your many valuable insights into the practice of journalism in the region. I hope you continue to advance the field of journalism, particularly in a rapidly changing environment, in pursuit of more transparent democracies and a better world.

I would also like to thank the people who provided feedback on various drafts of this manuscript. Special thanks to my sister, Mariette Storr, Pamela Moultrie, Denise Hughes Tafen, Tia Smith, and Nichola Gutgold, for your invaluable feedback; each of you helped me craft a better narrative. Additional thanks to Rebbeca Robinson, Shawn Townes, and Tia Smith, who helped me explicate the glocal perspective at a Caribbean conference in New Orleans.

I am also grateful to the undergraduate students who worked diligently to transcribe tapes, collect secondary data from libraries and online sources, and compile bibliographic material. Special thanks to Melissa Burnecke, Matthew Jones, and Alyncea Blackwell—your contributions to this project were immeasurable.

There are several institutions that assisted me, either through funding or other resources. These institutions are: the Bahamas National Archives, Pennsylvania State University, the University of the West Indies Mona and St. Augustine's campuses, and the College of the Bahamas. I could not have completed this book without their support.

Finally, it would be remiss of me not to thank my family and friends who have lent their support in numerous ways, especially my brother Darnell and his wife Judie, who provided the space I needed to reflect and write the first draft of this book. Thanks for providing a quiet backyard during my sabbatical in Nassau, Bahamas.

It is my hope that this project builds upon the work of other Caribbean media scholars and inspires others to continue where it leaves off.

Preface

In small places like the islands of the English-speaking Caribbean, journalism is being practiced in a complex, multicultural space amidst global developments, market-led reforms, and technological innovations. In the United States and Western Europe, journalism has an uncertain future. Howard Tumber and Barbie Zelizer believe journalism today "is expected to wither in an age of financial volatility, decreased revenues, porous borders, layoffs and buyouts, chipped prestige, diminished audiences, concerns about physical safety and variable content."[1] At the same time, it "is expected to flourish: information abounds and is more accessible than ever before, the varieties of content and form are unequalled in history, and more people are involved than at any other point in time as both journalism's producers and its consumers."[2] In the English-speaking Caribbean, for now, journalism has a more certain future as the volatility of changes brought on by market-driven logic, technological innovations, and globalization have not yet reached critical mass; Caribbean media organizations are not trending towards closures. However, Tumber and Zelizer's bleak assessment of American and European journalism remains a concern in this part of the world.

Despite the mixed messages about journalism's future in large countries like the United States, the Caribbean's principal trading partner and the largest media market in the world, journalism is still a profitable business in the Caribbean. But journalism as a craft or profession is facing many challenges as the newsgathering and dissemination process becomes more open and accessible to the public. Civil society is questioning Caribbean journalism—specifically, how it is being practiced in the region and its relevance to these small developing democracies.

This book describes the political, economic, social, and technological factors driving the new trends in contemporary Caribbean journalism. It examines the state of Caribbean journalism at a time when the profession is undergoing rapid changes. Central to this analysis of Caribbean journalism is a reflection on the following questions: What is the purpose of journalism in small Caribbean countries? What are the challenges of practicing journalism in the Caribbean in the twenty-first century? What is the role of journalism in advancing Caribbean democracy? What is the future of journalism in the Caribbean? This book also provides a theoretical and practical response to concerns of professional ethics, responsible performance, and the training and education of journalists.

Despite the rich intellectual history of the region, reflected in the works of various thinkers across a variety of languages over more than three hundred years,[3] the academic field of communication and journalism is not very well developed in the region. The first academic course on journalism began in Jamaica in the 1970s, at the University of the West Indies' (UWI) Mona campus. The UWI's Mona campus affirmed the importance of communication programs to the region when it created the Caribbean Institute of Mass Communication (CARIMAC) in 1974. CARIMAC emerged from a research project sponsored by the United Nations Educational, Scientific, and Cultural Organization (UNESCO) "and a partnership between the University of the West Indies and the Friedrich Ebert Stiftung Foundation (FES)."[4] The institute changed its name in 1996 to the Caribbean Institute of Media and Communication and expanded its focus to reflect global changes in the field. The institute is currently undertaking a phase of growth under the leadership of its new director, Hopeton Dunn.

When the institute was created it was tasked with giving "regional communicators a Caribbean orientation with professional grounding while ensuring that Caribbean media and communication performed while assisting with the region's development."[5] Politicians, media practitioners and owners in the region have criticized CARIMAC for not fulfilling this mission. At the time of this research, much of CARIMAC's work was languishing in obscurity because of the lack of resources for proper record keeping and the lack of interest in building a scholarly community. During its first twenty years, CARIMAC focused on the theoretical more than the practical and professional needs of journalists, which resulted in complaints that journalists were not receiving the kind of training and skills needed to function effectively on the job. When the institute expanded its mission and educational programs in 1996, it tried to address these deficiencies. However, complaints remained about job preparedness and professionalization. Professor Dunn indicated in 2015 that these deficiencies would be addressed under his leadership through an extension of CARIMAC's mission.[6] Several other programs have emerged throughout the region at UWI's Trinidad and Tobago campus, the Ken Gordon School of Journalism and Communication Studies at the College of Science, Technology, and Applied Arts of Trinidad and Tobago, Barbados Community College, St. George's University in Grenada, the College of the Bahamas, the University of Guyana, Northern Caribbean University, International University of the Caribbean, and University of the Virgin Islands. The majority of these programs are still young; many lack accreditation and are trying to find an academic footing in the field. The formal study of journalism and communication in the Caribbean remains inadequate for the growing regional and global demands in the field of communication. There is no adequate description and explanation of the media's role and responsibilities in these microstates—that is, there is no normative theory to guide the practice and profession of journalism and communication throughout the region. This book attempts to address this need through the propositions of communication and development's participatory paradigm and hybridity theories that emerged in the postcolonial era, and more specifically within the last twenty-five years of globalization. I find it troubling that there is still very little academic research and scholarship in the region for a field that is becoming more synonymous with globalization, development, and the advancement and protection of democracy.

Core components of the term hybridity emerged from biological, ethnic, and cultural definitions of mixed breeding—among humans, animals and plants, automobiles, multiracial people, dual citizens, and postcolonial cultures. In 1981 and 1994, Mikhail Bakhtin and Homi Bhabha, respectively, relocated the concept of hybridity, moving it from biology to language to culture. Bakhtin's theory of hybridity is based on the concept of heteroglossia, "a diversity of voices, styles of discourse, or points of view"[7] that come together through language to cocreate reality or "a blending of world views through language that creates complex unity from a hybrid of utterances."[8] Homi Bhabha's influential work on hybridity, *The Location of Culture*, provides a rich discourse on hybrid identities.[9] According to John Hutnyk, Bhabha uses hybridity as an "in-between" term by which he refers to a "third space," or an ambivalence and mimicry in postcolonial cultures.[10] Bhabha's thesis explains why the culture of Western modernity must be relocated from the postcolonial perspective. In *The Location of Culture* he explores those moments of ambivalence that structure social authority. This ambivalence is echoed in Jamaica Kincaid's description of her Caribbean home, Antigua,[11] as a small place that lives with ambivalence and contradiction, as well as the work of Dick Hebdige, whose *Cut 'N' Mix: Culture, Identity and Caribbean Music* examines the interaction of Caribbean sounds and ideas with those of the United Kingdom and North America to explore Caribbean cultural identity through music.[12] Paul Gilroy, in his book *The Black Atlantic*, adds the history of "the instability and mutability of identities"[13] that emerged from the movements of people and ideas between Africa, Europe, and the Americas as "an inescapable hybridity and intermixture of ideas."[14] Hybridity in the cross-cultural experiences of the Americas is also explored in the work of Rosario Ferré, Maryse Condé, and Toni Morrison.[15] Caribbean social critic Rex Nettleford described a process of "creolization" that emerged out of slavery and its consequences—plantation societies, colonization and decolonization, neocolonialism, racial and ethnic relations, and class distinctions.[16] For Josef Raab and Martin Butler, the concept of hybridity is a "useful metaphor for conceptualizing and analyzing cultural contact, transfer and exchange, especially in the field of postcolonial studies."[17] Like Néstor García Canclini, they contend that hybridity is an ongoing condition of all human cultures with no zones of purity because it is an ongoing process of "borrowings and lending between cultures."[18]

In 2005, Marwan Kraidy proposed that, instead of holding steadfast to an all-purpose definition of hybridity, theorists should "find a way to integrate different types of hybridity into a framework that makes connections between them that are both intelligible and usable."[19] I attempt to develop such a framework in this book. However, Kraidy sees hybridity is "a risky notion, since it comes with neither guarantees nor a single idea or unitary concept."[20] This perspective fits well with the descriptions of postcolonial Caribbean identity put forth by scholars such as Stuart Hall, Paul Gilroy, and Derek Walcott.[21]

The notions of hybrid cultures and normative theories of the press, along with the theories of the participatory paradigm for communication and development, are used to locate a theoretical position for journalism and communication in the daily lives of Caribbean people. In time, theories of hybridity could help Caribbean societies to reposition themselves from their ambivalent space to a determined position. Theories of hybridity could empower them to deconstruct their contradictory spaces and create—on a local, regional, and global level—a clear picture of who they are, what they want to be, where they want to go, and how to get there.

This book emerged from a study of journalism in six countries of the English-speaking Caribbean. Seventy-five journalists, talk show hosts, editors, media owners, policymakers, media scholars, and cultural critics were interviewed over a period of ten years. The participants came from Bahamas, Barbados, Belize, Grenada, Jamaica, and Trinidad and Tobago—or one-third of the English-speaking Caribbean. I also made a cursory examination of the news industry in Cuba, Curaçao, the Dominican Republic, and Haiti for comparative purposes. Although there are many similarities in the practice of journalism in the English-speaking and non-English-speaking countries of the region due to population size and historical similarities, I wanted to limit this analysis to the English-speaking countries. Journalists in the contemporary English-speaking Caribbean could be divided into two groups—the older generation, which encompasses journalists with more than ten years of experience, and the younger generation of journalists with less than ten years, and who comprise the majority of practitioners in the field. This is not an arbitrary marker, as historically many persons who start off as journalists in the Caribbean do not remain in the profession for more than ten years. Also, according to the journalists interviewed for this project, the average career has been reduced over the last decade to between one and five years. I maintain a ten-year time frame to distinguish between stability and instability, experience and inexperience, and continuity and discontinuity. Most of the older journalists received their training on the job with some of them later obtaining tertiary degrees or certification, while most of the younger journalists are coming to the profession with tertiary degrees. This division helps to explain some of the tensions among two generations of Caribbean journalists as they practice in a rapidly changing environment.

The interviews, along with secondary sources, such as archival documents, internet, newspaper, and journal articles, provide an analysis of Caribbean journalism. Initially, I began with a list of known journalists, media owners, and educators; these individuals in turn provided referrals to other journalists, editors, media owners, and scholars who they felt should be included in the research. The themes identified from the interviews and other source materials form the basis of this book.

As a former journalist from the Caribbean myself, I had previous knowledge and experience about the practice and profession. This background helped me to place my research within the cultural context of the region. An inductive approach was used to link the themes that emerged from this research to those in the global literature, as well as to provide a framework for identifying and comparing the practice and profession of journalism in North America and Western Europe to journalism in the Caribbean. A triangulation of data was used to recommend normative approaches for journalism in the Caribbean. Together, the interviews and the secondary data helped me to present a detailed description of the characteristics of Caribbean journalism, and a normative frame for understanding the role of journalism and communication in the region. The themes that emerged from the interviews coalesced around the concepts of changes and challenges in Caribbean media markets over the first one and a half decades of the twenty-first century.

The book is divided into two parts. The first part presents a historical context for the evolution and the purpose of journalism in the region, as well as its current economic successes. The second part outlines major challenges in Caribbean journalism in the twenty-first century and provides a theoretical perspective on how journalism should be practiced in small democratic countries to meet the current needs of those societies. Specifically, this work relies on the theoretical and practical understanding of journalism and communication provided by Bill Kovach and Tom Rosenstiel's book *The Elements of Journalism*, Clifford Christians, Theodore Glasser, Denis McQuail, Kaarle Nordenstreng, and Robert White's *Normative Theories of the Media: Journalism in Democratic Societies*, Frederick Siebert, Theodore Peterson, and Wilbur Schramm's *Four Theories of the Press*, Jennifer Ostini and Anthony Y. H. Fung's *Beyond the Four Theories of the Press: A New Model of National Media Systems*, and the works of Auksė Balčytienė and Halliki Harro-Loit, Howard Tumber and

Barbie Zelizer, James Carey, Brian McNair, Sarah Oates, Bob Franklin, Michael Schudson, Robert McChesney, and John Nichols, David Weaver and Lars Willnat, Marlene Cuthbert, Stuart Surlin and Walter Soderlund, Aggrey Brown, Roderick Sanatan, Mark Alleyne, Hopeton Dunn, Ewart Skinner, and other American, European, Caribbean and Latin American media scholars to provide a framework for understanding journalism as practiced in the Caribbean space, a hybrid or third space along the lines proposed by Homi Bhabha, as well as Marwan Kraidy, in his *Hybridity: The Cultural Logic of Globalization*.

Ultimately, it is my hope that this book sheds light on the relationship between media and Caribbean societies in a way that will help to diagnose problems and encourage reforms based on principles that guide public communication and democracy. Specifically, examining journalism in small places like the islands of the English-speaking Caribbean provides an opportunity not only to determine the purpose of journalism and describe the challenges of practicing journalism in small geographic spaces; it also enhances practitioners' ability to assess the future of journalism in a complex, multicultural region amidst global developments, market-led reforms, and technological innovations. According to Howard Tumber and Barbie Zelizer, "the key problems facing journalism as it moves into the future [are] globalization, changing business pressures, the internationalization of the study of journalism, diminished work conditions, and definitional ambiguity."[22] This book describes how these problems are reflected in the Caribbean. It also provides a historical context for the practice of journalism in the Caribbean and identifies the purpose of journalism in these democratic societies in the twenty-first century.

This book begins by examining the purpose of journalism in the English-speaking Caribbean. Journalists there are experiencing a variety of changes spurred on by technological revolutions and marketplace ideals. Hence, there are many parallels between the evolution of journalism in the Caribbean and rest of the world, with particular emphasis on the United States and Western Europe. But there are also many differences. These are based mostly on socioeconomic and political factors that have influenced the development of journalism in the region. This book discusses these differences as it examines the practice and profession of journalism in the English-speaking Caribbean as it evolves through a period of rapid technological and economic changes.

The book also describes the paradigm shift in the Caribbean marketplace from public service to commercialization. It examines the current challenges in the practice and profession of journalism in the last decade in relation to increased commercialism, audience fragmentation and segmentation, and digital technology. The second part of the book discusses a variety of emerging issues shaped by the new forms of public communication, forms that affect journalistic practice and the meaning of news and news culture in the Caribbean. These issues include the impact of commercialism, the blogosphere, citizen journalism, professionalism, media regulation, technological convergence, and conglomeration. This book presents much-needed discussion of journalism in the Caribbean and the future of journalism and democracy in the region. Much of the global analysis of journalism's future concerns the apparent demise of journalism around the world. However, at the start of the second decade of the twenty-first century, Caribbean journalism, despite predictions to the contrary, continues to exist. Bonnie Brennen believes that "in a time of plunging circulations, reduced viewership, and limited employment opportunities, one of the primary issues facing traditional media is their on-going relevance in our postmodern society."[23] With questions of relevance and economic sustainability at the heart of European and American discussions on the future of journalism, it is fair to raise these questions in smaller markets where rapid changes in technology and market structure are also propelling microstates to address the issues of relevance and sustainability. Does journalism have a future in the Caribbean?

The Caribbean is a multicultural space. Broadly speaking, it encompasses all the countries "below the Florida peninsula, from the Bahamas in the northwest to Trinidad and Tobago in the southeast, including Bermuda, the French and Dutch territories, and Guyana, Belize, Surname, and French Guiana in mainland South America. The majority of these English-speaking countries are former British colonies,"[24] and it is on these countries that this book focuses. They are small, independent and dependent microstates with population sizes ranging from 2.8 million (Jamaica) to a mere 5,100 (British-administered Montserrat). St. Kitts and Nevis is the smallest independent country in the region, with 41,000 people. The majority of the Caribbean is made up of independent states with a few remaining European dependences—British: Bermuda, the Cayman Islands, Turks and Caicos, Anguilla, Montserrat, and the British Virgin Islands;

Dutch: Aruba, Bonaire, St. Eustatius, and Saba; French: Guadeloupe and Martinique—as well as the American territories of the US Virgin Islands and Puerto Rico.

Current discourse on the future of these Caribbean countries emphasizes the complex problems that affect them—from high crime, corruption, and economic inertia, to inadequate educational systems, illiteracy, poverty, chronic diseases, and flailing leadership. In his book *Britain's Black Debt*, Hilary Beckles provides a sweeping analysis of how these issues are related to the region's colonial past.[25] According to Beckles, whose argument for reparation has ties to Eric Williams's seminal work *Capitalism and Slavery*,[26] the causal link between the crimes of slavery and the ongoing harm and injury to slavery's descendants is everywhere in the Caribbean.[27] He posits that the pain of slavery and the injury of its injustice continues to haunt citizens in the Caribbean, weakening their capacity to experience citizenship as equals with the descendants of slave owners. Consequently, the region still struggles to redefine itself and relocate Western modernity to a postcolonial perspective. Journalism and media's role in the development of Western societies are part and parcel of colonial history. This book examines the relevance of journalism in the Caribbean and how it engages with these issues to construct postcolonial narratives on the lived experiences of Caribbean people. Ultimately, the book tries to answer the question, What is journalism's role in relocating the region's identity and position in the world? Another way to phrase this is: What is journalism's role in the rehumanization project to restore the power that was stripped from native Indians and enslaved Africans more than four centuries ago, who remain entrenched in the Eurocentric worldviews of Western philosophies and ideologies?

This book reviews some of the major challenges of the practice and profession of journalism in the Caribbean. Chapter one begins with a brief overview of mercantile and capital commercialism, the evolution of journalism and its purpose in colonialism and post-colonization, particularly focusing on the role journalism plays and will continue to play in these currently competitive media markets. The peculiarities of small states, the constraints placed on a small group of practicing journalists, and the implications for regional and national development are the subjects of chapter two. It examines the arguments of scholars who advance the thesis that smallness impacts the purpose of journalism and the character of journalism in small states. This includes a discussion on the constraints of market size—both in the number of journalists and the size of audience—professionalism, resource limitations, dependency, and vulnerability. Throughout most of its history in Western societies, journalism has been imbued with the power to protect and advance democracy. Chapter three discusses journalism's role in democratic societies. The rise of the commercial model of journalism and questions about its ability to advance democratic ideals of equality and justice for all are the concerns of chapter three. It identifies the current economic trends in Caribbean journalism and the factors that influence these trends, reviews international media scholars' arguments for the necessity of journalism as a public good or service, and posits the need to refashion journalism to fulfill the needs of Caribbean societies.

The principle of making the news comprehensive and proportionate is the focus of chapter four. In small Caribbean states, the need to be comprehensive and proportionate is important to advance the democratic project began in each of these countries after independence. Caribbean journalists acknowledge the value of providing comprehensive accounts to the public and they agree on the value of journalism to democracy. However, as Henrik Örnebring and Epp Lauk argue, this need is difficult to achieve in states where the emphasis is on collaboration, compromise, and group cohesion. Journalists who were interviewed for this book explain the challenges of providing balanced, accurate, and full accounts of their societies. The constraints of acquiring sources, accessing information, and negotiating a culture of secrecy make this goal difficult to achieve.

The need for Caribbean journalism to be relevant to its public in a rapidly changing media environment is salient for small societies with a history of authoritarian governance. Chapter five discusses relevance and engagement, which are particularly challenging in the current competitive and commercialized markets where the gravitation to sensational and salacious coverage is becoming the norm. Journalists discussed the challenges of striking the right balance between relevance and engagement as media owners push for higher ratings and larger circulations. Effective storytelling is also challenged by smallness—the size of journalism as a profession, the number of resources, particularly sources, and access to information. Engaging Caribbean citizens is perhaps easier to achieve because, as Kincaid notes, the people in these societies make the small issues or everyday issues big and ignore big issues, perhaps because they do not know how to resolve them. But engagement without relevance results in sensational, salacious coverage. Issues of accuracy and the skills of journalists are included in discussions of making the news relevant and engaging. As Manuel Puppis and others argue,[28] small states are constrained by lack of resources and small audiences, both of which lead journalists to rely on few sources and limited know-how in presenting more balanced accounts and pursuing investigative journalism, which is costly to maintain even in large markets.

The principle of independence is an enduring value in professional journalism. Chapter six examines the need for journalists to separate themselves from the influence of those they cover, uphold the value of monitoring the powerful, and provide a voice for the voiceless. Caribbean journalists agree that this principle is important and necessary for journalism to achieve its purpose of providing the information people need to be free and active participants in a democratic society. The size of these markets, the number of journalists, and the sociocultural history of the region also affect the principle of independence. These factors make it difficult for Caribbean journalists to be independent from those they cover. In this chapter, Caribbean journalists recount their challenges in meeting this important need. Örnebring and Lauk's argument that small markets have fewer employers, fewer senior positions, and fewer alternatives in terms of career routes and career progression, is salient here.[29] Further, their claim that small markets result in small social groups and more social control is also relevant to this discussion.

Finally, chapter seven reflects on the evolution of journalism in Caribbean societies, the current challenges of practicing journalism in the region, and speculates on the future of the profession at a time of increased commercialism and advancing technologies. It prescribes a hybrid normative thesis with radical, advocacy, and community journalism as the core of the practice while not excluding the monitorial role of presenting accurate, well-balanced facts so that these small countries can evolve as more effective and transparent democracies in the twenty-first century.

PART I

The people in a small place cannot give an exact account, a complete account, of themselves.

—Jamaica Kincaid, *A Small Place*

Journalism and Media in the Caribbean

Since the beginning of the twenty-first century, journalism in North America and Western Europe has been saddled with an uncertain future. This uncertainty has led to the emergence of a discourse concerning the demise of journalism and the underlying threat to democracy. Though journalists and media scholars in these regions view journalism as a vital component of democracy, the profession finds itself struggling to stay relevant. This has come about through the spread of two major forces: market-driven principles that usurp social responsibility and co-opt the monitorial, radical, facilitative, and collaborative roles of journalism,[1] and new communication technologies that provide citizens with direct access to information. Though in the Caribbean, journalists and media scholars face similar challenges, they have had to face them within a specific context that includes both the smallness of their countries, as well as the centralized political structures, archaic media laws, dependent economies, and cultural peculiarities under which they operate.

Each of these challenges—commercial and technological—are perceived as threats to journalism. Because of the former, journalism is often seen as a commercial product more concerned with making a profit than being a pillar of democracy, while the latter is often seen as an encroachment on the exclusive rights of journalists to gather and disseminate information. As more people gain the ability to gather and disseminate information without the filtering effect of media organizations, the question "who is a journalist?" has emerged in Western media markets. Scholars such as Marc Raboy, Robert McChesney, and Jon Nichols predicted these commercial and technological changes would bring about the demise of journalism, imperiling democracy in the process.[2] In the Caribbean, these changes are happening at a slower pace. The present chapter provides a brief description of the history of commercialism in the Caribbean, as well as a brief look at journalism and the media, its origins and present-day status, in the small states of the English-speaking Caribbean.

Mercantilism, Capitalism, and Commercialism

The first experience of commercialism in the Caribbean was characterized by mercantilism, an economic system that emphasized the accumulation of massive wealth by individual nations. During the colonial period (from the seventeenth to the twentieth century), this wealth was concentrated in the metropolises of the colonizers—Britain, France, Spain, Portugal, Belgium, and the Netherlands. In Western countries, capitalism supplanted mercantilism as the prevailing theory of economic development at the end of the colonial period. Mercantilism and capitalism are related in that they both support a system of competition, but the latter emphasizes a system controlled by corporations, which is best expressed in Adam Smith's philosophy of the invisible hand of the marketplace. Mercantilism is also referred to by some economists as early commercial capitalism, but it differs from commercial capitalism to the extent that it was set up by European nations to amass wealth through the plundering of natural resources—gold and silver, and later, slaves, cotton, and sugar—from their colonies. In their book *Theory of Games and Economic Behavior*, economists John von Neumann and Oskar Morgenstern refer to this form of economic activity as a zero-sum game whereby participants either win or lose. In capitalism, the means of production are privately owned and production is guided and income distributed mainly through the operation of markets.

Mercantile capitalism, as exemplified by such countries as China, Japan, South Korea, Brazil and Russia, among others, still exists. Economic theorists like Ian Bremmer, Daron Acemoglu, and James Robinson view today's models of mercantile capitalism as state capitalism or cronyism. They argue that these systems do not produce the type of liberalism that promotes deliberative democracy.[3] Bremmer describes state capitalism as antithetical to the ideals of liberal capitalism. In the former, he argues, the state functions as the leading economic actor and uses the markets primarily for political gain. Acemoglu and Robinson agree that the problems with state capitalism are not economic but political; they believe these models will fail, "as the power of the state will interfere with the development of democratic ideals, particularly in an era of growing public access to information."[4] They conclude that "state capitalism is not about efficient allocation of economic resources, but about maximizing political control over society and the economy. If state managers can grab all productive resources and control access to them, this maximizes control—even if it sacrifices economic efficiency."[5]

Other economists, like James Fallows, Alice Amsden, and Aldo Mussacchio and Sergio Lazzarini, view state capitalism differently.[6] They see it as a sustainable model that will help nations to advance their economies. While state capitalism has been around for centuries, the state either owns the companies or plays a major role in supporting or directing them in contemporary dispensation.

James Fallows, in his book *Looking at the Sun: The Rise of the New East Asian Economic and Political System*, argues that the idea that the state prevents growth and general happiness is an Anglo-American prejudice. MIT economist Alice Amsden, in her book *The Rise of the Rest*, believes India, China, Turkey, and Brazil had no choice but to intervene in their local markets. Fallows and Amsden see state capitalism as a viable alternative to market capitalism.

As independent, postcolonial states, the English-speaking countries of the Caribbean shifted their commercial mercantile systems to capitalist economies that emphasized marketplace ideals,[7] but the development of commercial capitalism in the Caribbean was influenced by the social, political, and economic structures that were created under colonization. Therefore, although operating in capitalist marketplaces, Caribbean social, political, and economic institutions are still bastions of the former colonial empires that created them for mercantile purposes. The remnants of colonialism are most notable in public service institutions such as broadcasting, education, financial investment, and the judiciary. Despite the neoliberal policies of the 1980s and 1990s, which ushered in the deregulation of markets and the privatization of state institutions in the region, many of these institutions are still nationalistic corporations set up under British colonial government. In many Caribbean countries, the state still has either majority shares or minority shares and political influence in public utilities such as telecommunications, water, and electricity. Mussachio and Lazzarini describe this is as either a "Leviathan majority" or "Leviathan minority" approach, and define this type of capitalism as a hybrid form of state capitalism in which the government exerts considerable influence over the economy.

Fragano Ledgister attributes the current Leviathan institutional structures and systems in the Caribbean to colonization.[8] He believes colonization in the Caribbean "created authoritarian government at the hands of bureaucrats whose primary concern was social discipline in the interest of the colonizer, but also social amelioration (in part as a means of securing social discipline, in part as a way of providing the state with suitable recruit) in accordance with late nineteenth- and early twentieth-century liberal norms."[9] Ledgister explains: "the people of the region did not engage in heroic armed struggles for independence nor did they make a radical break with the colonial past and immediately seek to redefine who they were and their relationship with the rest of the world. Instead they took the institutions of democracy, which developed in the tutelary period, and kept them going."[10]

Consequently, in the present-day Caribbean small states are caught between state cronyism and neoliberal capitalism. This is exemplified by the centralized structure of the political systems in these countries, which allows the state to retain considerable power in the decision-making process and often pits the state's political agenda against the socio-economic agenda of liberal capitalism. This conflict makes it difficult for these states to progress with the advance of deliberative democracy.

This state of conflict is also reflected in journalism and media industries throughout the region. Tensions between journalists and government have escalated since the liberalization of these markets in the 1980s, with journalists pushing for less government control over public information, as well as the revision or elimination of the archaic media laws for libel and defamation that have allowed state representatives to penalize journalists for publishing information that public figures deem damaging to their images and reputations, or which, they claim, threaten national security. The International Press Institute's (IPI) 2012 mission to the region resulted in the IPI Declaration of Port of Spain, which identified Caribbean countries as being "subjected to a panoply of repressive measures, from jailing and persecution to the widespread scourge of 'insult laws' and defamation, which are sometimes used by the powerful to prevent critical appraisal of their actions and to deprive the public of information about misdeeds."[11] These efforts at state censorship undermine journalistic values, freedom of speech, truth and transparency, and the principles of democracy.

Throughout the English-speaking Caribbean, print media has had a long history of private ownership while broadcasting, with the exception of the private British firm Rediffusion, was owned and controlled by the state until the last two decades of the twentieth century. State broadcasting in the colonies began as public service broadcasting under colonial administration. However, unlike their parent model, the British Broadcasting Corporation (BBC), these broadcasters had to become commercial entities very early in their existence. Colonial broadcasters were not successful in establishing the same financial infrastructure as the BBC, and by the late 1940s and early1950s they had become commercial entities. These systems were further challenged when deregulation, liberalization, and privatization policies were implemented in the 1980s and 1990s, opening these markets to intense competition.

Caribbean media evolved with a mixture of private and public entities until the late 1980s. Although many states liberalized their markets, particularly with regards to broadcasting, most of them retained a state broadcast entity, some under the guise of public service broadcasting, while others continued as state broadcasters. Few opted out of broadcasting completely. Today commercialism is blamed for many of the ills affecting Caribbean journalism, both print and broadcast. These include marketization, tabloidization/sensationalism, fragmentation, and a decline in professional ethics. Other threats to journalism's integrity have emerged from new technologies such as the internet, which has provided the public with more access to information and created a competitive forum for citizen journalists and bloggers. Like its global counterparts, the media environment in the Caribbean is faced with the double threat of commercialism and new technology. But the intervening factors of market size, low-to-moderate internet penetration, and culture are sustaining these markets—for now.

It is important at this point to discuss the history of media and journalism in the region. The following historical background is not exhaustive, but it helps to explain how the current state of journalism continues to constrain and challenge journalists to make the news more relevant, accurate, comprehensive, and independent from those it monitors.

A Brief History of Caribbean Media and Journalism

Journalism in the modern-day Caribbean is prefixed by the global history of journalism, which is as old as the history of people's need to know. Human societies have always found a way to pass on stories about who, what, when, where, why, and how. Storytellers, formal and informal, were the forerunners of modern journalists. As societies evolved from preliterate to literate, we gathered and disseminated our stories about ourselves and our activities, near and far, with the aid of various technologies. The history of journalism thus began with the written word. The earliest traditions of gathering and disseminating written news reports began with the first handwritten dailies in Rome and China between 59 BC and about 222 AD. Later, in the fifteenth and sixteenth centuries, handwritten weeklies became common in European countries like Italy, Germany, Holland, England, and Russia. The modern-day newspaper was of course created with the invention of the printing press. Henceforth, journalism became a structured activity designed to record the daily events of society: gathering, analyzing, interpreting, creating and disseminating news and information.

Mitchell Stephens, in his book *A History of News*, identified the modern-day newspaper as a European invention.[12] He posits American journalism got its start from British contributions, in the form of the first newspaper owners and the style of news reporting. The British had a penny press before the Americans, and the early term associated with newspapers, "the gazette," was inherited from the British, though it can be traced to the early Venetian newssheets known as *avisi*. The origins of journalism in the English-speaking Caribbean are similar. As colonies of the British Empire, newspapers in the Caribbean were started by British citizens.

In addition to the printing press's contribution to journalism's history, many Western journalists regard John Milton's "Areopagitica," a speech delivered to the Parliament of England in 1644 against the licensing of printed material and censorship, as the precursor for the modern philosophy on the right to free expression and freedom of the press. It was delivered during the English Civil War and in the wake of the English Reformation; it was in the furor of this period that print journalism was born. Since the seventeenth century, the British Parliament has been committed to the ideals of freedom of speech and the exposure of ideas to open debate. Today, British journalism's first principle is "press freedom." These core values of free speech and press freedom were passed onto British colonies.

In the English-speaking Caribbean, the history of journalism is also intertwined with the history of discovery, piracy, colonialism, slavery, indentured labor, and long periods of conflict. The printed press was introduced throughout the region in the 1700s, and was owned and operated by members of the white oligarchies found throughout these colonies, most of whom were British or American businessmen and women. Free blacks, or "coloreds," introduced some of the printed press during the latter years of the nineteenth century, but the majority of the newspapers, whether daily, weekly, or monthly, were owned and operated by white mercantilists, and landowning oligarchic elites. Howard Pactor presents a historical sketch of newspapers in the English-speaking Caribbean in his bibliographic directory, *Colonial British Newspapers*.[13] John Lent provides more details of some of the newspapers in his work on Caribbean media.[14] Other Caribbean scholars, such as Aggrey Brown, Ewart Skinner, Mark Alleyne, Erwin Thomas, and Omar Oliveira, include brief sketches of the media history of Jamaica, Trinidad and Tobago, Barbados, Grenada, and Belize in Stuart Surlin and Walter Soderlund's edited volume *Mass Media and the Caribbean*.[15]

During the colonial period there was little concern for keeping a historical record of the daily happenings in these colonies; a lack of archival facilities existed until well into the middle of the twentieth century, which meant that few records of newspapers survived. According to Pactor, British settlers started the first newspaper in the region, the *Weekly Jamaica Courant*, in Jamaica in 1718. There were more than six hundred and fifty newspapers in the English-speaking Caribbean, but none of those started in the eighteenth century are in print today. Only five newspapers from the nineteenth century are still published: the *Royal Gazette* (founded in Bermuda in 1828), the *Daily Gleaner* (Jamaica, 1834), the *Nassau Guardian* (Bahamas, 1844), the *Voice of St. Lucia*, (St. Lucia, 1885), and the *Barbados Advocate*, (Barbados, 1895).[16]

The second longest-running publication in the region is the *Gleaner*. According to Jamaican communication professor Hopeton Dunn, the *Gleaner* was been owned by a succession of slave-owning and oligarchic families. Currently the region's largest newspaper publishing group, the Gleaner Company Ltd. is owned by the Clarke/Ashenheim family.[17] The Gleaner Company owns the *Gleaner*, the *Star*, a weekly tabloid, and the *Sunday Gleaner*. White businessman Gordon "Butch" Stewart started Jamaica's second-largest daily, the *Jamaica Observer*, in 1993. In the Bahamas, Barbados, Belize, Grenada, and Trinidad and Tobago, the histories are similar.

The longest-running publication in the Bahamas is the *Nassau Guardian*, which was established by a white oligarch family, the Moseleys. Today, the *Nassau Guardian*, along with the *Nassau Tribune*, which was started by white businessman Leon Dupuch in 1903, is one of two national dailies in the Bahamas. Dupuch's mulatto son, Etienne, was editor of the *Nassau Tribune* for fifty-four years. In 2012, the IPI and the Guinness Book of World Records named him the longest-serving newspaper editor in the world. A black businessman is now part owner of the *Nassau Guardian*. There is a third daily, the *Bahamas Journal*, owned by black businessman Wendall Jones, but it is not nationally distributed.

In Barbados, the longest-running paper, the *Barbados Advocate*, was started by the British newspaper conglomerate Thomson Newspapers. A white oligarchic family, the McEnearneys, bought the newspaper in 1985, and it was bought in 2000 by Anthony Bryan, a black businessman. The *Barbados Advocate* "enjoyed a long run as the most prominent newspaper in the country, at various times having a monopoly on the daily newspaper market."[18] It was not until the emergence of the *Barbados Nation* in 1973 that the *Advocate* had serious competition. Local businessmen Fred Gollop and Harold Hoyte started the *Nation* to compete against the *Advocate*. Today, the newspaper industry in Barbados is divided between the two newspapers, though the *Nation* is now the largest-selling paper. There are also a number of smaller monthly circulations and online publications.

The first newspaper in Grenada was the *Royal Grenada Gazette*, which began in 1765 and ended in 1788. According to Pactor, none of the colonial newspapers in Grenada have survived. The oldest newspaper there today is the *Grenadian Voice*, which began in 1982 and is owned by Spice Island

Printers, Ltd. The *Informer*, started in 1984, has become the weekly *Grenada Today*, which is published online.

Ewart Skinner describes contemporary national dailies in Trinidad and Tobago as "conservative entities that promote themselves as independent voices. Their editorial positions support capitalism, middle-class consumerism, upper-class social and cultural aspirations; and foreign, conservative governments, principally the US."[19] Trinidad and Tobago has three national dailies: the *Trinidad Express*, the *Trinidad Guardian* and *Newsday*. The oldest surviving newspapers in Trinidad and Tobago are the *Catholic News*, a specialty weekly that began in 1892, and the *Trinidad Guardian*, a national daily newspaper started in 1917 by a group of white businessmen. The *Trinidad Express* was started in 1967 by a group of local businessmen as a competitor to the *Trinidad Guardian*. Therese Mills, a black businesswoman and former editor in chief of the *Trinidad Guardian*, started *Newsday* in 1993.

Belize's media history is similar. Newspapers were started in the colonial period, were first owned by white oligarchs, and later, blacks and other ethnicities became media owners; in the mid-twentieth century, political parties became publishers of national newspapers as well. In August 2012, the columnist Janus provided a brief history of newspapers in Belize in the newspaper *Amandala*.[20] According to Janus, there was only one newspaper in the 1940s, the *Daily Clarion*, and it was started in 1936 under colonization. Phillip Goldson and Leigh Richardson turned the 1940s newssheet *Oh Yaeh* into the newspaper the *Belize Billboard* in 1950. Richardson and Goldson were members of the People's United Party (PUP) and the newspaper, which functioned as the voice of the PUP, became the *Belize Times* in the 1990s. Today, Belize has no daily newspaper. The major weekly newspapers in Belize are *Amandala*, the *National Perspective* and the *Reporter*. The *Guardian*, another significant newspaper, was established in 1969, and it is also published once a week. The *Belize Times* and the *Guardian* are the official newspapers of the PUP and the United Democratic Party (UDP), respectively. *Amandala* was started in 1969 by the United Black Association for Development (UBAD) and is the most widely circulated newspaper in the country. It is published twice a week. The *Reporter* was founded in 1967 by Harry Lawrence and is published weekly. The *National Perspective*, a weekly founded in 2008, is the latest newspaper. The history of journalism in Belize is not included in Pactor's account, which he claims is more comprehensive than earlier accounts of journalism in the region. However, in *The Making of Belize*, Anne Sutherland notes the first newspaper in the country appeared in 1852; she credits John Lent, one of the most well-known and disputed scholars of Caribbean mass media, as her source. She also acknowledges that in Belize, "there is no historical tradition of an independent press, and little attempt to promote one today."[21]

The emphasis on the ethnic and racial identities, as well as the political affiliations, of media owners is important in a region still encumbered by its colonial past. Race relations and political clientelism are complex and complicated in these hybrid societies. Caribbean nations are still very young, with fifty years of experience (and sometimes less) as independent states. This has not allowed sufficient time for them to evolve into mature democratic states, resolve the tensions among racial and ethnic groups who reside in these small spaces, or dissolve clientelistic practices and patronage-ridden politics. While the majority of these countries have a dominant African population, indentured laborers from East and South Asia (or East India, as it is known in the English-speaking Caribbean), as well as Europeans and people from many other countries, have created a complex multicultural space. In some Caribbean countries, such as Trinidad and Tobago or Guyana, there are two dominant ethnic groups, Africans and East Indians. Belize is a racially mixed society; Latino, Creole, Maya, Garifuna, and Mennonite are its five largest ethnic groups.

The issue of race relations is particularly relevant to the economic, political, and social development of these countries. The fact that these relations were created during the colonial era, and were only rarely addressed publically, underscores some of the challenges journalists face when it comes to covering economic elites in Caribbean countries, as the majority of the wealth still remains in the hands of white oligarchs. The emergence of a black oligarchy has provided some economic diversity, but social life remains stratified along class and race lines.

Since its inception, journalism in the Caribbean served the mercantile class and the metropolitan centers of the British Empire, which has advanced the wealth and culture of the British colonizers, and not the economy and culture of the colonies themselves. Although within the truncated history of the English-speaking Caribbean, journalism has often focused on disseminating news from external centers, it has also provided a rich portrait of social, economic, and political life in these "often obscure" and "nonessential" colonies. However, much of the content has focused on the concerns of the ruling elites, with very little attention, especially during the colonial era, paid to the internal or domestic social, economic, and political needs of the majority black, Indian, and indigenous populations. The content of newspapers during the colonial period and well into the middle of the twentieth century came directly from European centers, especially London, and later, from American cities like New York and Miami. Many of these early newspapers filled their pages with duplicated copies of foreign news stories; many also shared their content with each other, such that few local news reporters were hired. This outward focus superseded the need to focus on the injustices of colonization and slavery. The editors or publishers, along with a handful of additional persons put most of the newspapers together. Local news reporting in the region did not begin until the 1930s and 1940s, and even then a limited number of local stories made it into Caribbean papers. There were no local bylines in the newspapers until the late 1950s and early 1960s—and even then, most of the news reporters or journalists, particularly in broadcasting, were foreigners. It was not until the 1960s that more locals were hired at newspapers and radio stations. Of course, the amount increased after these countries became independent states, yet as Yvette Stuart noted in her 2001 study of Bahamian national dailies, a significant amount of news content—more than 50 percent—was still foreign or international; it focused mainly on the United States, the United Kingdom, and Canada.[22]

The black press in these countries also made significant contributions to the development of democracy, but unfortunately very few of these early efforts have survived. After slavery was abolished, the metropolitan-centered approach continued, but there was a shift to local news as more black or colored newspapers appeared in circulation during the latter part of the 1800s and early 1900s. These early black publications provided a context for reflections on black social, economic, and political life. By the start of the twentieth century, there was more domestic news in the local white-owned newspapers, but the content remained predominantly foreign. By the time radio broadcasting started in the 1930s there was a definite shift to local news, though foreign news was still dominant.

According to Howard Pactor, the earliest colonial papers "present a detailed record of the life and concerns of the colonists of the region. The individual papers reveal their own purposes in each colony at particular times in the colonial period. Reflective of oligarchic opinion, many of the journals serve as valuable records of European struggle to survive in the region."[23] However, as Pactor recounts, "by the late nineteenth century, newspapers established by and for the black communities began to appear. While many of these journals did not survive, their presence helped instill confidence and pride in the black populations, which contributed to the establishment of successful newspapers and to the eventual end of social disabilities and colonialism."[24]

While Pactor provides a positive description of the impact of black journals in the late nineteenth and early twentieth centuries, it took several decades before these newspapers were financially successful or succeeded as major contributors to the end of social injustice under colonization. Further, there were other factors that led to the end of colonization. The trade union movement of the 1930s, the early attempts at regionalization through the creation of the West Indian Federation in the 1950s, the American civil rights movement of the 1960s, the regional independence movement of the same decade, along with other global events after the end of the Second World War, contributed to the demise of colonization. These additional factors also led to shifts in the purpose and function of journalism throughout the region. The domestic or national needs of these former British colonies began to take precedence over international and colonial concerns. However, the long history of external leadership and focus continued to influence the profession and practice of journalism. As the need to be informed of their own domestic concerns grew, spurred on by early trade union, federation, and independence movements, Caribbean journalists shifted their focus from the external metropolitan centers in Europe or North America to the internal centers of these growing nations. By the 1950s and 1960s, journalism, particularly through the black press, emerged as an advocate for the majority black population in most of these countries, as educated black elites took political control of their countries and propelled them to independence. In countries like Trinidad and Tobago and Guyana, where the population is divided between Africans and Indians, the independence movement was dominated by members of the educated black and Indian elite, such as Eric Williams and Forbes Burnham, the first prime ministers of Trinidad and Tobago and Guyana, respectively. Indian leaders like Guyana's Cheddi Jagan and Trinidad and

Tobago's Basdeo Panday also played a significant role in the development of these countries. When black-led political parties replaced the oligarchic white minorities during the independence movement of the 1960s and 1970s, journalism—both print and broadcast—shifted its purpose to nation building.

Broadcast journalism's beginnings in the region are similar to that of print (though while broadcast media also began under colonial administration, slavery had been abolished by the time it developed). The earliest radio station, VIBAX, began operating in the Bahamas in 1930. Private citizens from the white mercantile class, colonial governments, or Rediffusion, introduced radio throughout the region. Because the colonies were so dependent on external centers to survive, broadcast radio went the way of newspapers, focusing mostly on the needs of the external metropolises rather than local populations. The goal of colonial broadcasting was to advance the values, standards, and beliefs of the British Empire, and the education and enlightenment of the rural areas of the region, particularly in the realm of public health and agriculture.[25] Broadcasting throughout the English-speaking Caribbean was guided by the public service ethos of the BBC, and early broadcasting in the colonies thus reflected the political, economic, and social policies of colonialism.

When radio broadcasting began in the 1930s, "it provided the citizens of the colonies with a faster means of disseminating information; it also ameliorated the fears and isolation of the people who lived in the rural communities: radio allowed them to learn more quickly about impending threats like hurricanes and tropical storms, and it informed them about other activities that were important to the economic and social wellbeing of their communities."[26] American communications scholar Harold Lasswell identified three additional functions of early broadcasting: surveillance of the environment (knowing what is going on), correlation of the parts of society in responding to its environment (having options or solutions for dealing with societal problems), and transmission of cultural heritage (socialization and education).[27] Charles Wright added a fourth function: entertainment.[28] These functions were encapsulated in the BBC's motto "to inform, educate and entertain."

In the early years of radio broadcasting, colonial stations—those owned both by the state and by Rediffusion—did not meet all the needs of these Caribbean societies.[29] Their primary focus was meeting the needs of the British Empire, namely the expansion of colonialism and the mercantile system. In the colonies this translated into news and information services that concentrated on public service. This condition changed when these state institutions "shifted their goals in the 1940s and 1950s to commercialization. Commercialization brought state broadcasting's sole dependence on the government for economic survival to an end. Decision-making powers were shared with advertisers who demanded that the stations attract larger audiences. These demands resulted in improvements in technology and quality of service and increases in staff."[30] However, state control of broadcasting remained.

The independence movement of the 1960s also influenced radio broadcasting in the Caribbean. In post-independent states, colonial radio stations were taken over by the newly elected national governments and henceforth became state-run entities; independence thus shifted the focus from external to internal. Yet while local programming increased, foreign content was still high. Also, Rediffusion continued to own private radio stations throughout the region until the 1990s, so external control of information continued. During the early days of independence, both print and broadcast journalism focused on nation building. This form of journalism was prominent throughout the region and is referred to by many scholars as development journalism. Later the term "communication for development" became the preferred term in the literature, and has since been used to describe media's role in development.

The term "development journalism" emerged at the Press Foundation of Asia in the 1960s. Asian journalists were concerned that foreign news organizations were covering socioeconomic developments in their countries in a superficial way; many journalists simply reported government press releases and quotes verbatim, rather than provide meaningful analysis to help citizens understand the impact or consequences of development projects. In the 1970s and 1980s, development journalism became very popular with African and Caribbean governments, who used it to foster national growth, and today it continues to focus on social conditions in developing states in an attempt to improve them; it identifies and examines socioeconomic problems such as poverty, researches its causes and consequences, and explains how to address it in developing countries. Despite its usefulness, development journalism lost its prominence in Caribbean states in the late 1980s, and was subsumed by commercial journalism.

One of the key goals of development journalism is to help government institutions implement positive socioeconomic change, especially in rural or remote areas of developing countries. Journalists are called upon to collaborate with government agencies to raise awareness of public projects through the stories they tell. Development journalists also propose changes and solutions. Their work therefore stands as a powerful advocate for positive change in the lives of millions of poor people. Clifford Christians, Theodore Glasser, Denis McQuail, Kaarle Nordenstreng, and Robert White describe this type of journalism in their description of the collaborative and facilitative roles of journalism.[31] Other scholars, like Michael Schudson and Silvio Waisbord, refer to this type of coverage as advocacy journalism.[32] In the facilitative role, Christians et al. explain, "the media is relied on by other institutions for certain services in areas such as politics, commerce, health, education, and welfare."[33] They believe "the media provide access for legitimate claimants to public attention and for paying clients. But they also make a virtue of the facilitative relationship, provided that it is voluntary and does not compromise their integrity, credibility, or independence."[34] In developed countries, collaborative journalism "supports the national interest, is patriotic, and respects authority."[35] In developing countries, collaborative journalism takes the form of development journalism and supports development goals: "The collaborative role specifies and values the tasks for media that arise in situations of unavoidable engagement with social events and processes."[36]

Michael Schudson links the history of advocacy journalism to the "partisan press" and "partisan journalism," which was popular in the US throughout the nineteenth century. Schudson discusses the vilification of advocacy journalism and its critics' strong belief that it taints the normative values of truth, objectivity, and balance. He identifies advocacy journalism as a tool for political mobilization, whereby the news media serves as an advocate for particular political programs and perspectives and mobilizes people to act in support of these programs. Despite the argument that equates partisan journalism with propaganda, Schudson believes that advocacy journalism or partisan journalism could be useful in democratic states: "if different partisan viewpoints are well represented among institutions of journalism, then a journalist-as-advocate model may serve the public interest very well. Partisan journalism enlists the heart as well as the mind of the audience. It gives readers and viewers not only information but also a cause."[37] In contrast to advocacy journalism, Schudson explains, "the objective, informative, and non-partisan investigative functions of today's leading news organizations may have de-mobilizing effects. They provide people with information, but they do not advise people what to do with it. If anything, they seem to imply that nothing can be done, that politicians are only interested in their own political careers."[38]

A second definition of development journalism aligns more closely with the collaborative role of journalists. Government and the press join together to spread important information throughout the country, especially crisis situations like terrorism, natural disasters, crime, health, and safety. Christians et al. point out that even without crises, "there is usually a latent or partial system of cooperation between the media and organs of government and the state that produces voluntary collaboration."[39] They acknowledge that this type of journalism "impinges on the independence of the press and other media"[40] but is legitimate and absolutely necessary. Governments need the media to help them educate and inform citizens and also to enlist their cooperation on major development projects. The danger to journalism comes when government uses "development" to restrict freedom of speech and journalists are told not to report on certain issues because it will impact the "development" or "security" of the nation. This limits the journalist's role in democratic states of providing citizens with the truth, and it impedes effective decision-making.

As a result of mid-twentieth-century political changes in Caribbean states, "broadcasting became a significant medium for transmitting culture, mediating politics and economics, selling products and services, and extending communication capabilities throughout the region and beyond. After independence, merchants and politicians paid more attention to radio's ability to reach a large audience simultaneously with the same message. Listeners, and later viewers, became more interested as the quantity and quality of programs increased after 1950."[41] Although Caribbean radio programs still had a lot of foreign content, particularly from Britain and the United States, there was a significant increase in local input. "Music programs became more entertaining; radio personalities became more endearing; and news programs were more informative and interesting. Government agencies and departments began to use radio and television to disseminate information to the public, particularly on education and public health."[42] As radio broadcasting, and later television, developed, it "cut across physical, economic, and social barriers to provide a variety of common cultural experiences."[43]

Internal and external forces also facilitated these changes. While European colonization gave broadcasting its structure and function, "American technology, and British and Canadian training and programming, changed its format and content; Caribbean and Commonwealth cooperatives gave it a regional focus; and nation building brought social, economic, political, and cultural changes to Caribbean societies and an indigenous focus to broadcasting."[44]

Caribbean media markets have evolved through two additional periods since the 1970s—the period of liberalization, deregulation, and privatization, which started in the mid-1980s, and the period of new digital technologies, which began in the mid-1990s. The region is still reacting to the changes brought on by both periods, which include intense commercial competition and increased digital communication. These changes will be discussed in more detail throughout the remainder of this book, but it is important to note that they have had a profound influence on the profession and practice of journalism throughout the region.

The Purpose of Journalism

The function of the press in modern societies rests on our understanding of the relationships between media, culture, and society. Many scholars have developed theories to explain these relationships. The most famous emerged from the various committees to establish and govern the BBC, which created the public service ethos that formed the basis of Caribbean colonial broadcasting, as well as the American Hutchins Commission report, which established the requirements for a free and responsible press.[45] Other significant contributions came from Fred Siebert, Theodore Peterson, and Wilbur Schramm's *Four Theories of the Press*, which identified media's role in four political systems—authoritarian, libertarian, social responsibility, and communism[46]—and theories of development—democratic-participant, postcolonial, media economics, and elite power groups. While these normative theories try to explain media's role or function in postmodern societies, they fall short to the extent that they rely on how things should be rather than how things actually are. Although debunked by scholars such as John Merrill and Ralph Lowenstein, in their article "Media, Messages and Men: New Perspectives in Communication," and Jennifer Ostini and Anthony Fung, in their article "Beyond the Four Theories of the Press: A New Model of National Media Systems,"[47] *Four Theories of the Press* is still highly regarded in journalism and communication schools in the United States and beyond. However, it has been criticized for its idealism, lack of empiricism, obsoleteness, and inapplicability to contemporary societies. International media scholars Ostini, Fung, Merrill, Lowenstein, John Keane, and others, have argued for more grounded theories that reflect the current variations in media systems, cultures, and societies. Ostini and Fung believe that "although journalism is contextualized and constrained by press structure and state policies, it is also a relatively autonomous cultural production of journalists negotiating between their professionalism and state control."[48] They propose a new model incorporating the autonomy of individual journalistic practices into political and social structural factors to reflect current global press practices more accurately. This is the perspective that I embrace in this work. But instead of using the conservative and liberal categorization of Ostini and Fung, I propose a more open model that incorporates the theory of hybridity, a mixing of various global perspectives with local and regional realities to explain the function and purpose of journalism in small Caribbean states.

My proposed model also builds on the earlier models of Caribbean media scholars such as Stuart Surlin and Walter Soderlund, Aggrey Brown, Ewart Skinner, Mark Alleyne, Erwin Thomas, John Lent, and Omar Oliveria. In Surlin and Soderlund's 1990 edited volume on mass media in the Caribbean, five major characteristics of Caribbean media are identified: government-press relations, mass media ownership, media imperialism, growth of mass media industries, and journalism education.[49] Building on Picard's 1983 elaboration of *Four Theories of the Press*, Surlin and Soderlund identified these systems as either "authoritarian-tending" or "liberal-tending."[50] Authoritarian-tending systems are those "which exert direct or indirect government pressure to 'restrict' the reporting of news (authoritarian), or conscious government use of the media to portray a particular social and political reality (communist systems)."[51] Liberal-tending systems are those with "minimum government interference regarding the information the press disseminates, the operative principle being that truth will win out in the free marketplace of ideas."[52] The cultural domination theses, particularly the one proposed by Humphrey Regis that encompasses the key framework of domination by importation/exportation with the addition of reexportation, are also included in this proposition for an open theoretical framework.[53] The reexportation framework complements theories of hybridity and is important for understanding current practices. Also, particularly salient for modern Caribbean societies are the theories of Bill Kovach and Tom Rosenstiel, as well as Christians et al., on the role and responsibilities of journalism in the twenty-first century.

The dictates of the marketplace are contravening the general consensus that journalism should serve the needs of the people of the Caribbean by providing citizens with the information they need to be participants in their own governance and make informed decisions that affect their daily lives. Kovach and Rosenstiel articulate this position in their book *The Elements of Journalism*. They see journalism as "storytelling with a purpose. That purpose is to provide people with information they need to understand the world. The first challenge is finding the information that people need to live their lives. The second is to make it meaningful, relevant, and engaging."[54]

In the introduction to the book *What is Good Journalism? How Reporters and Editors Are Saving America's Way of Life*, editors George Kennedy and Daryl Moen examine the value of journalism.[55] Kennedy and Moen believe that

> Journalism tells us most of what we know about the world beyond our own experience, and that it goes where its audience cannot or will not follow. Journalism keeps daily watch on the actions of government and the other powerful institutions of society. Journalism exposes wrongdoing and injustice. Journalism explains in everyday language the findings of science and the arguments of philosophy. Journalism pulls together and organizes obscure but important facts to create useful knowledge. Journalism tells stories of heartbreak and heroism, of triumph and disaster, of the endless fascinations in ordinary life. Journalism is the glue of information that holds a complex nation together.[56]

The American Project for Excellence in Journalism argues that the central purpose of journalism "is to provide citizens with accurate and reliable information they need to function in a free society."[57] American journalists who contributed to the project believed this definition encompassed "myriad roles, such as helping define community; creating common language and common knowledge; identifying a community's goals, heroes, and villains; and pushing people beyond complacency."[58] There are other requirements, too, "such as being entertaining, serving as a watchdog, and offering a voice to the voiceless."[59] To accomplish this task, American journalists identified nine core principles: obligation to truth, loyalty to citizens, discipline of verification, independence from those they cover, the independent monitoring of power, a forum for public criticism and compromise, making the news interesting and relevant, keeping the news comprehensive and proportionate, and the exercise of personal conscience. In the second edition of *The Elements of Journalism*, Kovach and Rosenstiel added: "the rights and responsibilities of citizens."[60] This last principle is particularly important in a digital environment where citizens can also gather and disseminate information.

Caribbean journalists have also articulated similar versions of the purpose of journalism in their societies. Bahamian journalist Tosheena Robinson Blair believes "the purpose of journalism is to educate, to inform, to keep our people abreast on what is happening in society, why it is important to them, why they need to know this, and why they should care."[61] Veteran Bahamian journalist Nicki Kelly also explained that "journalism has a very big responsibility ... to inform people, to investigate, to expose wrongdoing, and to initiate positive changes."[62] Karen Herig, editor of the *Nassau Tribune*, holds similar views about journalism's role in keeping "people informed about things that they have the right to be informed about, holding people and a government accountable, warning people if there is crime."[63]

In its 2010 code of ethics, the Press Association of Jamaica noted that all members of the press have a duty to maintain the following professional and ethical standards:

> 1) The rights of freedom of expression and the freedom to receive and impart information are fundamental rights of all human beings. 2) The agencies of mass communication, private and public, are carriers of public information, opinion and discussion essential to give practical effect to the right of freedom of

expression and right of all individuals to access information. 3) Those rights carry obligations that require media organizations to represent and reflect the public interest at all times and journalists to perform their professional duties with intelligence, objectivity, accuracy, and fairness.[64]

Barbadian journalists uphold similar values. As Eric Smith has explained, "We have a commitment to the people who don't have a voice … we have a commitment to try and seek out truth and justice and even where people wield a lot of power in advertising or they may wield a lot [of power] in politics or the legal system we still have a duty despite the legal hurdles that we may encounter to ensure that there is always right and justice and fair play."[65] Journalist and radio talk show host David Ellis said he would like to see "more individuals within the profession who see themselves and the role that they play as being absolutely vital to society."[66] One of the owners of the *Barbados Nation*, Harold Hoyte, believes the role of the journalist is to "ensure that the less fortunate in the society are protected, that the leaders in society are kept honest at all times."[67]

In Trinidad and Tobago the sentiments are similar. As Omatie Lyder, editor of the *Trinidad Express*, explained, "The ultimate reward for me is when people get useful information from my stories that they can use to make important decisions in their lives."[68] A young Trinbagonian journalist, Peter Christopher, believes journalism is not just a profession but a duty. He identifies the current practice of journalism in the Caribbean as weak and lacking quality because many young reporters treat it as merely a nine-to-five job. He thinks journalists need to think seriously about what they do and how it impacts society. "I don't consider journalism [as] just a profession because in a way … it's almost like … it's a duty that you have to the public because you have to get the facts out. You are basically the voice of the people in a way." He believed "you have to get the information they need. It's not just about writers or just to say hey Peter wrote the story that's in the newspaper. It's about how this affects the people, what does this mean to the public. It's a vocation, that's what I believe journalism is."[69]

Another aspect of the journalist's role in Trinidad and Tobago, Christopher added, is to

> highlight an issue, be it [a] public issue or public figure, an event that happened, and relay the facts, the information and implications to the public. That is the role of a journalist to me. I'd say very few [of us] are [doing this]; many of them would just cover the event and say this happened. They wouldn't go into why this happened or what will happen if this happens and the few that do, they sensationalize what happen[ed] and try to swing an angle that would cause controversy.[70]

In 2012, Belizean journalist and professor Holly Edgell posted an article on her blog entitled "Journalism in Belize: It's time to temper guts and gore with balance and context."[71] Edgell's comments came amidst a growing concern for the sensational nature of crime coverage in Belize and the region as a whole. "I believe Belizean journalists should temper their coverage," she argued, since "balanced storytelling that respects privacy and allows members of the public to retain their dignity in times of crisis can still be compelling."[72]

Based on these comments, one could conclude that Caribbean journalists hold similar views to those of their American and European counterparts on the central purpose and value of journalism. How well Caribbean journalists apply these fundamental principles in the current milieu of technological innovation and market-led reform will be examined later in this book.

The English-speaking Caribbean is experiencing a period of rapid change in broadcast and print journalism. While there are some parallels with changes experienced around the world, there are also areas of divergence. In the midst of the shift to commercialism, Caribbean journalism is flourishing economically as the overall circulation of tabloids, broadsheets, and specialized magazines multiplies and the number of news formats (free dailies, broadcasting time, online news portals) increases. From Jamaica—the largest independent English-speaking country in the region, with a population of 2.8 million and geographic space of 4,111 square miles, five terrestrial television stations, twenty-two radio stations, fifty-two cable television stations, and four newspapers—to St. Kitts and Nevis—the smallest independent English-speaking country, with a population of 41,000 on a landmass of 133 square miles, and three terrestrial television stations, twelve radio stations, two cable television stations, and three newspapers—these micro states have created oversaturated media markets. And these figures do not even include the availability of foreign media channels through satellite, internet technologies, and spillover signals.

Despite the increase in media channels and the attendant rise in profits, the homogenization of journalism, the rise of sensationalism and more entertainment-oriented reporting, as well as the blurring of boundaries between news and advertising, has resulted in a backlash against journalism. Much of this backlash presents itself in the form of public criticism and challenges to the profession. Robert Picard, a British professor of media economics, argued in a 2009 lecture at the Reuters Institute for the Study of Journalism at Oxford that in the current dispensation, journalists in Britain deserve low pay because they were not creating much value. Professor Picard explained the instrumental value of journalism—things that facilitate action and achievement including awareness, belonging, and understanding—has been usurped by contemporary communication developments whereby any ordinary person can observe and report the news, gather expert knowledge, determine significance, and publish this information using a variety of audiovisual aids. Further, most of the people doing these activities are doing them without pay. Accordingly, Picard believed journalists must redefine the value of their labor beyond this level. This lecture was reprinted in the 7 June 2009 *Jamaica Sunday Observer*. According to Byron Buckley, president of the Press Association of Jamaica, members of the association were upset with Professor Picard's statements.

For Caribbean journalism to survive and advance, practitioners need to center journalism so that it emerges as a more effective pillar of their democratic societies. Three significant areas that could be improved are comprehensiveness, relevance and engagement, and independence. And, as Professor Holly Edgell of Belize has argued, journalism in the Caribbean should focus on the three *Rs*: reality, responsibility and restraint.[73]

Comprehensiveness and Proportionality

In *The Elements of Journalism*, Kovach and Rosenstiel argue that one of the main principles of journalism should be comprehensive and proportionate news coverage. This principle rests on the notion that journalists should pay more attention to what stories to cover in their communities. Christians et al. argue that this principle is even more important in the current age of internet and wireless technologies.[74] According to Kovach and Rosenstiel, journalism is our "modern cartography; it helps citizens to navigate society: that is its utility and its economic reason for being."[75] Based on this responsibility, Kovach and Rosenstiel believe journalism's value depends on its completeness and proportionality.

The absence of both is one of the great areas of weakness in Caribbean journalism. The ideal of more complete and balanced news coverage comes from American, Caribbean, and European media scholars, but it is best articulated by Kovach and Rosenstentiel, who believe this is one of the core principles that journalists should practice in the twenty-first century. As citizens, they note, we should ask the following questions: "can we see the whole community in the coverage? Do I see myself? Does the report include a fair mix of what most people would consider either interesting or significant?"[76] These questions are particularly important in the Caribbean context as these microstates encompass multicultural societies; in such an environment, issues of media diversity and media literacy are becoming more prevalent. This principle will be examined in more detail in the second part of this book.

Relevance and Engagement

Another principle that is equally important to the practice of journalism in the Caribbean is the principle of relevance and engagement. Kovach and Rosenstiel's seventh principle of journalism requires journalists to make the significant interesting and relevant.[77] They note that much of the debate on engagement and relevance is positioned in relation to one or the other—engagement versus relevance. But this is a false dichotomy; news should be relevant *and* engaging, particularly in an oversaturated information age. Kovach and Rosenstiel ask: "Should we emphasize news that is fun and fascinating, and plays on our sensations? Or should we stick to the news that is the most important? Should journalists give people what they need or what they want?"[78] They claim that understanding these two as either/or, storytelling or information, need versus want, distorts the overall purpose of good journalism. Most people want storytelling *and* information, facts *and* fascination, entertainment *and* information. The "journalist's task is to find the way to make the significant interesting in each story and finding the right mix of the serious and the less serious that offers an account of the day."[79] This position moves journalism towards the middle of the continuum between storytelling and information. Seen through Kovach and Rosenstiel's argument, "journalism is storytelling with a purpose." They believe "that purpose is to provide people with information they need to understand the world ... [to find] the information that people need to live their lives ... [and] to make it meaningful, relevant, and engaging."[80] An interesting question to ask in contemporary journalism, both globally and in the Caribbean, is, "If journalism can be both significant and engaging, if people do not basically want it one way or the other, why does the news so often fall short?"[81] Within the Caribbean context there are numerous problems that stand in the way of news being presented engagingly and relevantly, including "haste, ignorance, laziness, formula, bias, cultural blinders."[82] Each of these issues contributes to the current "if it bleeds it leads" focus of journalism, and they will be explored in the Caribbean context later in this book.

Independence

Kovach and Rosenstiel's perspective on the principle of independence starts with the question: What makes something journalism? The answer, they argue, goes beyond the elements of truthfulness, commitment or loyalty to the facts, and extends to citizens playing the watchdog role, verification, and providing a public forum. They believe that while journalists must maintain a "fidelity to accuracy and facts," they must also remain independent from those they cover. This principle applies to hard news, soft news, commentary, opinion, or criticism. "It is this independence of spirit and mind, rather than neutrality, that journalists must keep in focus."[83] This is responsible journalism.

The central issue for journalists is determining to whom or what they owe their allegiance. Does their loyalty lie "with friends, colleagues, their political ideology or party, with the news medium or organization for whom they work, with cold facts or with the truth?"[84] In giving citizens the information they need to understand their world and make important life decisions, journalists must understand this important principle and decide where their loyalty should lie in a given situation. Yet ultimately, journalists, no matter what type of journalism is practiced, owe their loyalty to accuracy and hard facts.

Achieving journalistic independence is complicated in small places like the Caribbean, but it is an important part of advancing the public interest and providing citizens with the information they need to be free in a democratic society. In the Caribbean, this principle is closely related to journalism's mandate to be an independent monitor of power and a voice for the voiceless. These principles are often captured by the act of "investigative reporting," but there is a lack of this in the small countries of the Caribbean.

American and British journalism has a tradition—although not always evident or implemented when most needed, such as during times of war—of pursuing and exposing corruption that has been largely absent from Caribbean journalism. Perhaps the most famous example is the Watergate scandal of the 1970s, which was reported by American journalists Carl Bernstein and Bob Woodward in the *Washington Post*. This coverage culminated in the resignation of President Richard Nixon. Similarly, the 2012 phone hacking scandal in London, reported by British journalist Nick Davies in the *Guardian*, caused the demise of Rupert Murdoch's newspaper, *News of the World*. According to Kovach and Rosenstiel, after the Watergate story, investigative reporting in the United States gained "celebrity status and sex appeal and redefined the image of journalism."[85] The effect was seen everywhere from the *New York Times* to CBS, with its creation of the television program *60 Minutes*, to the creation of local investigative teams, or "I-Teams." The independence required of the press to perform its monitorial role is not new: it predates the Watergate scandal. In the United States, investigative journalism has its "roots in the earliest notions of the meaning of a free press,"[86] as well as the First Amendment. For the British, a free press can be traced to the early days of reporting with the founding of the press and the movement for reconstruction later borne out in the advocacy of John Milton, Thomas Hobbes, John Locke, John Stuart Mills, and other philosophers who agitated for liberty and equality. This history was transferred to the English-speaking Caribbean through colonization.

It is difficult, and at times impossible, to follow the American or British (or for that matter Canadian, Australian, or any other) tradition of investigative reporting in the Caribbean. Therefore, it is important for the region to develop its own style of investigative reporting. In the following chapters, I will discuss the reasons for the lack of investigative reporting in the English-speaking Caribbean and the challenges of implementing the principle of independence. I will also recommend a hybrid style of investigative journalism that may be more conducive to the Caribbean context.

These principles—comprehensiveness and proportionality, relevance and engagement, and independence—should become the core of the practice of journalism in the Caribbean. Using these principles, journalists might advance the role of their profession in the region.

Practicing Journalism in Small Places: National and Regional Implications

The literature on the effects of a country's size on its economic and political performance indicates that size matters in some areas but not in others.[1] For example, economic theorists argue that a larger population is more effective for economies of scale, while political philosophers believe that a smaller population is more conducive to democratic governance. In their book *The Size of Nations* Alberto Alesina and Enrico Spolaore identify five benefits of large population size: lower per-capita costs of public goods (monetary and financial institutions, judicial system, communication infrastructure, crime prevention, and public health, etc.) and more efficient tax systems; cheaper per-capita defense and military costs; greater productivity due to specialization; greater ability to provide regional insurance; and greater ability to redistribute income within the country.[2] Economic and social theorists at the World Bank and United Nations regard small states as economically disadvantaged or handicapped because of size. Plato, Aristotle, Rousseau and other philosophers posit that smaller countries have more effective democracies as citizens know each other, and therefore are more likely to support and protect each other. Governance in such countries is more likely to be effective because the impact of policies and programs are more visible in smaller populations and can thereby be more easily adjusted to affect greater benefits.[3] These benefits are also often equated with strong national identity, strong interpersonal relations, and greater transparency.

The arguments for the advantages and disadvantages of small states continue to shadow the economic, political, and social development of these countries. There are successful stand-alone models, like Iceland and Singapore, but the majority of small nations are hampered by limitations of size. One of the many challenges of small nations is the overreliance on the model of large nations to solve their problems. Small nations should reduce this dependency and develop more endogenous models that fit their complex ecosystems and distinctive characteristics. While the Caribbean is a region of small states, and thus shares many of the characteristics of other small states, it also has distinct characteristics.

Vulnerabilities of Caribbean Small States[4]

Small markets like the English-speaking Caribbean, as Jamaica Kincaid elucidates in her essay *A Small Place*,[5] have had a difficult time providing accurate and comprehensive accounts of their societies. While many read Kincaid's description of her place of birth, the island nation of Antigua, as an angry indictment against colonization, government corruption, postcolonial societies, and tourism, she successfully illuminates many of the sociological and psychological postcolonial issues and conditions of many of the Caribbean island nations. Kincaid's book is an important text on postcolonial theory. One of its major themes—expressed at the beginning of chapter one of this book—is the enduring trait of ambivalence common throughout the region. This is expressed in the internalization and resistance of cultural dominance, described throughout postcolonial theory as "the colonizing culture," and economic dependency. Kincaid's description of ambivalence supports Bhabha's theory of a hybrid third space—a space that requires Caribbean people to "cut 'n' mix," that is, to bring together all of the components of the various cultural influences found in these spaces to create a new model that incorporates multiple perspectives. Such a model, which helps Caribbean people to relocate their identity, is based on Bahktin's idea of heteroglossia.[6]

The small states of the English-speaking Caribbean were forged by a history of extermination, piracy, colonization, slavery, indentureship, geography, and state control models of economic, social, and political development. This historical trajectory has also been influenced by various internal and external influences, many of which—globalization for example—continue to complicate the region's development. These inherited characteristics permeate all levels of Caribbean society; it is therefore not surprising to find them in the present-day practice of journalism and the coverage of everyday life.

"Antigua is a small place. Antigua is a very small place. In Antigua, not only is the event turned into everyday, but the everyday is turned into an event."[7] Here Kincaid explains how the people of Antigua live trapped between the domination of their colonial past and the domination of American consumer culture. She believes Antiguans, and Caribbean people as a whole, have a distorted perspective of their lives: "small things loom large, and major events are reduced to an 'ordinary' occurrence."[8] Kincaid repeatedly asserts the phrase "a small place" throughout her book to emphasize the physical, psychological, and sociological constraints that overwhelm the people who live in Antigua. It is a colonized society that cannot, nor wants to, escape its colonial history, and ultimately, according to Kincaid, lives with and struggles with its ambivalent existence. For Kincaid, Antigua, like other Caribbean countries, becomes the ultimate "small place" as it struggles to define itself against the larger places of the world. It is from this context that questions arise concerning the role of journalism in sustaining and advancing democracy in small postcolonial Caribbean societies. How can journalism play a central role in advancing liberty and equality in Caribbean democratic societies when it remains trapped by the constraints of small states? How can journalism become relevant, comprehensive, and independent when it remains confined by the ambivalent nature of the region? How can journalism function to advance democracy in these microstates when commercialism and new technologies are challenging the relevance and significance of journalism throughout the region?

The vulnerabilities of small states theses, as advanced by Lino Briguglio,[9] Lino Briguglio and Eliawony Kisanga,[10] and Manuel Puppis[11] reveal the constraints in the development of Caribbean media, particularly broadcasting. Whereas smallness, based on population size, as Manuel Puppis argues, is an absolutist approach to defining small states, as state size interacts with other variables, population size is still a useful measurement for characterizing media systems, but its effects are complex.[12] Smallness is not the only factor in the development of these countries and their media systems, but it remains one of the forces that drive the dependent relationships that continue to characterize the development of Caribbean states. Other factors include geographic dispersion, vulnerability to natural disasters, fragility of ecosystems, isolation from external markets and the limits of internal ones, migration of highly skilled citizens, limited commodities and dependence on imports, and limited abilities to reap the benefits of economies of scale.[13]

These societies have been trapped by the circumstances of smallness. Kincaid maintains that Caribbean people have learned the ways of their masters very well and those elected to govern repeat the exploitations of their past slave masters by visiting those exploitations upon their own citizens. Why? The answer, according to Kincaid and other postcolonial theorists, lies in the fact that they have had no other model to follow, and they are hard-pressed to create their own. They assimilated the ways of their former colonizers and it is this "model" that continues to constrain the daily lives of Caribbean people, and leads to continued issues of corruption and abuse of power, clientelism, dependency, and cultural dominance—first by the old colonizers, and now by the new colonizers, the United States of America and China. The people's seemingly passive acceptance of these issues angers Kincaid. Although there are those who disagree with her premise by pointing to exceptional aggressors such as Cuba, Jamaica, and Haiti, collectively, the region has exhibited more passive inclinations. Caribbean peoples' passivity, though propagated in the malaise of colonization, is symbolic of their passive participation in effective governance in democratic societies. Although these states are lauded as highly participatory, as evidenced by free elections, open political debate, religious tolerance, constitutional government, and free press, citizens abdicate their responsibilities once the electoral die has been cast. Their homophobic and xenophobic inclinations also call into question their ability to advance the ideals of liberty and equality for all.

But Caribbean citizens are not alone in this critique of passivity. Contemporary democratic theorists, such as Benjamin Page, Robert Dahl, and Jürgen Habermas,[14] provide comprehensive explanations for public apathy and lack of participation and question the effectiveness of modern democracy, particularly in the United States and Europe, in providing the major tenets it aims to deliver: liberty and equality for all citizens. Kincaid's anger is also symptomatic of other scholars and theorists throughout human history who have questioned the power of ideologies to dominate and control the masses (see Marx, Althusser, Hall, Foucault, Gramsci, and Freire et al.).[15] The spread of democracy after the Second World War, as well as the recent movement for democratic rule known as the Arab Spring, continues the debate on the actual fulfillment of the ideals of democracy and the role of journalism in sustaining and advancing democratic ideals (see Barber, Hayek, and Schumpeter).[16] One of the symbols of democratic societies is a free and independent press that holds elites accountable. However, according to Robert Dahl, Jürgen Habermas, John Keane, and Benjamin Barber,[17] the model of democracy that emerged after the Second World War, and journalism's role in safeguarding it, have not lived up to the ideals of liberty and equality as outlined in constitutions throughout the democratic world. One of the reasons for the failures of journalism is the overreliance on commercialism or market-driven ideals and the rise of consumer culture. Media scholars Aukse Balčytienė and Halliki Harro-Loit, Ben Bagdikian, James Carey, Robert McChesney and Jon Nichols, Herbert Schiller, and Michael Schudson,[18] have lamented the demise of effective journalism in the face of growing media conglomerates and commercialization. In his work *Journalism and Democracy Across Borders*, John Keane warned of the dangers of communication poverty and market censorship that result from market-driven forms of media.[19] Keane makes the case for strengthening global journalism, the global public sphere, and global civil society to function as vital checks and balances on powerful institutions—whether for-profit, nonprofit, or governmental. He labels this new form of global monitoring power "cosmocracy": "a global civil society that monitors the globalization process through journalism and makes power publicly accountable."[20] The issue of growing media conglomerates and the rise of commercialization is becoming a prevalent issue in the Caribbean. However, at the time of publication none of the governments of the region were addressing this issue. Mark Alleyne discussed this in 1990 in his review of media in Barbados, concluding that there was a need to create comprehensive public policy to address this issue.

The vulnerabilities of small states theses are also prevalent in the work of Caribbean scholars such as Norman Girvan, an economist and staunch advocate of regional integration, and Mark Alleyne, a media scholar and former journalist. Alleyne isolated smallness as a continual influence in the structure and control of media, the liberal democratic standards of media, legal environment, media policy, professional standards and media ownership.[21] In the twenty-first century, Girvan believes, the small states of the Caribbean remain encumbered by size-related macroeconomic vulnerabilities, lack of economies of scale, natural disasters, and capacity constraints. One of the region's most defining features, and its greatest limitation, is the archipelago of islands, which are scattered over a wide area, encouraging isolationist tendencies. Girvan outlines other challenges, such as the distinctions between English-speaking and non-English-speaking nations, CARICOM (Caribbean Community) members and non-CARICOM members, larger and smaller island states as well as those on the mainland, and independent and dependent states.[22] These distinctions are part of the region's uniqueness.

Other Caribbean scholars, like Keith Nurse, recognize the challenges facing small states but express more optimism about future opportunities in the creative industries. Since the beginning of the 2000s, one of the areas gaining more attention for economic diversification is the creative or cultural industries. However, as Nurse points out, these industries "are not seriously regarded as an economic sector, the key stakeholders are poorly organized, and its economic value remains largely undocumented."[23] Journalism and communications are recognized as key components of the cultural industries. However, these industries remain scattered, hit-and-miss attempts due to poor infrastructure and lack of policies, regulations, legislation, and economic support.

Practicing Journalism in Small States[24]

How do small state theses apply to the field of journalism and communication? Henrik Örnebring and Epp Lauk, in their recent work "Does size matter? Journalistic values and working conditions in small countries,"[25] conclude population size is less of a factor in explaining value orientation differences among journalists in small, medium, and large countries, but found indicators that size does matter in other areas, like the basic working conditions of journalists as related to job market size and the skills valued by journalists. Örnebring and Lauk also found some support for the notion that social control and consensus are greater in small nations. They acknowledge the size of the market, as well as the number of practicing journalists, could affect levels of cultural and social organization in journalism.[26]

This research is helpful in identifying some of the challenges and complexities of practicing journalism in small markets. However, Örnebring and Lauk focus on small European states with populations of one million or more; they do not provide a structured or detailed analysis of the practice of journalism in places like the Caribbean, where national populations can be as little as fifty thousand, and where a long history of colonization and external dependency prevail.

The challenges of practicing journalism and operating media organizations in small markets are made more complex by the globalization of these markets. Caribbean countries represented here range in population size from Jamaica, with 2.8 million—the largest population in the English-speaking Caribbean—to Grenada, with 104,890. Barbados has a population of 286,705, Belize 321,115, the Bahamas 377,374, and Trinidad and Tobago 1.4 million. In the six countries discussed in this book, the number of journalists working in print (newspapers and magazines), radio and television broadcasting and online (though not playing a significant role at the time of this research, this field is expected to grow) and freelance journalists working in the English-speaking Caribbean does not exceed a few hundred in even the largest countries, and in many cases is as low as fifty. These are estimates, as there is no official registration of journalists in these countries. All of the countries represented in this book have some form of press association but not all practitioners are members, and not all associations are active or effective. The Press Association of Jamaica, founded in 1943, is the oldest, largest, and most active press association in the region. Grenada's Media Workers Association, founded in 1981, is the second-most active association. The Barbados Association of Journalists was relaunched in 2009. The Belize Press Association started in 1995, but at the time of this research it was defunct. With the help of the author, the Bahamas reestablished a press association near the end of 2012 (it was replaced by the "Bahamas Press Club" in 2014), and Trinidad and Tobago's press association was in the early stages of revival in 2009; it had been defunct for several years.

The journalists in these countries, regardless of their numbers, uphold certain values. Although there are some variations in value orientations, Caribbean journalists' values are similar to their global counterparts. No matter the size of the population, journalists value truth, accuracy, balance, fairness, loyalty to citizens, the monitoring of the powerful, providing a voice for the voiceless, independence, and providing a public forum for critical discussion of important issues.

Manuel Puppis argues the economic realities in small states have significant implications for their media systems. Currently, these economic realities present themselves as challenges in the form of global and local market competition, funding of state broadcasting systems, audience appeal, audience fragmentation and segmentation, and advances in telecommunication and audio-visual technology.[27] Perhaps the greatest challenge in the current media landscape is the power of external actors to force changes in policymaking, market structure, and local media culture. According to media scholars, four structural peculiarities of small states, as identified by Werner Meier and Josef Trappel,[28] Peter Humphreys,[29] and Gabriele Siegert[30] (and summarized by Manuel Puppis in his article "Media Regulations in Small States"[31]) have influenced small media systems. These four peculiarities include shortage of resources, small audience market and advertising markets, dependence, and vulnerability.

Örnebring and Lauk posit each of these peculiarities influences the way journalists do their everyday work in small countries as well as their general value orientation. They believe it is not unreasonable to assume a small occupational collective will have different sociocultural characteristics compared to a larger one. "A small job market generally means fewer employers, fewer senior positions, and fewer alternatives in terms of career routes and career progression. And, as in any small social group, social control is likely to be greater: there may be formal and informal pressures and incentives for homogeneity within the group, and an emphasis on collaboration and consensus."[32] The practitioners in each of the six countries in this book would likely concur with these findings. These countries have small job markets with a fixed number of employers and senior positions. Thus, career routes and progression are limited. This leads to high turnovers, with average career spans of three to five years. Journalists described these markets as "merry-go-rounds" where journalists, taking advantage of the increased number of media houses, move from one employer to another to obtain better salaries or positions. There is also frequent movement from journalism to public relations. In the 1980s and 1990s a large number of seasoned journalists left the profession for public relations positions, to work as communication specialists in other business sectors, or to pursue other career opportunities altogether. This left these markets with a decrease in the number of senior journalists, which has led in turn to a number of challenges: the hiring of young, inexperienced journalists, increased criticism of the practice, defunct professional associations, and a decline in training and mentoring.

Small Caribbean states are constrained by shortage of resources, which creates limitations in production, especially audiovisual, based on unit costs. As Norman Girvan and Manuel Puppis explain,[33] "shortage of resources occurs not only with respect to capital, but also with respect to know-how and creativity."[34] Shortage of resources "impedes the successful establishment of a domestic audiovisual industry"[35] in most of these small states. In Surlin and Soderlund's *Mass Media and the Caribbean*, media scholars identified similar limitations. Sales are limited within these small markets by audience size and constricted advertising markets. Also, Puppis points out that "while production costs are essentially the same in small and big media markets, audience markets in small states are too small to realize economies of scale."[36] Consequently, small states have very costly media production and the small size of the audience sets limits on advertising revenues.[37]

These endogenous constraints, along with new technologies, have caused many in the region to rethink their markets and seek exogenous means to expand economic growth. However, Jean-Claude Burgelman and Caroline Pauwels believe this deficit cannot be offset by export, as "media productions from small countries are too culturally specific."[38] This economic reality provides some explanation for the limited local production throughout the region. Since the 1980s, Caribbean media scholars such as Aggrey Brown, Hopeton Dunn, Lynette Lashley, and myself, have lamented the economic, political, and social factors that have given rise to the lack of a vibrant local production culture throughout the region.[39] These factors include cost of production, lack of production skills, limited markets, lack of government incentives or initiatives, availability of low cost of foreign productions, and the development of audience taste for foreign production quality. In some of these countries local production is as low as 5 percent, if it exists at all; in others it is 25–30 percent. There may be some changes in local production on the horizon, as Keith Nurse points out, with regional governments renewing their interest in the cultural industries.

Also, the strength of Burgelman and Pauwels's argument is being tested through the use of new communication technologies, which are lowering production costs and providing alternative distribution channels. So, although this limitation in audiovisual production is still prevalent throughout the region, new technologies are providing professionals and ordinary citizens with the opportunity to create and disseminate audiovisual material online. There is renewed interest in local production and this may result in an increase in audiovisual production. Much of this new activity has emerged because of advances in technology, and it will take some time to create a profitable cultural industry. There is more audiovisual content on YouTube and other internet portals, but so far this has not translated into a successful production industry. Despite Nurse's optimism and the Caribbean Institute of Media and Communication's (CARIMAC) new programs, the cost of production may have shifted as more people gain access to technologies, but the control of the distribution in the global market remains with external multinational corporations like Sony, Disney, and Universal. Further, it will take some time to develop a demand for culturally specific audiovisual production from the region. Unlike the growing markets for Mexican telenovelas, Japanese anime, or Asian dramas and soap operas now available at Viki.com and Hulu.com, the Caribbean, in spite of the increase in audiovisual output in countries like Jamaica, Barbados, and Trinidad and Tobago, has yet to develop sufficient audiovisual content for a global market. African countries, led by Nollywood, are developing audiovisual content; India has Bollywood. But the Caribbean hopes to develop a successful industry over time as a cultural foundation has been created through reggae, calypso, carnival, and Caribbean food. Over the next five to ten years, Hopeton Dunn anticipates the emergence of a "Jollywood."

Despite the optimism for the development of the cultural industries, one of the prevailing factors that continue to affect all levels of Caribbean society is dependency. Success in the cultural industries will depend on the region's ability to contain external dependency and create demand for indigenous products.

Caribbean Media and Dependency[40]

The dependency thesis emerged in the region in the wake of the colonial period, and it is useful as a framework for understanding political, economic, and social development in the region after independence. The dependency debates were prominent for about two and a half decades, from the 1960s to the early 1980s. They were replaced in the mid-1980s with neoliberal ideas of development, particularly deregulation, liberalization, and privatization. Since the 2000s, theories of globalization have dominated the literature. One of those theories, hybridity, is used as the framework for this book. The dependency thesis is also experiencing a rebirth throughout the region in the wake of disappointments with neoliberalism. "A core component of the dependency thesis is the understanding of the issues of asymmetrical power relations, the core issues of which are economic, epistemic, sociological, psychological, technological, political, functional, and regional considerations."[41]

Since media shares a reciprocal relationship with society, the core issues of the dependency school of thought are also reflected in media systems throughout the region. In the second half of the twentieth century, media systems scholars examined dependency from the perspective of the relationships among media, audiences, and the larger social system in which they operate.[42] Thus, the media dependency thesis emerged simultaneously with the major discourse on economic dependency after the Second World War, culminating in a field of study that examined the global flow of news and information and the resultant dependency. The discourse of the global imbalance in the flow of news and information posits similar arguments as the dominant literature on dependency and was purposefully advanced after independence. The core issues of these debates were cultural imperialism, cultural domination, and media imperialism. Many of the new countries that came into existence during this period examined the role of the mass media in the development process and protested the unfair technological advantage of advanced countries like the United States and Britain, which led to their global dominance over the news and information flow. The most radical thoughts on this type of dependency were advanced in developing nations, not only in the Caribbean but also throughout the world, who viewed this global imbalance as unjust. This opposition climaxed in the 1980s, with debates over the new world information and communication order.[43]

Global imbalances in the flow of news and information still persist. Advances in new communication technologies have shifted some of the power relations but overall control of production and distribution remains with powerful nations like the United States, Western European countries, and Japan. Advancing economies like Brazil, China, India, and Russia, along with Mexico, South Korea and Nigeria, have added new dynamics to the global flow of information,[44] but the majority of information is still controlled by American, European, and Japanese conglomerates such as Time Warner, Disney, Viacom, News Corporation, CBS, Universal, Google, Apple, Microsoft, Facebook, Bertelsmann AG, Sony Corporation, Associated Press, Reuters, Vivendi, Lagardère Group, and newcomers like Mexican Televisa and Brazilian Organizaçċes Globo. As a result, media systems in small countries are still controlled by dominant external centers.

Manual Puppis[45] and Thomas Steinmaurer[46] believe that while small media systems "are strongly affected by developments in commercialization and globalization, they are less able to influence these developments than big countries."[47] Small states are also held hostage to the political decisions of their bigger rivals—the United States in particular—which then "influences their media systems and media regulations without taking their peculiarities into account."[48] Werner Meier and Josef Trappel contend media regulation in small states is therefore reactive, as they are forced to rely on ad hoc decisions instead of deliberate strategies.[49] In the Caribbean region, throughout the liberal 1980s and 1990s, domestic broadcasting, particularly television, became, as Manuel Puppis wrote, "victims of wide scale imported deregulation."[50] To compete, Hopeton Dunn explains, "public service television throughout the region pandered to domestic commercial interests with increased foreign commercial content, leading to the devaluation of public broadcasting."[51]

The overall impact of this trend, along with access to direct foreign content through satellite, cable, and internet technologies, led to low domestic and regional production and the demise of state broadcasting in Jamaica and Belize, and a redefinition of state broadcasting in Bahamas, Grenada, and Trinidad and Tobago. The latter two countries have shifted toward public service, but the entity is still owned and operated by the state. Jamaica reinstated state radio and television broadcasting with the creation of its public service radio and television operations in 2009. State broadcasting continues in Barbados without any major changes. While the Bahamas has a public service orientation, it is also still controlled by the state.

Barbados presents a slightly different model of broadcasting. It retains control of television through the state. Cable is also distributed in Barbados through the state broadcaster, the Caribbean Broadcasting Corporation (CBC), which operates radio and television stations. Private radio broadcasting exists in Barbados but television remains controlled by the state. In all of the other countries television broadcasting comprises a mixture of state and private enterprises. The cable industry is solely private in Jamaica, Bahamas, Belize, Grenada, and Trinidad and Tobago. Barbados has a mix of state and private cable enterprises.

The mix of private and public broadcasting reflects an interesting shift in the internal control and flow of information, but much of the content is still foreign: external dependency and control continues. Yvette Stuart's 2001 study of the flow of international news in the Bahamas national daily newspapers found a continued dominance of foreign news, especially US news, in local coverage.[52] Ewart Skinner drew similar conclusions a decade earlier.[53]

This type of dependency makes small media systems vulnerable to exogenous threats. Puppis outlines three areas of vulnerability.[54] The first threat was identified by both Gabriele Siegert and Josef Trappel as the foreign takeover of media companies and a resulting decline of domestic influence.[55] The second concerns national media's tendency to conform to foreign media. And the third is the presence of foreign media products in the media markets of small states. The first threat has appeared in the Caribbean telecommunications market, 80 percent of which is under foreign ownership.[56] Conformation to foreign media has been a trend throughout the region since the introduction of radio broadcasting; with the introduction of television came an increase in conformity. In the 1980s and 1990s, Robert Martin[57] and Aggrey Brown[58] drew our attention to the prevalence of foreign media content in Caribbean media markets and the adoption of foreign production values and formats. Both Brown and Martin determined that high foreign content, particularly American cultural products, exert a direct influence on the culture of the region. But while they argued for more control of foreign content, new technologies like the internet has only abetted the spread of foreign content. In 2013, Keith Nurse recommended to the heads of CARICOM governments that they impose content regulations.[59] Currently, as Jean-Claude Burgelman and Caroline Pauwels argue,[60] national and regional sovereignty is threatened by the abundance of foreign television channels via satellite, highly developed cable networks, and internet technology.

A good example of recent challenges to sovereignty emerged when Wikileaks released "sensitive" information about Caribbean countries in 2011. Caribbean political actors were not pleased with the release of this information; they regarded it as a threat to national security. While some Caribbean media critics believe Wikileaks represents a controversial use of new media, particularly when it comes to issues of ethics, others say it is useful because it provides valuable information to the public, information that would not have otherwise been released by Caribbean governments. At the symposium on "New Media, Journalism and Democracy" held in Jamaica in July 2011, Jamaican political critic and blogger Paul Ashley noted the release of information by Wikileaks about the decisions of Caribbean political actors had a positive impact on society as it exposed how governments, political actors, and power brokers in the region operate. "It is really a stark exposé as to the 'loyalties' and dependences of our political actors and how they relate to superpowers in the region. For me it is the most revealing bit of data that has come forth in my lifetime and I'm looking forward to more."[61]

Also present at the 2011 symposium was Mark Beckford, online content coordinator of the *Jamaica Gleaner*, who agreed with Ashley's assessment of Wikileaks as a useful source and acknowledged that it has caused a lot of debate in the newsroom about issues of morality and whether it is right, ethically, for Caribbean journalists and citizens to have access to this information. Despite issues of ethics, Beckford believed "while it has not dented many politicians' aspirations, it has just revealed what we have known or suspected all along. It is very good for discussion. … People are really passionate about their country and the Wikileaks cables help to shed a different light for people."[62]

The convergence of digital technologies is transforming the control of information flows. Yet while they are circumventing traditional hierarchies of institutional power, there is still some control being imposed by corporations and governments. Companies like Google, Facebook, Yahoo, among others, still control the distribution of content. Governments throughout the world—China in particular—have created laws to police these new activities and they are also using technologies to control the flow of information. However, because of the nature of new technologies, citizens are finding ways around the technological blockades to communicate freely. Wikileaks' use of information to expose corruption in the Caribbean in 2011 provided citizens in the region with an opportunity to understand how political actors were making decisions on their behalf, something to which Caribbean political actors reacted negatively. Some analysts predict governments will try to impose new laws to deal with the perceived threats to national sovereignty. For example, in 2013, Grenada created new electronic communication laws to police these activities. These laws, and the subsequent protest against, will be discussed later in this book.

CARIMAC, CANA, and CBU

In the English-speaking Caribbean, the history of media and journalism has developed in the context of foreign dependency. Media systems in the region were started by people who arrived under colonization. Media in the region evolved through many social, political, and economic changes during and after the colonial period. However, it was not until the middle of the last century, when the region began to see itself as one entity, that a regional emphasis was placed on the role of media and communication in development. Because of their common historical development, the peoples of the English-speaking Caribbean placed significant emphasis on regional integration. "This culminated in 1965 with the creation of the Caribbean Free Trade Association (CARIFTA) following the signing of the Dickerson Bay Agreement."[63] (CARIFTA later evolved into CARICOM in 1973.) The creation of these two entities was an attempt to protect the Caribbean from international threats—economic, political, and cultural.

Shortly after gaining independence, Caribbean state actors, recognizing the need to protect regional cultures and identities, partnered with United Nations agencies and the German Friedrich Ebert Stiftung to create institutions that would promote the role of media and communication in the development of these Caribbean countries. To this end, several

UNESCO projects were created in the 1970s to protect the region from external dependency and cultural domination, and to foster a media and communication agenda that was focused on the needs of the region. These projects culminated in the creation of the Caribbean Broadcasting Union (CBU) in 1970, CARIMAC in 1974, and the Caribbean News Agency (CANA) in 1976. These institutions were established to strengthen regional cooperation and integration.[64]

The CBU started with a mix of private and state broadcasters to advance the regional integration agenda through the exchange of radio and television programs throughout the region. According to Aggrey Brown, the initial efforts of the CBU focused on "collective concerns such as the cooperative purchasing of internationally distributed material, the sharing of technical expertise in areas such as engineering and program production, and the ad hoc live broadcasting of regional events—sports such as the Olympic Games and cricket."[65] Brown believes the CBU met the challenge of regional broadcasting by combining the collective resources of its members. Since its inception, the CBU coordinated the transmission of daily news programs between its member systems and live coverage of regional events.

Despite its initial success, the structure of the CBU created many challenges. One of its handicaps was the fact that the majority of its members were government-owned stations. This relationship, according to Brown, resulted in the CBU's inability "to implement collective decisions expeditiously."[66] Further, the membership structure resulted in financial woes, as smaller states were sometimes unable to meet their financial obligations. As a result, the CBU relied on external funding sources for assistance. One of its most successful programs, Caribvision, was launched in 1989 with assistance from the Friedrich Ebert Stiftung. "The CBU also produced a weekly television news magazine program, Caribscope, and a number of weekly entertainment and educational programs designed to promote and develop regional cultural expression."[67] Based on my research on the development of media and journalism in the region, I believe the CBU has had very little influence on Caribbean regional identity. These countries remain isolated and parochial in their approach to development.

Four years after the creation of the CBU, CARIMAC was established. It began with the objective of providing homegrown training to people who had been practicing as journalists without formal instruction. Prior to 1974, most of the journalists in the Caribbean were trained on the job; those journalists who had some formal training had had to go abroad, primarily to England. Patrick Prendergast, one of the current professors at CARIMAC, points out that in 1974 the idea was to work with the University of the West Indies in Jamaica to provide journalists with training from a Caribbean perspective.[68] The institute, which began with a diploma program, now offers undergraduate and graduate programs in media and communication studies, including a doctoral degree.

There were two major challenges that hindered CARIMAC's development and the fulfilment of its mission. First, like the CBU, the governments of the region fund the University of the West Indies, and by extension CARIMAC. This financial arrangement constrains autonomous decision-making and as a result journalism and communication programs, as well as all other programs, are heavily dependent on state resources. Second, CARIMAC was hindered by the continued lack of understanding about the role of journalism and communication in the development of the region. Prendergast believes the institute and the region needed to understand the role of the journalist, "and the role of communication in general, the journalist more specifically and in the new dispensation, the role of communicators in the development of the region. If we continue to see that role as primarily one of information sharing and information dissemination, then I think we are putting ourselves at a disadvantage."[69]

Prendergast admits that in some areas, for example technological research, the region did not have the capacity for the type of research that it needs. However, he believes the region could advance a more comprehensive research agenda, though it needs financial resources to do so. Caribbean governments have not yet fully embraced the role of academic research in national development—economic, political, and social—and have therefore not invested in research and development institutions nor in building human capacity to do so. They still rely on the old model of colonization—that is, bringing in the foreign consultant. In an interview in June 2015, the new director of CARIMAC, Hopeton Dunn, explained how the new goals of the institution would address these deficiencies. CARIMAC's new goals include the addition of several new undergraduate and graduate programs—the Bachelor of Fine Arts (BFA), Master of Fine Arts (MFA) and Master of Arts (MA) in integrated marketing communications (or IMC) to prepare students to work in the cultural industries, create a new research agenda targeting governments, institutions, and organizations in the region to assist with regional development, fashion new training programs for practicing professionals, and build collaborative partnerships with other media institutions in the region.[70]

However, it will take more than a new set of goals for CARIMAC to change the attitudes of Caribbean people and decision-makers. The Caribbean, despite its close proximity to the United States, with its rich history in journalism and communication, still does not appreciate communication as a field or professional discipline, and this shows in the level of research that has been done in the region. Some Caribbean scholars believe this is due to the geopolitics of the region and its continued external dependency. Prendergast explained that until Caribbean people learn to think more independently, they will continue to be beholden to external actors:

> We have not fully gone past the idea that we are [independent], we remain too dependent on those who we have given pride of place to determine our destiny. We're just too dependent on that process still. ... We are not doing enough ... [research] to support the way we see things, the way we think the region can go. We're just not. And if we have become so dependent on this external way of doing things, and accepting that, in a sense we have to basically produce the way they would want to see us produce as part of that ... demonstration that we know what we are doing. ... It's always a challenge.[71]

Prendergast argues that, because of the region's orientation towards journalism and communication as information dissemination, there was very little value placed on media and communication from the perspective of development. He described the region as having a "big country" way of looking at things while not responding to what was on the ground. "We tend to look down on some very small but important things and we don't know that it's important until somebody [external] gives it some kind of validation."[72] As long as the Caribbean has this external orientation, it will not place emphasis on important areas like research and development and thus all sectors of society will continue to react to external actors' determinations of what is and is not important. Decision-making in media and communication will therefore continue to be driven by an external agenda.

With the help of UNESCO, a regional media institution, the Caribbean News Agency (CANA), was created in 1976 in an attempt to balance the flow of news and information in the region and between the region and the world. CANA failed in this mission. A former general manager of CANA described it as "a real interesting experiment of private enterprise and government enterprise."[73] The main objective of CANA was to circulate news and information in the Caribbean that would bring Caribbean people closer together. The former general manager conceded that this was a very idealistic approach, especially for those who worked at CANA during the 1980s and 1990s and believed in the idea of uniting Caribbean people through the exchange of news and information. This idealism is reflected in Marlene Cuthbert's 1981 description of CANA as a unique third world model because it was "jointly owned by [the] private and public mass media of its region, and is independent of both government and foreign news agencies."[74] However, because of its organizational structure, there were built-in tensions from the start between journalists and the Caribbean governments that financially supported CANA. Journalists were interested in presenting the news that was relevant, accurate, balanced, and engaging. Caribbean governments were more interested in publicity that framed their agendas in a positive way—as one of public relations. The former general manager of CANA describes the conflict in the following terms:

> We were working on the premise that if we know more about one another we will be able to come together in a sensible and sensitive way. I am not sure that that really panned out as we thought because I found that our countries were so singular, so narrow in their outlook that really and truly what the governments were interested in was in getting their own public relations out and very often what the people [who worked there] were interested in, as distinct from the government, would be something entirely different and nobody wanted to build a community based on just government handouts.[75]

CANA's failure was also related to economies of scale. The news agency began with sixteen subscribers, a mixture of government and private entities. The market did not grow rapidly and therefore the news agency had to rely on the financial support of its subscribers, who were asked to pay more as the cost of operating the agency increased. Operating the news agency for a Caribbean domestic audience became too expensive. The agency did make some attempts to gain subscribers from the Caribbean diaspora, but most of the targeted subscribers were in the United States, and they did not see their contributions to CANA in the same way the initial subscribers did. Several attempts were made to rescue the news agency in the 1990s, but CANA closed its doors in 2000. The former general manager of CANA believes it "would still have been in existence today if we had looked forward and change ... from just being a distributor of news ... to go into a whole host of other things—news and advertising and the whole media gamut."[76] That is, if it had been allowed to diversify.

CANA not only failed because its rates were too high for subscribers to continue their support; there was also competition from the Associated Press and Reuters, who were offering their services at a cheaper price. These factors led the news agency to shift its focus to the electronic media in an attempt to survive. CANA merged with the CBU in 2000 to form the Caribbean Media Corporation (CMC).

One of the valuable lessons that came out of the CANA experiment was that Caribbean journalists and governments learned it takes more than news and information to integrate people. Today, there is still a Caribbean regional media institution, the CMC, but the goals and objectives of this organization are different. Some of the Caribbean journalists that I interviewed saw the failure of CANA as a setback for regional integration because the information from other countries in the Caribbean was no longer readily available, as it was under CANA. When CANA and the CBU joined to form the CMC in 2000, some practitioners and media scholars were against the merger. They felt that the two entities should have been allowed to continue separately. Others felt that the merger would bring about a clearer mission and consolidate the financial costs of operating these two institutions. However, neither position has brought about regional integration. If the Caribbean integration project is to succeed it will have to rethink the role of its regional media and communication institutions. The success of the integration project requires a daily flow of news and information about the region, and collaborative journalism and communication projects—scholarship and praxis.

In conjunction with the challenges of sustaining and advancing such institutions, the region is also affected by its strategic location, close to the world's largest economy and most dominant media empires, which has limited its ability to resist the influence of external agents, especially foreign media. The influence of CNN, BBC, FOX, Associated Press, Reuters, Google, YouTube, Twitter, Facebook, and WhatsApp is highly visible in contemporary Caribbean societies. While there have been changes in the channels of influence, with technological shifts from wireless services to online services through internet and other telecommunications media, the overall level of dependence remains high. The era of convergence has shifted the distribution pipeline but the content owners remain the same. The technological and commercial changes of the last three decades impose continuous threats to the region's plans for regionalization and integration. New digital technologies are creating more fragmented audiences, while commercialization continues to trump public service and public interest.

The World Summit on the Information Society, the United Nations, UNESCO, and other world organizations, along with CARICOM, believe the only way to balance the dependence of the region is to forge new relations among these countries to enhance their bargaining positions on the world market. To achieve this goal the region has to rethink not only how it utilizes communication and journalism to advance regional integration but also give up on the neoliberal model of integration. Regional institutions like the CMC and CARIMAC will have to be restructured to advance a sociocultural integration agenda. New ideas for how to use new communication technologies in the integration process must emerge.

CARICOM has had some success in bringing the region closer together, but it still suffers from parochialism and isolationism. Norman Girvan describes CARICOM's four pillars of integration as economic integration, foreign policy coordination, functional cooperation, and security.[77] In 1989, CARICOM revised its goals for Caribbean integration. The primary focus consisted of the creation of the CARICOM Single Market and Economy (CSME), a neoliberal Open Regionalism integration scheme. But the CSME is still far from completion. According to Girvan, the CARICOM Single Market was formally inaugurated in 2006, "but some elements are still not yet in place; and there has been but little progress towards implementing the CARICOM Single Economy."[78] Implementing the CSME requires a great deal of work; particularly challenging is the quest to bring together the policies, laws, institutions, and regulations that all member countries can agree on. Not all of the countries have signed on to the new policies of CSME, which are especially troubling for countries with the strongest economies. Most of these countries' economies are characterized by monoculture (agriculture, tourism, and petroleum) and the new policies for the free movement of people throughout the region and a common currency are worrisome for countries with strong economies.

The CSME is a daunting task because it strains the human and institutional capacities of most of these small member states. Also, some countries believe there are limited economic benefits to be derived from the new agreements. As long as intraregional trade is dominated by energy-rich Trinidad and Tobago, with its strong manufacturing base,[79] some Caribbean economists believe there is little hope for the success of CARICOM's economic integration. Further, Girvan explains, "the majority of member countries have very little to export to one another, and their exports consist mainly of primary products, tourism, and international financial services oriented toward international markets."[80] As Havelock Brewster and Clive Thomas,[81] and Moreira Mesquito, Mauricio and Eduardo Mendoza[82] have shown in their work, market integration by itself is likely to bring few benefits in regional groupings that consist of small and undiversified economies with competitive, rather than complementary, structures of production and trade. According to Girvan, "the neoliberal model of integration is therefore of limited relevance as a strategy of development for CARICOM."[83]

Since the start of the twenty-first century, Caribbean integration policies have become more complicated with new agreements emerging between various countries in the region, as well as with the European Union (EU) and alternative partnerships. "In 2008, CARICOM states, along with the Dominican Republic, signed a new Economic Partnership Agreement (EPA) with the EU."[84] The EPA brings new restrictions to Caribbean governments' ability to control their own economic policy and protect local market initiatives or pursue alternate south-south partnerships. Alternative economic partnerships have also emerged within the region. These new agreements include Alianza Bolivariana para los Pueblos de Nuestra América (ALBA), an economic partnership created by Venezuela and Cuba to counter and balance the impact of restrictive agreements like the

FTAA (Free Trade Area of the Americas) with the United States and the EPA agreement with EU, and growing partnerships with the People's Republic of China.

Caribbean countries struggle to implement these new strategies for integration and economic development, what Girvan calls "asymmetrical neoliberal integration,"[85] mainly because very few citizens in the region understand these agreements. Caribbean journalists have lagged behind in providing an accurate and comprehensive account of these policies and their effect on the region. This benightedness was particularly apparent during the 2008 negotiations between CARICOM and the EU over its EPA agreement and the collapse of 2003 negotiations for the extension of the American FTAA policies. Caribbean journalists did not present a detailed, comprehensive, and accurate account of the social, economic, and political implications—both negative and positive—of these agreements for Caribbean societies. The limited coverage, mostly talk show commentaries and editorials, raised important questions about the relevance of Caribbean journalism in disseminating information concerning regional integration. One of the responsibilities of journalists is to help their communities make sense of important policies like CSME, EPA, FTAA, and ALBA. Caribbean journalists have not done this, nor are they discussing the region's new relations with China.

Although some of the blame for this lack of public understanding came from a lack of information on EPA from official sources, journalists should have provided information on the agreement and its impact on Caribbean societies. Journalists play a pivotal role in disseminating critical information to the public about policies that could affect the daily lives of people. When they fail to do this effectively, the public is ignorant of the changes that are being made on its behalf by policymakers who have a tradition of making decisions in secret or closed sessions without apprising the public of their decisions. This approach diminishes the citizen's role in democracy. The media could help to raise awareness of policymakers' decisions on new policies before they are implemented.

One of the major critiques against journalism throughout the region is its failure to make sense of complex political, economic, and social issues. Wendall Jones, owner of Jones Communication Network in the Bahamas, believes journalists have an obligation to educate the people so that they understand what these issues mean to them personally. "For instance, the whole question about EPA ... we need to get people to understand where the Bahamas is in matters of trade," Jones explained. "It is the role of the media ... in my opinion, to get them [Bahamians] to understand that we have to be competitive in the global market and we have to move with the times because we have in our country many people who are phobic and many people that believe that we don't need outsiders to help us to develop our country."[86] He feels citizens are harmed when the media and journalism fail to fulfill this obligation.

With regard to salient national and regional issues, veteran journalist Nicki Kelly explains the importance of journalism in the region in the following terms:

> I think today's journalists need to take another look at the profession, to understand what it is to be a journalist. I don't think many of them understand what it is. I mean, doctors have a Hippocratic Oath and they pretty well know that their job is to save lives. What is a journalist's job? I don't think many of them fully understand what it is they are supposed to do. To me, journalism is one of the most responsible and also most significant jobs or professions that anyone can undertake because you are the recorder of history, and that, believe me, is a very, very responsible job. When you write, you don't just look at the immediate thing: twenty-five years from now somebody is going to read this. Am I presenting the truth? Are they going to be able to count on what I say? Have I told it the way it should be told, the way it is? They need a broader outlook, and a greater appreciation of their profession. I don't think they fully appreciate the job. I think until they have that appreciation, I don't think anything is going to improve.[87]

Related to issues of integration is the impact of new technologies on journalism. The new communication revolution is granting unprecedented access to information and providing citizens of the region with more opportunities than ever to circumvent national and regional control and form new alliances in regional and global markets. Unfortunately, most of these opportunities also aid the spread of commercialization and consumption, which some scholars blame for the decline in civic-mindedness.

Contemporary Threats to Journalism

Beate Josephi identifies modernization, secularization, and commercialization as "the three endogenous forces of change." Later she added technological innovation, which has produced its own communication culture that cuts across national boundaries.[88] Of these, Josephi believes commercialization in particular is shifting media systems away from the world of politics to the world of commerce. Like Daniel Hallin and Paolo Mancini,[89] Josephi concludes this changes the social function of journalism, as the journalist's main objective is no longer to disseminate ideas and create social consensus around them, but to produce entertainment and information that can be sold to individual consumers.[90] As a result, scholars like Josephi, Hallin and Mancini believe journalism has to guard against the possible "subordination of the media to the political interests of business,"[91] which could turn out to be the most serious threat to the professional autonomy of journalists worldwide since it "could diminish [the] political balance in the representation of social interests."[92]

This assumption threatens Jürgen Habermas's and Benedict Anderson's position on journalism: a communal force to provide a public sphere in which an issue can be debated.[93] Stig Hjavard believes continued political, economic, and technological pressures will lead to "the convergence, homogenization, and denationalizing of news."[94] These pressures jeopardize journalism's role in regional integration. The market-centered approach, which focuses on commercialization and consumption, puts at risk national and regional concerns, and threatens to erode the normative values of journalism. These issues are discussed further in chapter three.

Perhaps the most significant threat to the survival of journalism today comes from the technological sphere, the rise of citizen journalism and the use of new technologies such as blogs, Facebook, Twitter, and YouTube. Although, at the time of this research, citizen journalism as expressed through new media did not yet have the same impact in the Caribbean as it has had in the United States and Europe, it is bloggers, Twitter, YouTube, Facebook, and WhatsApp users who are undermining the professional model in the United States and Europe. A similar trend is now emerging in the Caribbean. While most of the journalists interviewed for this book did not feel threatened by citizen journalism, blogging, tweeting, and other internet activities were becoming competitive sources of news. For a region that has already had a difficult time telling its own stories, these new versions could be both beneficial and harmful to journalism's progress.

One recently created news organizations that represent both sides of this debate is the controversial On the Ground News Report (OGNR). Founded in Jamaica in 2010, OGNR immediately caused a sensation. It uses ordinary citizens as reporters and claims to be first with many news reports. Using new technology, Twitter and Facebook, citizens gather and disseminate information on OGNR's Facebook page, website, and Twitter feed. While some citizens, particularly journalists, criticized OGNR for inaccuracies, unethical practices, and defamation, others have welcomed this new media player, readily turning to it as an information source. There are several similar online news sources throughout the region, and their impact on traditional media and society will be discussed in the second part of this book.

Organizations like OGNR, with its offer of a higher rate of participation in public debate, raises questions about journalism's relevance. The majority of the journalists in this research were more inclined to agree with Peter Dahlgren, Ari Heinonen, and Klaus Bruhn Jensen, who raise the question, If journalism is to foster the public sphere, how then can communication facilitated and shared by the internet, and also text messaging (SMS), not be seen as contributing to that exchange?[95] Heinonen suggests that the "loci of journalism as a practice" are moving and that these "new loci should be embraced."[96] But not all journalists embrace this perspective. Dane Claussen, outgoing editor of the *Journalism & Mass Communication Educator* in the United States, does not place citizen journalism on the same level as traditional journalism; he warns against its use to supplant professional practices:

> Overall, you will excuse me if I think that the term citizen journalism, while perhaps a noble ideal and something that a few will strive for and achieve, is almost entirely an oxymoron. (This goes for the other silly concepts—stand-alone journalism, participatory journalism, open-source journalism, crowd-sourced journalism, and representative journalism—that assume that more than 1 or 2 percent of the population has always been dying to be journalists, if only professional journalists would

allow them or assist them.) The reality is: citizen fact-gathering, yes, citizen fact-transmitting, yes, citizen-opinion-about-news-and-trends, yes. In the old days, average people did these things through writing letters to each other, keeping dairies, having conversations, taking notes, writing letters to the editor, and many other activities, none of which were called "journalism." But we have "citizen journalism" now, all of a sudden? Yes, but it is extremely rare and likely to remain so if one defines journalism the way it should be defined, and is defined, by good professional journalists such as those who met with Kovach and Rosenstiel and whose discussion formed the basis of their fine book.[97]

Claussen's perspective reframes the importance and relevance of professional journalism. His warning comes at a time when there are debates on the accuracy and credibility of the information disseminated by citizens via digital technologies. Old ethical issues have reemerged in the new free-for-all distribution of content. To date, these cautions and ethical concerns have not been addressed within the citizen-centered approach to journalism. Journalism educators, lawmakers, and civil society will have to address these issues and find solutions to the problems that have emerged under citizen journalism if democratic principles are to be upheld.

While Claussen sounds the alarm bells on citizen journalism's effect on the future of professional practice, Denis Weaver predicts economic pressures will bring about the demise of journalism. In his assessment of the future of US journalism in the twenty-first century, Weaver is pessimistic.[98] In the current climate of cuts and layoffs, buyouts and closures, he believes journalism in the US will have a very hard time surviving in the future. As Weaver concludes, this will lead to less effective monitoring of society and less dissemination of important information. Nowhere was this more evident than in the 2014 downgrading of US and UK press freedom by the international monitoring organization Reporters Without Borders. According to the 2014 report, there was "a profound erosion of press freedom in the United States in 2013."[99] (The United States dropped thirteen spots from its 2012 ranking.) The report cited several cases of increased crackdown on whistleblowers, from the trial and conviction of Bradley (now Chelsea) Manning, to Edward Snowden's leak of National

Security Agency documents, to the Justice Department's seizure of Associated Press phone records in an attempt to find the source of a CIA leak. The United Kingdom was downgraded by three points for its harassment of the *Guardian* newspaper. Reporters Without Borders warned American and British journalists to perform their duties as monitors of the powerful in the public interest and recommended a federal "shield law" to protect journalists in the United States.

David Cuillier, president of the Society of Professional Journalists in the United States agrees with the findings of the 2014 report and believes journalism in that country is becoming more imperiled. "The main problem," says Cuillier, is that "the public no longer trusts journalists and believes it is acceptable for government to intimidate reporters, hide information, and threaten journalists with jail time for doing their jobs."[100] This trend should sound warning bells in the Caribbean, a region with a long history of state control of information and political influence.

The impact of economic stresses and government control of information are major concerns for Caribbean journalists, as well as for all democracies where journalism plays a watchdog role. If these stressors are unchecked, journalists will not be able to perform the role of analyzing complex problems, investigating government claims, and avoiding stories where facts cannot be verified. This is particularly important in the current acrimonious relationship between journalists and politicians in the Caribbean. This may be an opportune time for journalists throughout the region to advocate for their own shield laws. So far, citizen journalists are not held to the same standards as professional journalists. There is an increase in the dissemination of distorted, untruthful information; a lot of this information is coming from people's increased access to new information technologies. Some Caribbean governments have created new laws to protect citizens from harmful information. But these activities do not bode well for advancing the democratic process.

On a more optimistic note, Weaver believes "nonprofessional" journalism may provide a more optimistic picture of the future, but it relies on professional journalism as its source and professional journalism is under attack from the breakdown of the old paradigm. This book is concerned with how Caribbean journalists respond to these threats and advance democracy.

Caribbean Journalism's Media Economy: Advancing Democracy and the Common Good?[1]

Caribbean journalism has always occupied a contested exogenous and endogenous space. Bordered by its British colonial past and its dominant northern neighbor, the United States, Caribbean journalism has developed in a milieu that has been constrained by both external and internal forces. The region has accepted the historical dependency that has been foisted on it since colonization and has subsumed everything under its power. In the postcolonial period, American domination has added new layers to the region's dependent nature. Despite the external controlling forces of core states, as described by Immanuel Wallerstein,[2] contemporary Caribbean journalism exists amidst a perplexing paradox: rapid technological and market-led reforms are changing the practice and the profession, but the current successes have stopped the closure of media organizations. At the time of this research, countries in the English-speaking Caribbean had increased their number of media outlets, their advertising revenues, and their circulation numbers in the midst of a global decline in the news industry. But these economic successes may not last long, and we must ask, at what cost are they achieved?

American and European media scholars blame the commercial success of media organizations for the failures of journalism and its decline as a public service. Some scholars see the dictates of the market in every facet of the media, from hybrid discourses, mixed genres of journalism and advertising, to convergence in broadcast and internet media. Other critics believe American and European media firms are competing with the same content and blame increased competition for the increase in program duplication in broadcasting, and a decline of content diversity and quality in other fields.[3] Are these trends now visible in the Caribbean, and do they raise concerns for the common good? Are news industries in the Caribbean putting profit ahead of serving the public?

Journalism's Global Trend

At the turn of the twenty-first century, journalism, especially as practiced in the United States, Australia, Canada, and Western Europe, has been subject to dire predictions as to its imminent extinction. According to Rick Edmonds, 142 newspapers were shut down in the United States in 2009.[4] As newspapers throughout the United States ceased their operations, journalism's demise dominated the discourse on the future of journalism.[5] Academics and practitioners began advocating for new models of journalism in a rapidly changing media landscape.[6] Amidst these rapid changes Michael Schudson, a professor of journalism at Columbia University, "sees the promise of a better array of public informational resources emerging."[7] The 2010 Pew Center report on the state of the news media predicts "this new ecosystem will include different 'styles' of journalism, a mix of professional and amateur approaches and different economic models— commercial, nonprofit, public and 'university-fueled.'"[8]

Every year since the beginning of the twenty-first century, the most debated question among American and Western European journalists has been "will journalism survive?" The old economic model of the news industry was centered on advertising—that is, selling readers, listeners, and viewers goods and services, everything from real estate, automobiles, apparel, and food, to employment opportunities, dream vacations, and prescription medication. But that model is in free fall in the United States and Europe, with a rate of decline that grows every year. The 2009 figures for advertising revenue in the United States reveal how urgent the situation has become. According to the Pew Center's 2010 report, "newspapers, including online, saw ad revenue fall 26% during the year, which brings the total loss over the last three years to 41%."[9]

Further, the report notes "local television ad revenue fell 24% in 2009; triple the decline the year before. Radio also was off 18%. Magazine ad revenue dropped 19%, network TV 7% (and news alone probably more). Online ad revenue overall fell about 5%, and revenue to news sites most likely also fared much worse."[10] Cable news had a better advertising performance; indeed it was the only sector of the news industry that did not experience a decline in revenue in 2009. However, future predictions for the news industry overall see advertising revenue continuing to decline as more people seek alternative sources of information. To further complicate this forecast, online advertising does not offer much hope, as studies have shown online advertising cannot sustain the news industry.

The Pew Center's 2012 report brought mixed news on the state of the US industry. The good news: New technologies such as mobile smartphones and tablets were increasing news consumption among adults. The not so good news: "New technological intermediaries continue to control the future of journalism."[11] Most significantly, these technological emissaries may control the future of advertising revenue.

In addition, the 2012 report highlighted two major trends, both of which overlapped and reinforced "the perception that the gap between the news and technology industries is widening: First, the explosion of new mobile platforms and social media channels represents another layer of technology with which news organizations must keep pace."[12] The second trend that emerged is "a small number of technology giants began rapidly moving to consolidate their power by becoming makers of 'everything' in our digital lives."[13] These companies—Google, Amazon, Facebook, Apple, and others—"are maneuvering to make the hardware people use, the operating systems that run those devices, the browsers on which people navigate, the e-mail services on which they communicate, the social networks on which they share and the web platforms on which they shop and play."[14] What does this mean? These companies now have the ability to gather detailed personal data about each consumer. They also have the ability to sell more products and services targeted specifically to an individual's needs and wants.

By the end of 2011, according to the 2012 report, five technology companies accounted for 68 percent of all online ad revenue, and that list did not include Amazon and Apple, which get most of their dollars from online transactions, downloads, and devices.[15] By 2015, Facebook was expected to account for one out of every five digital display ad sold.[16] Facebook's 2014 buyout of WhatsApp for $19 billion portends more control of the digital domain. The Pew Center's 2013 and 2014 reports emphasized the continued dominance of mobile news consumption, a year of small gains for newspapers in 2013, a 3 percent decline in circulation in 2014, and audience increases in broadcast news, both local and network. Cable television was experiencing declines by the end of 2014.

In Europe, the trends are similar. European Publishers Council (EPC) 2012–2013 *Global Media Trends Book* identified the news industry's growing use of social media to deliver content and engage with audiences. Despite this increased use, the EPC noted "the challenge of adapting to new media platforms, new trends in media consumption as well as the challenge of new areas of competition and a host of new players which are not bound by the same rules as the media and publishing industry."[17] According to the EPC's 2012–2013 report, the professional media may have strong, trusted brands, which created new audiences online, "where we find soaring popularity for quality news, comment and debate. But with more competition for less revenue, profits remain elusive."[18] The report noted that "profit comes more easily for some because of their investment in high quality content, often creating the illusion of 'everything for nothing.' Enticing though this might be to consumers, there is the risk longer term of a very impoverished media—generating less fact-based journalism and undermining our professionalism, threatening jobs, titles and future investment and innovation."[19]

The EPC based its findings on data gathered by the nonprofit international media research organization, World News Media Network. The EPC report also noted that since the devastating 2008 global financial crisis, a steady pattern of growth has emerged, particularly in the internet, television, and out-of-home advertising sectors. "While overall advertising rose 4.7 percent in 2011 and 5 percent in 2012, print media has experienced a decline both years, while broadcast and internet have enjoyed a rebound effect."[20]

The report also cited MAGNA GLOBAL data, a major media-for-profit organization, which indicated the most significant growth in advertising revenues has been happening outside of Europe and the United States. "The most spectacular advertising growth is happening in China, Peru and Argentina, with more than 21 percent growth from 2011 to 2012, followed by Russia, Turkey, Ukraine, India and Indonesia, which experienced an 11 percent to 20 percent surge in advertising revenue growth from 2011 to 2012."[21] The economic and technological challenges remain core elements of the EPC's 2013 report and the Pew Center's 2013 report, but both emphasize the continued growth in mobile advertising, the importance of strong trusted brands, and increased profits from paywalls amidst concerns for financial data safety.

This analysis focuses on the United States and Europe. What is happening to the news media industry in the rest of the world? In 2009, Bob Franklin, professor at Cardiff University in the United Kingdom, described the global media landscape more optimistically. Franklin believes the pessimistic tone concerning the imminent demise of newspapers in the United States and Europe is unrealistic for the rest of the world:

> The precocious pessimism and unwarranted hyperbole of those who wish to proclaim the imminent demise of the newspaper, is clearly unsustainable. It articulates a curiously North American and Eurocentric view of the press, which seems blinkered to the explosion of new titles and readerships in other parts of the world; the future of newspapers is more open and considerably more nuanced than some observers imagine. Globally, there is no cause for pessimism about the future of newspapers with the most recent data gathered by the World Association of Newspapers (WAN) detailing unprecedented growth.[22]

According to Franklin, this growth is evident in the fact that "daily paid newspapers, globally, have recorded an average 17% growth from 9,533 to a record breaking 11,142 titles between 2002–2006, although rates varied markedly across Asia (33.1%), Africa (16.7%), South America (12.6%), Europe (5.6%) and Australia (1.4%)."[23] Based on WAN data "the circulations of paid daily newspapers also increased by 8.7% across the same five year span to a record high of 510 million copies, while the distribution of free daily newspapers expanded three-fold from 13,795 millions to 40,802 millions."[24] Regional variations were noted in that some of these publications were relatively new free daily newspapers recording extraordinary growth figures of 77 percent in South America, 65 percent in Europe but only 18.4 percent in Asia:

Market share is uneven, however, with Europe claiming 66% of the free daily market by circulation, while Australasia manages only 1%. In some settings the growth of newspaper titles and readerships across all sectors has been striking. In India, for example, the 330 daily titles with 2.5 mn readers in the early 1950s mushroomed to an estimated 5,638 titles and 59.1 mn readers in 2001 (Bhaskar 2005, 19). These data offer a sobering corrective to the pessimists' case; the global newspaper business is booming.[25]

What do these trends mean for the Caribbean? The news is mixed. On the one hand, the Caribbean data, discussed below, indicates that the region is following the trends found in Latin America, India, China, and Africa with regard to the growth of the news industry. On the other, the region is so close to the United States that it is also feeling the impact of the growing use of new technologies and commercialism. The countries of the English-speaking Caribbean are caught between two major trends and fluctuate between cycles of growth and decline.

Further, as receiver cultures, countries that do not invent new information technologies, but rather consume foreign ones, especially from the United States, the technological and commercial trends will also impact their news industry. But even more daunting, the concerns about dependency, cultural domination, and media imperialism will continue to grow. Unless Caribbean countries find innovative ways to use these technologies to create something new, their dependency will continue and concerns for the erosion of cultural identity will be heightened. Theories of hybridity offer an opportunity for Caribbean societies to rethink their political, economic, and cultural relations, both internal and external. They should guide the development of the cultural industries in the region. Yet while these industries offer an opportunity to reverse external dependencies, regional decision-makers must include a long-term plan to change cultural taste for foreign products if their efforts to develop indigenous cultural products are to succeed.

In the United States and Europe, the decline of newspapers continues to raise questions about the civic responsibilities of journalism in the twenty-first century. As the traditional primary source for people in government and civic affairs, what will happen to this type of news, which is so important in democratic states? Despite the Western news conundrum, the 2012 Pew report predicted if the current trends continue, news and journalism will still have a more positive future. Journalism as a business in the United States and Europe is evolving rapidly and no one has come up with a good business model that could be applied to the whole industry. In other regions of the world, for now, journalism and media industries are experiencing a period of growth. However, questions remain about the relevance of journalism in the twenty-first century as more and more digital venues emerge for accessing information. News industries must continually reinvent themselves if they want to survive in the digital future. Journalism as a profession must continue to position itself as relevant to civic engagement and responsible governance; it must continue to serve the common good; most importantly, it must rethink how best to tell and sell its stories. The future is uncertain but most practitioners and scholars believe journalism will be around for a long time, albeit in revised forms. It is against this background that the present chapter focuses on the trends of the news industry in the English-speaking Caribbean and raise questions about the future of these receiver cultures.

Trends in the Caribbean News Industry

Media has become big business in the Caribbean. At the time of this research, the industry in the English-speaking countries of the region was experiencing a period of growing profits and expanding empires. This growth began with an explosion of new media channels, particularly in broadcasting, from the late 1980s to the present, which were ushered in through policies of deregulation and liberalization that opened these former state-controlled markets. These policies led to the privatization of many state-owned institutions, including state broadcasters, and an increase in the number of media organizations, particularly in broadcasting, within these markets.[26] Many Caribbean media markets went from one state radio and television broadcaster to as many as sixty private radio and television stations. These increases created highly competitive media markets. (See Table 1).

Historically, newspaper ownership in the region has been mainly private; the recent growth in media markets has not changed this. According to the World Association of Newspapers, the English-speaking

TABLE 1: LIST OF MEDIA IN FIVE CARIBBEAN COUNTRIES

	Newspaper Daily	Newspaper Other*	Radio	Television	Cable	Magazine	Internet Penetration
Bahamas Pop. 377,374	4	7	17	3	1	6	203,653 (45 %)
Barbados Pop. 287,733	2	2	18	2	5	4	205,756 (71.8 %)
Belize Pop. 327,719	N/A	11	22	2	7	1	60,000 (25 %)
Grenada Pop. 104, 890	N/A	5	11	3	1	N/A	37,860 (35 %)
Jamaica Pop. 2,889,187	3	10	25	9	52	30	1,158,100 (55.1 %)
Trinidad and Tobago Pop. 1,400,000	5	11	21	13	8	29	677,583 (55.2 %)

* Compiled from various sources in 2012: internet, media houses, local governments, chambers of commerce. Includes weeklies, special supplements, bi-weeklies, monthlies throughout each country.
For a complete list of sources for this table see page 222.

Caribbean's media growth follows trends in India, China, Latin America, and parts of Africa where newspapers are also successful.[27] But many of the editors and publishers interviewed believed it will be only five to ten years before these countries follow the pattern of the United States and Western Europe.

In addition to economic growth in the news industry, journalism in the Caribbean is experiencing a period of rapid change led by technological innovation and economic reform. But in the midst of these changes, journalism as a business is prospering as advertising revenue and the overall circulation of tabloids, broadsheets, and specialized magazines multiply and the number of news channels (free dailies, broadcasting time, magazines, online news portals) has increased over the last decade.

In 2009, Omatie Lyder, editor of the *Trinidad Express*, described the difference this way: "Trinidad, and by extension the Caribbean ... are somehow caught in a wave where ... newspapers continue to grow. The *Express*, our paper, has put out a 240-page paper on a Wednesday—240 pages is bigger than the *Sunday [New York] Times*. How is that possible? We are inundated with ads, we're actually refusing ads."[28] In 2014, these newspapers were still making profits. In 2011, the *Nassau Tribune* created a new weekly tabloid paper, *The Big T*, which sold out in its first two months of distribution, and remains profitable still.

Although some of the newspapers in the region were affected by the 2007–2009 global recession, which led to a decline in advertising profits, many have largely rebounded and circulations have increased. The impact of the economic recession was most visible in Jamaica, the Bahamas, and Barbados, while Trinidad and Tobago, Grenada, and Belize did not report a decline. In 2009, the Caribbean technology blog *Silicon Caribe* noted the *Gleaner*, Jamaica's largest newspaper, reported their worst financial loss in the company's one hundred and seventy-five-year history, noting a drop in 2008 of 444.69 million Jamaican dollars from the previous year's profits.[29] Among the factors that contributed to the decline in revenues was a drop in advertising revenues. "Advertising, which contributes 53% of total revenue, incurred a 7.3% decline due to shrinking advertising budgets."[30] The company also reported a loss in their publications (books and stationary), which fell by 16.9 percent when their contract to provide textbooks to the government of Jamaica was reduced in 2008. However, despite the loss in advertising revenue, circulation, which accounts for 20 percent of overall revenue, had increased by 13.8 percent, though this rise in circulation was attributed to increased prices. The *Gleaner* acknowledged that this reflected the global trend of dwindling demand for printed newspapers.[31] Despite the negative global forecast for print newspapers, company executives at the *Gleaner* expected significant future growth through online media usage. At the end of 2008 Caribbean media scholar Hopeton Dunn reported that overall newspaper readership had grown in Jamaica from 1.4 million in 2007 to 1.6 million in 2008.[32] In 2010, the Gleaner Company annual report noted an increase in profits of over $270 million compared to 2009 thanks to regained advertising revenue. The 2010 report also noted a significant growth in the company's online media products. The Gleaner Company continued to increase its profits in the second decade of the twenty-first century, despite the challenges of new technology, competitive markets, and the International Monetary Fund's (IMF) economic austerity plan.[33] In 2013 the Gleaner Company reported a profit of $86 million, and $118 million in 2014.

Other newspaper companies in the region also reported similar trends for the years 2007–2009, but by 2010 they had regained advertising revenues and increased circulation by implementing new strategies—mergers and acquisitions, the hiring of accountants, collaborative partnerships, global markets, and integrative online services. Some news organizations created joint operational agreements to share rising costs. In July 2007, in the Bahamas, the *Nassau Guardian* and *Nassau Tribune*, the two largest daily newspapers, and the *Freeport News*, a subsidiary of the *Nassau Guardian*, signed a joint operating agreement to share rising operational costs. According to media economists John Busterna and Robert Picard, joint operating agreements are entered into to save a newspaper from failure.[34] The joint operating agreement (JOA) strategy was applied to many news organizations in the United States in the 1970s and 1980s. However, since the 1990s, many US newspapers rescinded their JOAs as they were no longer economically viable, or one or both parties were no longer willing or required to continue joint operations.[35] The *Nassau Guardian* and *Nassau Tribune* dissolved their joint operation agreement in 2009 for similar reasons.

Under the joint agreement, both newspapers increased circulation. After the dissolution of the JOA the *Nassau Tribune* continued to report increases in its circulation, while the *Nassau Guardian* held stable circulation numbers. Since 2009, both newspapers reported increases in circulation (see Table 2) and advertising revenues. Although advertising revenues are better indicators of success, advertising data was not available from these private companies, and the present research relied on available annual reports and circulation revenue. The *Nassau Tribune's* daily circulation increased from 12,000 in 2002 to 21,000 in 2012, while the *Nassau Guardian* increased from 14,100 in 2002 to 17,000 in 2012.[36] In 2011, both newspapers added supplementary sections with increased advertising content. Using the Pew Research Center's formula—daily circulation number multiplied by the cost of the newspaper—the estimated annual circulation revenue for the *Nassau Tribune* increased from $825,000 (Bahamian dollars) in 2007 to $1,575,000 in 2012; the *Nassau Guardian's* was $450,000 in 2007 and increased to $1,275,000 by 2012. The Tribune Group, owners of the *Nassau Tribune*, is the largest media conglomerate in the Bahamas. It owns five radio stations, an online media news aggregate service, two newspapers, a broadsheet, and a tabloid. The second-largest media conglomerate, the Nassau Guardian Group, owners of the *Nassau Guardian*, has two newspapers, two radio stations, and a television station. Colina Holdings, parent company of Colina Insurance, owns 60 percent of the Nassau Guardian Group and has reported "continual profits" since it bought majority shares in the newspaper in 2002. There were no additional details on revenue dispersion. The Tribune Group, a family-owned company, has no public record of its revenues.

Barbados has two national daily newspapers, the *Barbados Nation* and the *Barbados Advocate*. The *Nation* merged in 2005 with Trinbagonian media giant Caribbean Communications Network to form the largest media conglomerate in the English-speaking Caribbean, One Caribbean Media (OCM). Since the merger, the *Nation* newspaper has increased its advertising revenues and circulation. In 2002 it had a circulation of 32,000; by 2012, circulation had increased to 35,000.[37] Its circulation revenue was estimated at $320,000 (Barbadian dollars) in 2002 and $350,000 in 2012. The *Nation*, now a subsidiary of One Caribbean Media, is the largest media conglomerate in Barbados. The Nation Corporation owns the radio stations of StarCom Network (seven radio stations—four in Barbados, one in Trinidad and Tobago, and two radio stations and a television station in Grenada), an internet service company, Nation Logic; and a real estate holding company.[38] Its rival, the *Barbados Advocate*, has also become a media conglomerate, acquiring Sun Printing and Publishing in Antigua, the parent company of the *Antigua Sun*, and the *Grenada Advocate*, and it owns radio stations in Barbados, Grenada, and Antigua. The *Barbados Advocate's* circulation increased from 15,000 in 2002 to 22,000 in 2012. Using the Pew Research Center formula, circulation revenue was estimated at $150,000 in 2002 and $220,000 in 2012.[39] The success of the news industry in Barbados was overshadowed in 2015 by the country's economic crisis. Since the 2008 recession, the Barbadian economy has been struggling to reverse a negative trend of indebtedness; the country has turned to the IMF to reduce its debt-to-GDP ratio. By the end of 2013, OCM reported that the economic climate in Barbados and the eastern Caribbean presented challenges, particularly in advertising revenue. At the end of 2014, OCM reported "Barbados however continued to face serious economic challenges and our operations in this market reported a 23% decline in profitability."[40] To stabilize its media operations in Barbados, OCM applied several strategies, including "the closure of a non-performing business unit, staff cuts and cost efficiency improvements."[41]

Trinidad and Tobago's media market is dominated by Caribbean Communications Network (CCN), which owns the *Trinidad Express*, TV 6, and four radio stations. As noted, in 2005 CCN merged with the largest newspaper company in Barbados, the Nation Group, to form One Caribbean Media. OCM owns newspapers, television and radio stations, and publishing companies in seven Caribbean countries—Antigua, Barbados, Grenada, Guyana, Jamaica, St. Lucia, and Trinidad and Tobago. OCM's third-quarter report for 2012 shows a net profit increase of 7 percent. The report also notes the company's newspapers, television and radio stations "continue to grow and extend their audiences."[42] OCM also acquired four new radio stations in the third quarter of 2012, three in Trinidad and Tobago and one in St. Lucia. Despite the economic turbulence in Barbados, OCM reported that 2013 and 2014 were profitable years for media holdings in Trinidad and Tobago, although there were only marginal profits for 2014.

According to Omatie Lyder, the editor of the *Trinidad Express*, Trinidad and Tobago has one of the highest per capita consumption rates of newsprint in the Caribbean. The country's four major newspapers—the *Trinidad Express*, the *Trinidad Guardian*, *Newsday*, and the *Tobago Evening News*—had a daily circulation of 240,000 in 2002; by 2012 this had

TABLE 2: DAILY NEWSPAPER CIRCULATION IN THE ENGLISH-SPEAKING CARIBBEAN (2012)

	Bahamas	Barbados	Belize* (No Daily)	Grenada (No Daily)	Jamaica	Trinidad and Tobago
	Tribune	Nation	Amandala	Grenada Today	Jamaica Gleaner	Trinidad Express
2002	7-14,000	32,000	N/A	N/A	259,000	51,000
2012	11-21,000	35,000	45,000	28,542	509,000 (est.)	75,000
	Guardian	Advocate	Reporter	Grenada Informer	Jamaica Observer	Guardian
2002	10-15,000	15,000	N/A	N/A	N/A	46,760 (est.)
2012	6-17,000	22,000	6,500	20,448	115,000	67,000
	Bahamas Journal			Grenadian Voice	Herald (weekly publication)	Newsday
2002	N/A			N/A	N/A	25,000
2012	2,000			6,816	20,000	40,000
	Freeport News			Grenada Advocate		
2002	N/A			N/A		
2012	3,000					

Source: The figures were compiled from various online reports in 2012—annual reports, special commission reports, country profiles of media systems.
*The figures represent weekly circulation numbers. Based on 2007 data.
For a complete list of sources for this table see page 223.

grown to more than 300,000. The most popular newspapers are the *Trinidad Guardian* and the *Trinidad Express*. The *Express* has 40 percent of the readership, while the *Guardian* follows closely, with 37 percent. In 2002, the *Trinidad Express* had a daily circulation of 51,000; the *Trinidad Guardian* had 46,760, *Newsday* 25,000, and the *Trinidad Evening News* 33,770. In 2012, the *Trinidad Express's* daily circulation had grown to 75,000.[43] The *Trinidad Guardian*, its major competitor, had an estimated daily circulation of 67,000 in 2012.

Of the six countries in this study, Jamaica's media organizations have the most detailed public records of their revenues. The *Jamaica Gleaner* and the *Jamaica Observer* dominate the country's newspaper landscape. In 2002, the *Gleaner* had a circulation of 259,000; by 2009 it was 432,000. The readership grew in 2010 to 509,000, an 18 percent increase. Its rival, the *Jamaica Observer*, had an estimated circulation of 115,000 in 2010. The *Sunday Gleaner*, a weekly edition published by the Gleaner Company, had a readership of 671,000 in 2008. This dropped to 640,000 in 2009, but increased again to 745,000 in 2010, a 16 percent growth. The Gleaner Company's tabloid publication, the *Star*, also had a high readership—653,000 in 2009 and 884,000 in 2010, for a 35 percent increase. In 2011, the Gleaner Company continued to make profits but reported flat revenues, with a $431 million (Jamaican dollars) profit in 2010. The Gleaner Company's 2011 profit was $118 million, a drop from 2010, but the *Jamaica Gleaner* increased its revenue by 1.5 percent. The company's 2013 annual report indicated that the company continued to increase its profits with a growth of 1 percent in its media services. The company's digital strategy expanded in 2013 with the introduction of mobile applications for Android and iOS operating systems.[44] By the end of 2013, the Gleaner Company had assets valued at $3.7 billion (Jamaican dollars), and it showed an increase in profit of $6 million over 2012. Profits also increased in 2014. That year, the *Gleaner*, following the model of the *New York Times*, added a partial paywall to its online edition. The Gleaner Company, recognizing the challenge of maintaining continued profits in the midst of the country's economic crisis, hopes to remain profitable by diversifying its financial portfolio.

The Gleaner Company is the largest media conglomerate in Jamaica, with assets of $3.6 billion as of December 2013. The Gleaner Company operates media services in Jamaica, the United Kingdom, Canada, and the United States, including newspapers, both online and print—the *Gleaner*, the *Sunday Gleaner*, the *Star*—two radio stations, and book and magazine publications. The Gleaner Company, like many of the larger media companies in the region—the Tribune Company, The Nassau Guardian Group, One Caribbean Media—has employed a global marketing strategy that focuses mainly on the Caribbean diaspora. The second-largest media conglomerate in Jamaica is Radio Jamaica Rediffusion Communications Group (RJR), with assets of $1.2 billion as of 2011. RJR owns Television Jamaica, Reggae Entertainment Television, TVJ Sports Network, Jamaica News Network, and radio stations RJR 94 FM, FAME 95 FM, and HITZ

92 FM, and it also owns shares in One Caribbean Media.⁴⁵ The *Jamaica Observer* comes third. Gordon "Butch" Stewart, owner of Sandals Resorts International, owns the *Jamaica Observer*.

The Jamaican media landscape will face another gigantic change when the Gleaner Company and RJR merge, making the former one of the biggest conglomerates in the region. The Gleaner Company announced the pending merger in the *Gleaner* in August 2015. The Gleaner Company also published details on its website, which includes a lengthy explanation of the merger in a twenty-nine-item Q&A section. The company explained that it was undertaking the merger with RJR, "to remain competitive in a rapidly changing environment and take advantage of economies of scale to provide better products and services."⁴⁶ The merger was approved by the shareholders at the end of 2015.⁴⁷

Belize and Grenada have a slightly different story. In 1990, Omar Oliveria described Belize's media context as "economic dependence, limited natural resources, no military forces, small population, and a lack of national integration."⁴⁸ There are no daily offline newspapers in Belize, though daily online newspapers started in the mid-2000s. In 2002, *Amandala*, a biweekly newspaper in Belize, had the largest circulation, with about 45,000. In 2013, its circulation remained the same and its estimated circulation revenues were $90,000 (Belize dollars). *Amandala* also owns one radio station, Krem. The *Reporter*, the second-largest weekly, had a circulation of 6,500 in 2012. There are thirteen additional newspapers in Belize that offer print and/or online versions and are published weekly, biweekly, and monthly. These include the *Ambergris Today* (which is now offered only online), the *Belize Times* (the political newspaper of the ruling PUP), and the *Guardian* (the opposition party's newspaper). The largest Belizean island, San Pedro, has a daily newspaper, the *San Pedro Daily*, and a weekly newspaper, the *San Pedro Sun*. Circulation figures were not available for these newspapers, but online sources estimate a range of approximately 5,000 to 20,000. In 2006, a new paper, the *Independent Reformer*, was started first as a print publication and then as an online newspaper as of 2011. In November 2014, Belize Media Group started the fast breaking online news service Breaking Belize News, similar to On the Ground News Report in Jamaica.

The largest private media company in Belize is RSV Media Center, which owns the largest private radio station, Love FM, three smaller radio stations, and Love Belize Television. The second-largest media corporation is Kremandala Limited, with major shares in the press, radio, and television, which includes *Amandala*, Krem FM radio, and Krem television station. Channel 7 and Channel 5 are the two largest privately owned television stations in Belize. Channel 7 is owned by Tropical Vision Limited and has been on air since 1981, producing its own news since 1994. Channel 5 is a subsidiary of Great Belize Productions (GBP), a company based in Belize. GBP was a subsidiary of Belize Telecommunications Limited (BTL), the largest telecommunications company in Belize. Prior to the nationalization of BTL, in 2009, BTL sold GBP so that it would remain a private company.

Like the other Caribbean countries, Grenada's media market has grown significantly over the last twenty years. Liberalization, deregulation, and privatization opened this market to intense competition. Given the country's size (133 square miles, with a population of 100,000), there is a lot of media in Grenada. While there is no daily offline newspaper, there are five weekly newspapers, eleven radio stations, three television stations, and one cable provider. Grenada's newspapers are also operating online versions with daily reports.

In 2007, Barbados-based Systematic Marketing and Research Services conducted a survey of local newspapers in Grenada. Based on those findings, the *Grenada Today* was identified as the leading newspaper, with 67 percent of the country's readership, which was recorded as 42,600, or nearly half of the population. The *Grenada Informer* came in second, with 48 percent, and the *Grenadian Voice* came in third, with 16 percent. The remaining newspapers, the *Spice Isle Review* and the *Grenada Advocate*, were ranked fourth and fifth, respectively. Weekly newspaper readership was fairly high, at 75 percent.[49]

Like Belize, political partisanship is evident in Grenada's media and its history is intertwined with the history of the 1979 revolution. At the time of the revolution, the two contending political parties, the Grenada National Party and the New Jewel Movement, had their own newspaper, the *Vanguard* and the *Jewel*, respectively. In 2013, Laurie Lambert described the role newspapers played in the revolution, concluding that "the Grenada Revolution was a discursive political process where branding and narration were necessary elements in securing the revolution's authority and legitimacy."[50] She argued Cuba functioned as a metonym through which the revolution was translated in Grenadian periodicals: "Even before the coup of 13 March 1979 Grenadian media represented the New Jewel Movement—the revolutionary party—as Cuban-inspired and socialist."[51] In order to examine how socialism in general, and the socialist character of the People's Revolutionary Government (PRG) in particular, were narrated, Lambert compared two newspapers—the government-run *Free West Indian* and the privately owned *Torchlight*. She examined competing discourses on Cuban communism "for the ways in which they stood in for the Grenadian people's hopes, aspirations, and anxieties in the midst of radical political change."[52] Issues including race, gender equality, property ownership, freedom of religious practice, and freedom of travel were examined in relation to capitalism and socialism, and the PRG's efforts to maintain narrative authority of the revolution. Political partisanship is still evident today in Grenada's newspapers and broadcast media.

OCM bought majority shares (60 percent) in the Grenada Broadcasting Network (GBN) in 2007, making it the largest media network in Grenada. The government of Grenada retained 40 percent of its shares in GBN. GBN has two radio stations and a television station. Grenada's media market was further divested when the *Barbados Advocate* bought the *Grenada Advocate* and two radio stations in the country.

The current wave of mergers and acquisitions is creating regional conglomerates that are controlling major portions of the Caribbean media market. In the English-speaking Caribbean, there are no media anti-trust laws, and this trend raises concerns for fair competition and good public information.[53] The creation of media oligopolies (the domination of the market by a few companies, which leads to high levels of concentration) has been criticized by American media scholars such as Herbert Schiller, Ben Bagdikian, and Robert McChesney, who have been concerned about the impact of concentrated media ownership on journalism's role as a public service.[54] McChesney and Bagdikian have criticized policymakers for the way in which antitrust laws have failed to control the mergers and acquisitions of multinational and transnational media corporations like Viacom and CBS, AOL and Time Warner, Time Warner and EMI, and Tribune and Times Mirror. In the UK and Australia, Rupert Murdoch's News Corporation has become a media behemoth. The fear is a few media oligopolies will control the content of global, regional, and national information and thereby impact editorial independence and content diversity. This fear is emerging in the Caribbean as well.

In 2000, Norman Solomon wrote an article, "Coverage of Media Mergers: Does it Provide a Window into the Future of Journalism?" in Harvard University's *Nieman Report*, in which he discussed press freedom in today's environment of mega-media mergers. Solomon believed the accelerating mergers are good for the profits of big business but "bad for journalism and democracy."[55] He summarized the impact of media mergers by quoting American journalist A. J. Liebling, who several decades ago wrote that "freedom of the press is guaranteed only to those who own one."[56] As noted earlier, eight (now seven, with the merger of the *Jamaica Gleaner* and RJR at the end of 2015) media conglomerates control the majority of the global news and information flow in the Caribbean. Solomon also quoted American media critic Mark Crispin Miller in the same report. According to Miller, "the implications of these mergers for journalism and the arts are enormous. It seems to me that this is, by any definition, an undemocratic development. The media system in a democracy should not be inordinately dominated by a few very powerful interests."[57]

In the smaller markets of the Caribbean, this concern is an urgent one. Having broken the history of state-controlled media over the last ten years, the emergence of the private control of information in the region may be even more damaging to regional democracy. To ensure the independence of the media, particularly the news, Hopeton Dunn believes Caribbean policymakers need to implement anti-trust laws to ensure fair competition, diverse content, and editorial independence.[58] Other media owners in the region agree with Dunn. In particular, Charles Carter, owner of Carter's Marketing and Communication in the Bahamas, identified media conglomeration as the other danger of free market enterprise, where it is really the survival of the fittest.

> Sometimes ... there is a player that is not playing as fairly as the other people ... or who has grown so big that he is the biggest bear in the cave, and the cave can only accommodate so much. Yes, we are facing that, and that is the danger, the vulnerability if you like, of markets of all sizes is that the major players, the ones who create media conglomerates ... those who are able to put together all the modes of communication under one umbrella,

the print and electronic, and say to the marketplace "more bang for your buck." ... After a while, that sense of democracy that you thought you created, you have created something that is undemocratic where the message is being shaped by just one medium."[59]

Carter believes that if regional governments are concerned about media democracy, more care should be taken to ensure that checks and balances "that ought to exist in a democracy, exist here [in media ownership] as well."[60]

Factors Influencing Media Growth in the Caribbean

What accounts for this economic success? There are several factors, perhaps the most significant of which is small markets. Size matters. International research shows that over the last decade, newspapers in small markets are faring better than their large-market counterparts. The 2012 findings of US research and consulting firm Borrell Associates confirmed this trend.[61] Prior to the recent economic woes of Barbados, the *Jamaica Gleaner*, has had the most significant loss, but it has presented steady financial reports since the significant losses of 2009, and revenues have increased since 2010. The World Association of Newspapers and News Publishers (WAN-IFRA) noted in its 2013 report that print newspaper circulations continue to rise in Asia, Australia, New Zealand, and Latin America, while they declined in mature markets in the West.[62] Vincent Peyrègne, CEO of WAN-IFRA, noted that "even if paid circulation declines, newspapers reach a vast number of readers—print, online and mobile—and the latest trends show that advertising engagement in print keeps performing well and improves in many countries."[63] WAN-IFRA's 2014 report on world trends revealed a robust industry that continues to evolve and grow. More than half the world's adult population—2.5 billion—were still consumers of print newspapers; more than 800 million were digital consumers.[64]

New economic strategies have also been employed. One of the major global strategies is revenue diversification. The editor of the *Nassau Tribune*, Paco Nunez, explained that beyond the hiring of a plethora of accountants, some media organizations also created new partnerships and expanded their markets globally to include the Caribbean diaspora.[65] The *Nassau Tribune* and *Nassau Guardian* experienced growth after their JOA and they have shifted their focus to a mixed marketing environment using a combination of online and offline advertising to expand growth. In Barbados, both national dailies, the *Nation* and the *Advocate*, increased circulation and revenues after mergers and acquisitions created media conglomerates. The same trend has emerged in Belize, Grenada, Jamaica, and Trinidad and Tobago, where mergers and acquisitions have created new media empires. Caribbean editors and media owners also noted that they have extended their markets by diversifying their financial portfolios. In 2013, OCM acquired a 51 percent share in Innogen Technologies Inc., a new energy company in Barbados.

Two other factors have contributed to this period of prosperity, and they are related to cultural aspects of the region: oral traditions and interpersonal selling. Caribbean societies have very strong oral cultures.[66] Caribbean societies still rely on interpersonal storytelling to disseminate information. This aspect of the culture plays a significant role in the newspaper industry, as those who do not purchase newspapers rely on those who do to tell them the day's events or pass on important information. This oral tradition is coupled with the culture of selling newspapers. In many of these countries, newspapers are sold on street corners by street vendors, at neighborhood convenience stores, or other public venues. In these spaces there is high interpersonal interaction and a lot of storytelling goes into the act of selling newspapers. Marketing scholars Paolo Guenzi and Ottavia Pelloni believe interpersonal relationships play a significant role in customer satisfaction and loyalty.[67] Many of the editors interviewed for this study indicated that because of these cultural factors, they expected newspaper readership to remain significant over the next five to ten years. But many also expected some changes with increased access to digital technologies. According to a 2013 survey of media in the Bahamas, access to the digital environment has grown significantly, and was presenting some challenges to traditional news media, particularly in breaking news.[68] By the end of 2014, the anticipated changes in readership behavior were happening rapidly in each of the countries covered as access to technology grew.

Omatie Lyder, editor of the *Trinidad Express*, has explained the cultural influence on media performance in the region in the following terms:

> It's all a part of the interesting paradox of why in a world of dying newspaper industries ours is still alive and healthy and making money, and again that goes back to connectivity. A significant number of the population depend daily on what comes out in the paper in terms of where [they are] from, what's happening in terms of traffic and getting to their flights an hour ahead because of the Summit [of the Americas] coming up, to where we going to lime this weekend.[69] So it's incredibly important in terms of our culture and social development.[70]

As of 2014, competition has increased in the countries with higher internet penetration. As previously noted, in Jamaica, OGNR became an instant competitor of traditional media when it began gathering and disseminating news using social media and citizen reporters. However, since its initial interruption, OGNR has become just another media channel as traditional, or legacy, media organizations continue to make a profit. In Antigua and Barbuda, *Caribarena* shook up the status quo when it started its online operation in 2007, and although it is still regarded as an "opposition press," its initial shock has worn off. Caribbean News Now, an online site based in the United States, has had a similar impact.

Another aspect of the cultural influence is the newspaper-reading culture in the region. Ken Gordon, one of the shareholders of OCM, explains this culture in Trinidad and Tobago:

> Whereas abroad, many newspapers have lost circulation because of the internet, and ... advertising rates have fallen ... many of them have had to close or merge or whatever. So your production costs have gone down because technology has made that possible, but your revenues have fallen so sharply that you have not really improved the net position of your company, and ... their profits have dropped dramatically. This hasn't happened here. ... My view is that this [the internet] has been around long enough now to see—to make a judgment about how it's likely to impact the habit of picking up the paper for your granddad

and your father on the street—is so strong. I waited for a while to see if that would disappear and it hasn't. … There's a habit of picking up that paper from that vendor, which is an easy thing. It's built in with the society, into the culture, into a whole host of things, and somehow, the fact that circulations … basically have grown by in excess of 40 percent … in spite of the internet and in spite of the fact that newspapers are available to read on the internet and so on. And I think that will continue to be so for the foreseeable future. So newspapers have benefited in a net way, because on the one hand the production costs have gone down and on the other hand they have not lost as a result of the same circulation adversity that the people have had [in other parts of the world].[71]

Another factor affecting the continued success of newspaper readership is demography. The Caribbean population has a high percentage of older people. However, much is still unknown about the demographic makeup of this group, as data on the elderly is still scarce throughout the region. But, as noted by a 2004 report from the Economic Commission for Latin America and the Caribbean, the region has, aside Europe and North America, the highest percentage of elderly people in its population.[72] A 2006 UN report also noted that by 2010, more than 10 percent of the Caribbean population would be over sixty, except in Belize, the Dominican Republic, Guyana, and Haiti: "It is estimated that the Caribbean will experience absolute and relative increases in the elderly population over the next 50 years and that the elderly population, which constituted 4.5% in 1950, will increase to 18% in 2050."[73] According to several editors and publishers interviewed for this book, this group of consumers still has a marked preference for print newspapers. The younger generation is shifting to the online/mobile environment for their information and entertainment. Roxanne Gibbs, editor of the *Nation*, in Barbados, believes that when the older generation dies out, the region will experience a significant drop in newspaper readership.[74]

Technological factors that are impacting these changes involve advances in digital technologies. At the time of this research, the relatively low internet connectivity in the region was also impacting the growth of Caribbean newspapers. According to Hopeton Dunn and Omatie Lyder the region has 100 percent wireless phone usage. In 2013, internet penetration was highest in Barbados (72 percent) and the Bahamas (65 percent), moderate in Jamaica and Trinidad and Tobago (55 percent), and low in Belize (29 percent) and Grenada (35 percent). Bermuda and St. Lucia had the highest penetration, at 88 percent and 81 percent, respectively.[75] By the end of 2014, internet connectivity had increased significantly throughout the region. The Bahamas increased to 90 percent penetration, Barbados to 77 percent, while Grenada and Belize remained low, at 35 percent and 31 percent, respectively. Jamaica remained the same (55 percent), and Trinidad and Tobago increased (64 percent).[76] Global media trends indicate that most of this digital consumption is being done through smartphones and most of the advertising growth is through mobile advertising. News organizations throughout the region could use these trends to their advantage and drive new market developments. The *Jamaica Gleaner* has incorporated this strategy in its marketing mix. Further, OGNR has also taken advantaged of Jamaica's high smartphone usage. Although there are ethical concerns when it comes to citizen journalism (such as issues of accuracy, accountability, privacy, and harm), OGNR's model has been extended throughout the region as citizen journalists participate in the dissemination of information in rural areas where traditional media has done a poor job. Andrea Polanco, a Belizean journalist attending the 2011 Commonwealth Broadcasters Association and Caribbean Broadcasting Union's two-day symposium on "New Media, Journalism, and Democracy in the Caribbean," indicated that they were currently implementing this strategy in the way they gathered information in remote parts of Belize.[77] These efforts should be organized and integrated in public journalism or community journalism projects.

The newspapers in the six countries included in this book have integrated online media into their operations. Caribbean editors and publishers in the Bahamas, Barbados, Belize, Grenada, Jamaica, and Trinidad and Tobago indicated digital technologies would play a major role in the future of their newspapers. Internet and wireless technologies are changing the practice and profession, allowing Caribbean journalists to research, access, and disseminate information quickly, providing interactive elements in news content, and increasing the competition for readers, viewers, and listeners as more citizens have the ability to publish information on the internet or disseminate it via wireless technology, Twitter, Facebook, and

WhatsApp, and other social media platforms. These are the strategies that Gunn Enli urged public service broadcasters to adopt to survive and succeed in the digital age.[78] Fortunately, for now, as a Bahamian managing news editor indicated, the credibility for news sources still lies with the professional journalists and traditional media, so the competition from bloggers, although making an impact, is limited.[79] However, change is occurring. In 2013, according to Juan McCartney, the editor of the *Nassau Guardian*, the impact of the internet and social media on traditional media in the Bahamas was more significant.[80] Editors of the *Jamaica Gleaner*, the *Jamaica Observer*, the *Barbados Nation*, and the *Barbados Advocate* also noted the increased impact of the internet and other social media on the consumption and distribution of news. However, despite the popularity of new online sources, such as OGNR, not everyone views these organizations as credible. For example, Karyl Walker, online news content editor of the *Jamaica Observer*, is not worried about the competition, "because we have a wider audience that we carried over from our traditional days and I believe we are seen to be a more credible source than OGNR. ... I think it's good they do this thing with alacrity but we do more checks sometimes we find the On the Ground News Reports not entirely correct."[81] Other journalists throughout the region share Walker's views.

The growing use of digital technology by citizens and the media industry indicates that Caribbean media markets are facing similar technological challenges as their American and European counterparts. The number of "mass self-communicators" is growing, and the amount of information produced by people who are not employed as journalists has increased substantially. American and European journalism scholars like Jay Rosen and Mark Deuze described the changing power relationships in media industries, especially journalism, as the emergence of "consumers as co-producers, the democratization of media access, and the redistribution of agency from news and creative producers to owners and employers."[82] Rosen and Deuze identified these changes from two perspectives—that of "the people formerly known as the audience" and "the people formerly known as the employers."[83] These changes indicate the kinds of challenges that have emerged in the newsgathering, editing, and publishing industries. Media critics and journalists in the region believe this new form of journalism is good for democracy. One of the areas in which journalism is being most notably affected is investigative journalism, as citizen bloggers and news aggregators publish stories online that traditional journalists are not able to publish. According to the Barbadian journalists David Ellis and Reudon Eversley,[84] citizen bloggers are filling a void in the Caribbean. However, despite these advances, investigative journalism throughout the region is still constrained by access to information laws, and other economic and cultural factors.

The Cost of Media Success: The Common Good?

Making a profit comes at a price. As news organizations in the English-speaking Caribbean become more commercially oriented concerns for the public interest have grown. Caribbean journalists believe many media organizations are placing profits ahead of good journalism. Competing in commercial environments, media organizations throughout the region are resorting to the tactics of their global counterparts to increase profits and cut costs. Over the last ten years, there has been a greater emphasis on sensational, tabloid-style journalism, increased mergers and layoffs. Journalists in Barbados and Jamaica discussed the issue of layoffs that came about as a result of mergers or acquisitions and overall decline in the economy. There was no accurate figure of the number of journalists who have been laid off in these countries, as much of this data has not been collated and this work relies on the anecdotal stories of journalists. While the absolute number is small in comparison to the United States and Western Europe, it is significant in terms of proportionality. Further, there have been few newspaper closures in these countries over the last five years. The trend in the English-speaking Caribbean is not closure but mergers and acquisitions, as new strategies are employed to ensure the future of the newspaper industry, and media industries in general.

Ken Gordon believed the change to market-oriented journalism has created a crisis in journalism throughout the region.[85] He has argued the crisis came about because the marketplace opened up quickly and the new competitors were unprepared to operate media organizations, particularly radio and television stations. Consequently, Gordon believes, this led to the erosion of standards. Other journalists throughout the region agree with Gordon's assessment. Peter Christopher, a journalist at the *Trinidad*

Express, believes the current crisis was not just the result of the way some journalists practice, but also of the emphasis owners placed on "quick, attention grabbing, salacious stories that sell in the marketplace."[86] He contends that media owners' emphasis on selling journalism in the competitive marketplace to get advertisers' support led to the current crisis in Trinbagonian journalism. Christopher believes there was a change in the type of journalism in that country after owners placed more emphasis on making money and less emphasis on the quality of journalism. Caribbean journalists are concerned about this trend as they believed the emphasis on sensational, tabloid-style journalism does not bode well for the advancement of democracy and the common good.

Another prominent trend, an increase in mergers and acquisitions, could also endanger democracy in the region. According to Roxanne Gibbs, editor of the *Barbados Nation*, senior members of that paper's editorial team were laid off when the company merged; they were replaced by young, inexperienced reporters.[87] As a result, what emerged in the Caribbean was a lot of "green" newsrooms. This change resulted in increased public criticism about the quality of journalism. Of course, this trend is not unique to the Caribbean, but is rather common in countries across the globe, from the United States to Australia.

Green newsrooms also exist because these competitive media markets created a high turnover of employees. This is largely a result of the movement of journalists from one media organization to another, where many are in search of higher wages and better benefits. This movement has led to a lack of continuity and professional development. A journalist in the Bahamas expressed concern over his meteoric rise from cub reporter to senior reporter to editor in the short period of one year. He agreed the high turnover was partially responsible for the quality of their work and the increased public criticism. But he also believed the fragmented, fast-paced media environment was also to blame.[88]

Clearly, Caribbean journalism is in transition. The profession is going through a period of rapid change brought on by the shift to commercialized markets and technological innovations. Like its global counterparts, the homogenization of Caribbean journalism, the rise of sensationalism, and the advent of more entertainment-oriented reporting, as well as the blurring of boundaries between news and advertising, has resulted in complaints about the quality of journalism. Roxanne Gibbs believes the market model may be good for selling products but not for providing the kind of information citizens need. Her concerns reflect those of media scholars such as Edward S. Herman and Noam Chomsky, John Keane, Herbert Schiller, and Bill Kovach and Tom Rosenstiel, who warned of the influence of commercialization on the democratic process. Here, Gibbs described what happened to journalism in Barbados when the business model became the dominant approach to news production:

> We were known as the people's paper and we did what we called people's journalism. ... [When] the *Nation* became a public entity ... some of the changes began to be apparent. ... First of all, the whole pace of journalism began to change. Not only here in Barbados but elsewhere too. The *Advocate* was actually taken over by a businessman who said quite plainly and frankly he was really not that interested in journalism, he was interested in the business aspect of it. ... The fight or the conflict between the advertising and editorial department has now become more intense because the advertising department is now saying, well you know, without us the paper's going out of business. ... It's changing the way journalists are beginning to think. What it is doing is making some of us traditional journalists very disheartened.[89]

In the region, traditional media have added new technologies to their operations and new players like OGNR, *Caribarena*, and other bloggers and online news aggregates have emerged as competitors of traditional media. The level of new media competition varies among the countries based on internet penetration, but smartphone technology is making up for low connectivity in many of the remote areas of the region. The increased level of new media usage in the region has resulted in a sporadic emergence of a discourse on the relevance of traditional media in advancing democracy in the region. The 2011 symposium "New Media, Journalism and Democracy in the Caribbean" is one of the few debates on journalism and its future in the region. During that symposium, all of the panelists acknowledged new media's impact on traditional media and society. They argued traditional media will continue to play a significant role in the gathering and dissemination of information, but that new media will create more competition, and hence more opportunities to disseminate public opinion. Paul Ashley, one of the panelists, believed traditional media would always have a place in people's lives, but that new media would be more influential because digital technology makes it easier to capture, manipulate, store, transmit, and retrieve data. Consequently, Ashley explained, digital technologies would lead to "a widening of freedom of expression, a deepening of democracy but with that comes invasion of privacy."[90] He conceded the manipulation of information would cause harm—defaming private citizens and politicians—and would lead the state to react. As Mark Beckford argues, "one of the ways the state will react is that the state will demand every user of a smartphone and every user of a computer be registered, so that big brother will know who you are and what you have said, and you will be held to account for your advent into unprotected journalism."[91]

Other panelists at the 2011 symposium believed that along with issues of privacy, new media can also lead to the distortion of information. One of the drawbacks of the speed at which information can now be disseminated is the increase in inaccurate and unreliable information. Caribbean journalist Karen Madden James argued that, though

> there is a place for such agents as On the Ground News Reporting and Twitter and Facebook and so on ... there's [also] an inherent danger in that these reporters don't have to substantiate their claims, there is nobody suing [them]. ... They are not liable to the same ethics of journalism that traditional media is obliged and obligated to. Somebody will sue you; nobody is going to sue OGNR, anonymity is bliss, nobody knows who you are. But I believe there is a place for social media, but we have to differentiate the positions and responsibilities, because they are different.[92]

Some scholars have lauded the use of new media to advance democracy; others are concerned about its inherent dangers. New technology has produced a new type of journalism. Anyone can become a journalist without formal training, but the lack of editorial oversight and control in the new journalism has caused many to pause and revert to traditional media to verify the accuracy and reliability of information. The new form of journalism is generated anywhere, involves new forms of writing, relies on a fragmented audience, is delivered quickly, and is interactive and participatory. While many of these characteristics could advance journalism and democracy, some practitioners fear they may also threaten them. Both advocates and opponents continue to weigh in on this debate as use of new media technologies continues to change our social, political, and economic interactions. No matter which side of the debate you support, the fundamentals of journalism—truth, accuracy, and good storytelling—should remain. Further, each society will have to determine what rules should be applied to the new disseminators of information.

In the midst of advancing technologies and the growth in commercialism, concern for the public sphere and the advance of democracy remains a focal point for journalists in the English-speaking Caribbean. What is at stake in a heavily commercialized news market? According to many scholars of democracy and media's role in it, the sacrificial lamb is the common good. Concerns for the common good date back more than twenty-five hundred years, and is centered on the ideas of early philosophers like Plato, Aristotle, Cicero, and later Hobbes, Locke, and Rousseau, whose general concerns were equality and liberty for all. In 1992, Manuel Velasquez, Claire Andre, Thomas Shanks, and Michael J. Meyer noted the common good consists "primarily of having the social systems, institutions, and environments on which we all depend work in a manner that benefits all people."[93] This is particularly important in democracies.

Most democratic theories propose that people are equal in some important ways and all deserve a voice in their governance. They hold that all democratic governance should be open and accountable to citizens. To accomplish these basic tenets, democratic societies turn to journalism to ensure governments and other institutions are accountable to citizens. Normative theories of media's social responsibility have filled the literature from the early days of mass media, from the printed press to the radio, from television to the current technologies driving convergence. The ideals of normative theories of the media come from a tradition of good public communication. This tradition can be traced to the doctrines of early Greek and Roman debates on the role of public discourse in democracy. At the core of these debates are issues of freedom of expression, truth, and citizen participation. Over the centuries, normative theories of public discourse have evolved to express more explicit ideals of public communication based on various cultural and political systems. Today this debate has become a global conversation.[94]

As part of that conversation, Clifford Christians, Theodore Glasser, Denis McQual, Kaarle Nordenstreng, and Robert White define the normative theory of public discourse or public communication as "the conceptual foundation, the explanatory rationale of a particular institutional organization of communication in a democracy."[95] From their perspective, democracy is seen as an essential form of communication in which citizens debate the decisions of governance and monitor the activities of those elected. Today, much has changed in terms of how citizens expect this to happen. There is more demand for direct participatory communication, and the theoretical foundations for public communication have become a major concern in many societies throughout the world. Christians et al. argue "that a foundation of normative theory is extremely important for the vitality of democratic communication and for the media that support and implement"[96] that process. Key elements of normative theories of public communication emerge in normative doctrines on communication ethics, communication policies, and professional leadership. Christians et al. organize these elements hierarchically, with the communication values of a culture (public philosophy) at the top, followed by social theories and normative theories of public communication as proposed by academics and philosophical community; national/international policies of communication including legislative measures that are designed and implemented by politicians; the social responsibility of the culture industries with media entrepreneurs as actors; a professional code of ethics proposed by professionals; and personal ethics/ideals.[97]

Arguments can be made in favor of each of these elements. However, it is my belief that all are equally important and should be placed on a continuum, not a hierarchy. As Christians et al. point out, there are dialectic tensions among and between each level. Communication values in a given culture impact the professionals who work in delivering public communication and vice versus. It is because of these tensions that each level should be weighed equally. For, as Christians et al. argue, "each normative element relies on personal ideals and values, as well as persons acting according to their conscience about the kind of public communication that represents truth, justice, and respect for human dignity."[98] Further, all of these elements should be weighed equally, not hierarchically, if democratic principles are to be upheld among people and nations.

How do these elements play out in the Caribbean context? What is news? What are the normative practices of the media in carrying out the kinds of public communication that impact democracy and the common good? The concern, as reflected in earlier comments about the quality of Caribbean journalism, indicate that the media, particularly the news media, have abandoned their social responsibility to provide good public information in favor of a market-driven model of communication that is more concerned with selling a product.

These concerns are dealt with in the remaining chapters, which focus on the ideals, values, and practices of journalists in the Caribbean, and their implications for the advancement of democracy.

PART II

Caribbean Journalism: Comprehensive and Proportionate

What is news in the Caribbean? Caribbean people have a basic understanding of what types of stories make the news. The news is about prominent people, events, and issues of the day. But the emphasis on relevance and significance is skewed towards their everyday lived experience, which reduces the importance of news stories to the sphere of the personal.

If we accept Jamaica Kincaid's argument, Caribbean people take an event and turn it into the everyday, and the everyday is turned into an event: "Small things loom large, and major events are reduced to an 'ordinary' occurrence."[1] Caribbean people, according to this logic, struggle with the significant. For societies that love to talk, it seems counterintuitive that they make small things significant and significant things small. This rationale goes against Western interpretations of what passes for news: the significant, the unusual, not the everyday. Nonetheless, Caribbean people weave the significant into the storytelling of their everyday lived experience.[2]

The legacy of Caribbean storytelling emerged from an African oral tradition, one filled with analogies and allegories for conveying important lessons and messages. African societies do not openly discuss social ills. According to Edward Hall's and Geert Hofstede's analyses of African cultural orientations, these societies are collectivist, high context cultures.[3] As such, group cohesion, kinship ties, and belonging are valued and result in deeper bonds which bring with them less direct, explicit communication; the rules of behavior are understood and do not have to be discussed. But Hall and Hofstede's models do not accurately describe Caribbean cultures, which, in post-independence have vacillated between collectivist and individualist dimensions and low context and high context orientations. (Anthropologist Edward Hall, in his work on language, places a culture's communication style on a continuum between low-context and high-context. These are based on a culture's preference for direct, explicit communication—low–or indirect, implicit communication—high.)[4] In democratic models of governance that push openness, freedom of expression, and personal liberties, Caribbean societies clash with Western interpretations of how these ideals should work in public discourse. Caribbean societies are comprised of closed, secretive, conservative groups that remain silent on many important political, social, and economic issues, ones that Western societies like the United States and United Kingdom disseminate as news. While there is public discourse on political, economic, and social issues, this discourse is usually controlled by political and economic elites who prefer to maintain the status quo.

Colonial history is integrated into the oral traditions and maintained in these conservative cultures. Under European rule, colonial administrators made decisions without consultation with, or consideration of, the majority of the colonized. The significant was determined externally. External actors continue to play this role in present-day Caribbean societies.

Caribbean people should be interested in pursuing comprehensive and balanced accounts of their social realities. These accounts require "careful weighing, careful consideration, careful judging, careful questioning."[5] To accomplish completeness and exactness, Kincaid believes, "would demand a reconsideration, an adjustment, in the way they [Caribbean people] understand the existence of time."[6] These demands should be made of Caribbean journalism as it seeks to fulfill the principles of comprehensiveness and proportionality. When these principles are upheld, they lead to more accurate accounts of the political, economic, and social realities in these societies.

If Caribbean journalists provide comprehensive and proportional accounts, they will help citizens of the region to understand clearly what is significant and important to know about their societies. According to Bill Kovach and Tom Rosenstiel, when journalists do this they are performing the cartographic function—that is, they are helping citizens to navigate their social world and make sense of it.[7] This task is the social responsibility of journalism, and it helps journalists understand what to cover and how to cover it. Although Caribbean journalists accepted the importance of their social responsibility, many believe economic, political, and cultural challenges inhibit their ability to uphold this responsibility.

Journalism in a Culture of Secrecy and Silence

Former director of culture in the Bahamas, Nicolette Bethel, referred to Bahamian society, and indeed that of the wider Caribbean, as one that suffers in silence and secrecy. "You don't speak it, because if you do then it is real," she explains. "If you are living it, it isn't as real as when you speak it."[8] This culture of secrecy was imposed on Caribbean society by colonial powers. It has left an indelible mark on the psyche of Caribbean people who are, the examples of Jamaica, Cuba, and Haiti notwithstanding, docile people resistant to change. Barbadian journalist David Ellis characterized this culture of silence as endemic to the region, and believes it influenced how journalists practice in the region. Ellis explained that David Thompson, the prime minister of Barbados, was very sick, though no one was talking about his illness as it was perceived to be a private affair. Despite the talk "on the ground" about the prime minister's illness, Ellis noted, "people did not want to be obscene, or they didn't want to appear to be. And these are the nuances of the culture that we talked about; they don't want it to appear as though we are not respectful of his private life, his children's situation, or his wife's, or his mother. Those things matter in this instance."[9] Ellis believes these types of situations are tempered by the culture of silence and fear, the fear of victimization, "which is a reality in this [small] environment which the journalists themselves live with."[10]

Another example comes from the Bahamas, where a prominent member of the bar, Rubie Nottage, was nominated in 2008 for the position of Supreme Court judge. Questions were raised by journalists about her fitness for this position based on the US government's indictment of her and her husband, Kendal Nottage. Juan McCartney, one of the journalists who questioned Mrs. Nottage's nomination for Supreme Court judge, explained that citizens were angry with him and his newspaper because of his story; they wanted to know why he brought it to light. As McCartney explained, people were really upset that we were questioning the fact that Rubie Nottage had an indictment against her in the US, and they thought it was just none of our business to say anything. No one ever stopped and asked, really how do we appoint our judges? What do we know about the people they are putting on the bench? Why don't we have open hearings? Why aren't we able to participate at least on a spectator level when these people are making these appointments? Right now, the legal and judicial commission does whatever the hell they want. We don't have any input; we can't even monitor them. All we can do is really speculate on what is happening.[11]

During the debate on this issue, the *Bahamas Press*, an online news distributor, ran a story with the heading "Nottages should sue the Guardian & Tribune for libel."[12] The *Bahamas Press* story blamed "foreign influence" for the local media's attack on Mrs. Nottage's character. Mrs. Nottage and her husband were stalwart members of the political party, the Progressive Liberal Party (PLP). The *Bahamas Press* is a partisan organization that supports the PLP, and its defensive stance on the issue was biased.

In addition to the social pressure by which topics are deemed "off limits," the difficulty finding reliable sources constrains Caribbean journalists' ability to be comprehensive and proportionate. McCartney explained that when he entered journalism, a lot of his subsequent disappointment came from people's unwillingness to talk on the record. This aspect of the culture remained one of his greatest challenges since "at times, it is very challenging to get people to open up and talk. Especially in a society … where everything is closed and people like to keep secrets about the things that matter. It is very difficult to get them to open up and talk [on the record]."[13] Based on his experience, McCartney believes that people love to gossip about what is happening, but they will not publicly go on record about issues they considered too sensitive to discuss in the open. McCartney's experience underscores the problem of maintaining anonymity and confidentiality in small societies.

Bahamian journalist and talk show host Quincy Parker also identified this aspect of Caribbean culture when he reflected on how some topics or issues were still taboo among Caribbean societies. In particular, topics like child abuse and incest are swept under the rug because no one wants to say anything about them; neither is openly discussed in Caribbean societies, despite the fact that, according to the United Nations Children's Education Fund (UNICEF), the World Health Organization, and World Bank, the Caribbean has extremely high levels of both.[14] The region also has a high prevalence of domestic violence, sexual assault/rape, and human trafficking. The culture of secrecy makes any discussion of these important issues difficult. Nonetheless, Caribbean societies will have to learn how to discuss significant issues openly and deliberatively in a public forum if they are to progress as healthy democracies. Journalism will have to embrace the advocacy role as proposed by Michael Schudson,[15] as well as the radical role prescribed by Christians et al.,[16] to change the beliefs, attitudes, and behaviors about culturally sensitive topics like incest, rape and domestic violence.

Although objectivity is the holy grail of most Western journalism, especially as practiced in the United States and United Kingdom, advocacy journalism, which "promotes a cause or expresses a subjective point of view,"[17] should be used to increase public knowledge and an understanding of the harm and injustice present in the Caribbean. In small societies that have a predilection for secrecy, silence, and authoritarian governance, journalism must advocate change. In some cases, this may require journalists to take on the radical role of airing "views and voices that are critical of authority and the established order"[18] so as to bring about change and reform. Some media scholars believe advocacy journalism is bad journalism or merely propaganda, but this is not always true: It depends on the purpose of the story and the integrity of the journalist. The purpose must fit the context of these small societies, where journalism has more to do with advocating on behalf of the people. Journalists must become more radical if these societies are to resolve some of their complex human problems and institute more democratic practices. The ideals of journalism espoused by Kovach and Rosenstiel—truth, loyalty to citizens, verifiability, independence, engagement and relevance, comprehensiveness and proportionality, and the provision of a public forum—could all be achieved while practicing the advocate and radical roles.[19] It will require journalists to function at the highest level of integrity, to be aware of their biases and influences, and to make their process of gathering, analyzing, and interpreting information open and transparent to the public.

In Western democratic societies, journalism obtained its legitimacy on the grounds of being neutral, gathering facts and analyzing them objectively. But no journalist is free of bias and they must be cognizant of these biases when performing the advocacy or radical role while upholding the principles of accuracy, fairness, and balance. Journalism in the Caribbean should be practiced not as a dichotomy of subjectivity versus objectivity, but rather on a continuum between subjectivity and objectivity to fulfill the needs of these societies and live up to the public's trust. The most trusted type of journalism is one free from political or economic influence, one that works on behalf of the people to provide them with the information they need to make informed decisions.

Quincy Parker conceded that a lot of progress has been made since the new forms of talk show began discussing challenging political, economic, and social topics in the 1990s.[20] However, he believes Caribbean societies still have a long way to go to become more open to critical debate on these issues. In the 1990s, liberalization, deregulation, and privatization engendered a more open kind of talk radio. When these new shows began they pushed the envelope on social and political issues and started to create societies that were willing to discuss these issues more openly. However, the early furor created by this new liberal environment lost its luster and influence. Many of the talk shows descended from their initial perch as effective mediums for discursive conversation and became infotainment-style shows relying on the lowest common denominator to maintain their audiences. Many of the hosts interviewed for this book believed their initial impact on democracy had been supplanted by economic imperatives.

As Bahamian talk show host Steve McKinney explained,

> when it started, when this new, modern talk radio business became the pining spirit of the Bahamas, people were able to call in and they led the discussion because most of them were like open lines. They would have led the discussion and say you know, "I want to talk about this, these roads gotta be fixed" and people power was actively at work. So, I would like to say that when radio talk show first began, people had this interest that they could change things and they expressed themselves through the power of the microphone and the telephone over the airwaves. And they did. The powers that be, government, church, state,

everyone, institutions, they listened. They sat up and listened because after all, this was a new phenomenon.[21]

But the euphoria of such liberty did not last long. Talk radio's ability to bring about deliberative debate soon died out. In Barbados, for example, David Ellis described the current environment this way:

> We now have a situation where the market forces are so dominant that to some extent it is diluting what is considered to be the important stuff. People are attracted more and more by what might be perceived as the trivial or what others might describe as the human-interest dimension. And in these Caribbean environments there is an excessive emphasis on politics and politicians and to a lesser extent economic dimension. The people-centered aspect of it still needs to come to the fore.[22]

In essence, the novelty faded and the audience dwindled as many people lost interest in talk shows. But beyond the shift to commercialism, another reason the radio talk show lost its potency was due to the phenomenon of the "chronic callers," individuals who called the shows numerous times each day. Many audience members grew weary of hearing the same chronic callers.

At first, politicians and other social actors were jolted out of their comfort zone when this new style of talk show emerged, but after the novelty wore off, they became more complacent and viewed this type of public feedback as loud, sensational talk, not effective debate. Politicians also learned how to contain the talk shows through increased legal action or the use of public relations. There was a significant increase in the number of lawsuits filed against radio stations and talk show hosts throughout the region, which will be discussed further in chapter six.

Although many of the talk show hosts still believe they were providing a vehicle for public debate on important issues, the effectiveness of these talk shows has declined. As McKinney explains, the initial commercial success of these shows created a competitive atmosphere, and talk show hosts became more extreme and outrageous in their presentations to gain or maintain audience shares. The content has therefore become more entertainment-focused and less informative. As McKinney put it, there was serious competition for the commercial dollar. And every entity that was selling a product in this country [the Bahamas] decided that they was going on More FM ... because it was cutting edge, it was innovative, it was stylish, we mixed it with music. It was very provocative, and it cut right to the questions. We didn't play around with it, because it was new. Because it was new we were free-wheeling, there were no kind of conditions that said "well you know you can't say this." It was unregulated in a way. While we have rules through the business licenses for having a radio station, there was no real regulations put in place that would have been able to deal with what you could say, how you could do things on talk radio.[23]

Krissy Love, a female talk show host in the Bahamas, provided a similar description of the early days of radio talk shows. While these shows are still influential, their descent into competitive practices to gain market share did produce negative perceptions. "One of the disadvantages when the government released the reigns," according to Love, "[was that] they did release the reigns. I was telling the current prime minister you know you gave us freedom but we didn't have any rules. So with rights come responsibility and a lot of station owners don't get that. This genre created some monsters too."[24] Despite this development, Love believes the good outweighed the bad, as she claims there were still some levels of accountability: "It made policymakers realize that they have to answer to the people. But sometimes they now believe that there is so much talk show nobody checking so 'I ain't got to answer to nobody,' so it made people a little cynical."[25]

Fear of victimization also impacted the effectiveness of the new talk radio shows. Barbadian talk show host David Ellis contends that the smallness of Caribbean societies restricts how journalists practice their craft. As a result, talk show hosts were not able to report on political and economic elites as liberally as their American counterparts, for fear of intimidation and victimization. Some of the journalists interviewed described how they were forced to leave their country to find employment because they were fired or blacklisted by political elites for exposing corruption or wrongdoing; others have been physically harmed or threatened. According to Freedom House, a nonprofit organization that monitors global press freedom, in Belize in October 2012 "the cars of two journalists who were critical of the government were vandalized in what opposition media deemed attacks on media freedom. In one case, the nuts securing the tires to a journalist's car were removed."[26] The report noted, however, that the motives for the incidents remained unclear. In August 2012, Guyanese journalist Freddie Kissoon reported he was assaulted after publishing a column in which he claimed he had been a victim of state oppression. Earlier that year, Kissoon was also dismissed from his position as lecturer at the University of Guyana.[27] In its 2012–2014 report, the Media Association of St. Lucia claimed that media freedom in the country was "somewhat weak."[28] The report cited intimidation, victimization, lack of free expression, political influence, and abuse of power as the main contributing factors: "Politicians and their party faithful are quick to criticise and use various methods of persuasion and coercion when the media does not report in their favour, but will not hesitate to use that same media as leverage against their opponents or to support their causes when convenient."[29] The 2012–2014 report also identified nine major threats to the free press: political pressure, the nature of press ownership, economic climate and technology trends, conflicting commercial interests, poor competitive practices/undercutting of the market, lack of training and guidance, poor leadership, regulations and laws, violence and unprofessional conduct.

The relationship between governments and media is often very contentious. Some politicians have labeled journalists as the "opposition press." Others have characterized news stories as "too sensitive" or "not appropriate" for publication. Also, the increase in the number of lawsuits has effectively muzzled talk show hosts and journalists, causing media owners to impose self-censorship as they become more concerned with the bottom line and staying in business.

The new style of talk radio that emerged in the region in the 1990s, also known as "talkback," is one of the most fascinating phenomena to emerge in the region in the last twenty years. In talkback radio the host invites the listeners to participate more actively in the program by phoning in, sending an SMS (Short Message Service), or emailing with their views and opinions. However, although talk radio shows became a popular phenomenon in the region, and the world, many scholars question their effectiveness when it comes to advancing democracy. In his analysis of the new talkback radio culture, Australian media professor Graeme Turner acknowledges that this format displaced conventional news and current affairs programs in many countries as ordinary people incorporated themselves into the production of journalism. However, Turner believes talkback radio represents the "demotic voice" at its most aggressive and cautions us not to confuse it with democracy. Further, he contends, "radio journalism has given way to the talkback host or entertainer at precisely the time when the political influence of the talkback format has become most pronounced, and when the regulatory control of that influence has become least effective."[30] Turner contends talk radio hosts have taken on some of the roles of journalists but few of the responsibilities.[31] He connects his analysis of the demotic voice and populism of talkback radio to Richard Hoggart's analysis of the "rise of opinionation" as a substitute for analysis and judgment which had become a populist tendency in media (among newspaper columnists and letter writers) and public life in the 1950s.[32] Turner agrees with Hoggart, who viewed this tactic as "a grotesque and dangerous flattery of the public—dangerous because it substitutes a rhetorically constituted 'people' for genuine democratic participation."[33] Turner believes this observation is still apposite today. He views today's public media environment as a "demotic turn" where talkback radio and new online media are lively expressions of popular culture. He therefore deems talkback radio and new media as "poisonous cultural and political functions."[34] The result of this, Turner claims, is a "type of entertainment that mimics the form and practice of journalism but which performs quite different social and political functions." Consequently, Turner posits talkback radio, and online media, are "limited deliberative platforms that do not serve democracy well."[35]

McKinney, Ellis, and Love agree with Turner that talk radio has produced a cacophony that is often interpreted as effective public debate. However, they also extended Turner's argument to include the peculiarities of Caribbean culture. Bahamian talk show host Eddie Carter believes the power of talk radio is limited because Caribbean societies are not yet mature enough to discuss important issues openly and publicly hold politicians and other important political and economic actors accountable:

> I honestly don't think we're truly able to handle open radio in our country. Perfect example is politics. Politics is probably the

easiest example you could get. Now you have a politician that speaks in the House [of Assembly] and he talks about morality and he talks about we have to do things the right way. We're such a small community that we know his dirt. We know the fact that he's got a family on the side and he's children with XY. We know that. But, we haven't matured enough as a nation yet where I can openly come out and say "well John Doe, you need to sit back down because we all know you've got Susan on the side with Tom, Dick, and Jane as your side children. You are not one to be talking morality and responsibility to me. You are not a good example." We haven't reached that stage yet. Which is funny, because we "sip, sip" it, you know. We will go outside and at the bar or the water cooler, or wherever, having lunch, and we will talk.

Funny, we all are willing to talk about "sweet hearting" to some extent and you know being playboys and players and all that. We'll talk about that. But, you know, we don't want to talk about incest. We don't want to talk about the murderers and the fact that families are out there protecting these people who are violating us and this country. They know who they are. We are too small for you not to know that guy is a criminal who is living next to you. We are too tiny. But yet we don't want to talk about [it].[36]

Trinbagonian journalist Peter Christopher presented a similar narrative for Trinidad and Tobago but added the people's appreciation for the journalistic version of the "news." He believes people do like to gossip about what is happening but, based on his experience, they also seem to like to know the truth behind these rumors: "I've always believed that our culture is very, as Dr. [Tia] Cooper would say, 'Bacchanalist.' We like to hear those saucy rumors ... but I do believe there are a lot of people who respect when people get to the bottom of the rumors and find out the truth."[37] He explained that he got more feedback from the public when his stories went in-depth: "There'd be a whole heap of volley and fuzz and then rile up and then after a while they'll stop talking the story because it has no basis for them to continue talking about it."[38] Christopher's review supports and contradicts Kincaid's analysis of Caribbean people and my earlier assessment that it is difficult for Caribbean people to identify what is significant. His position both supports and refutes the argument that Caribbean people live with contradictions, mixing rumors and facts to discuss the significance of issues or events, but still wanting to know the truth, the significant.

The issues of fear, intimidation, and victimization are related to the distribution of power in these patriarchal societies with matrifocal households. The hierarchy of power is most visible in the inherited centralized structures of governance. Most of the power is in the hands of the prime minister or president, the central controlling force in most of these countries, who along with his/her governing party tries to control the decision-making at all levels of society. As a result, the prime minister/president is the most powerful political figure, and has authority over all government institutions and agencies; the prime minister/president and the governing party also has tremendous control over the media in these countries: They apply their control or power through policymaking, governing bodies that implement regulations and policies, and the creation of laws.

As Nicolette Bethel explains, "the fact that we live in a society that is dominated by government policy means ... that [because of] cultural secrecy, real issues don't get discussed. You raise an issue, and there are standard responses. We really don't know how to deal with freedom of speech. ... It's a culture of not disseminating information."[39] Bethel does not believe a freedom of information act would resolve the culture of secrecy and allow access to public information because the problem is in the structure of the civil service. These range from lack of responsibility and accountability, hierarchy of power, especially in decision-making, to an exodus of qualified technocrats who reached a glass ceiling:

> The civil service is really not in place to facilitate the public in anything. That is why we need a complete redesign of our government structure. We should look at creating stand-alone agencies that get to hire and fire independently; they get to set their own qualifications independently. What we have now is an extremely lopsided administration, a lot of administrators that are not working in their area of expertise, if they have a specific area, and a shrinking number of technocrats. ... You

can't discipline anybody unless you go through the public service commissioner. You can't retire anyone, hire or fire anyone, promote anybody unless it goes through the public service commissioner. The centralization of everything is a problem.[40]

This is the environment in which journalism is practiced throughout most of the region. Bethel's description points out how challenging it is to work professionally in these environments and more specifically how challenging it is for journalists to obtain access to public information. To fulfill journalism's obligations in democratic society, practitioners in the Caribbean will have to advocate for media literacy programs to educate society about the role of media and journalism in advancing the ideals of democracy. They will have to encourage drastic change and reform at all levels of society and become a voice of criticism. For, as Christian et al. posit, without this participation democracy will not be possible.[41]

These roles require journalists to practice communication according to a participatory paradigm. This multi-perspective approach to communication and development embraces the theories of hybridity, mixing and matching theoretical approaches and practices to provide a framework to guide the region's understanding of communication, media, and journalism and the role they play in advancing democratic society. It is not enough to create elaborate policies or academic programs concerning information and communication technology (ICT) without also understanding how they ought to be used to improve equality, justice, and liberty for all citizens.

According to Christians et al., the radical role of media and journalism "insists on the absolute equality and freedom of all members of a democratic society in a completely uncompromising way."[42] Too often, these scholars believe, "great imbalances of wealth, education, and access to information and communication are accepted as simply the rewards of personal initiative in societies based on competitive market principles."[43] To reverse these imbalances, they explain, "radical journalism makes every effort to ensure that no injustice is tolerated. The radical democratic commitment works for the continual elimination of concentrations of social power to enable every person to participate equally in all societal decisions. Professionally, journalists are called on to encourage not just superficial changes, such as voting procedures, but changes in the core of the existing social institutions."⁴⁴ This description of journalism's radical role aligns with Nicolette Bethel's call for a complete redesign of government institutions and agencies. It also aligns with the call for the universal recognition of human rights for all members of society. This is particularly relevant for a region that is still overwhelmingly homophobic and xenophobic and has a high prevalence of corruption, domestic violence, child abuse, incest, human trafficking, crime, drug and alcohol abuse. Moreover, ethnic tensions exist in Trinidad and Tobago, Guyana, the Bahamas, Barbados and many of the other island nations. In this milieu, it is crucial that journalism comes to the defense of the voiceless and disenfranchised.

Caribbean Journalism and Democracy

Journalists' understanding of their profession's role in a democracy is crucial to the advancement and protection of democratic ideals. Media scholars and journalists throughout the Caribbean region believe journalists lack this fundamental understanding, which impacts the type of journalism that is practiced. According to Christians et al., journalism has three basic tasks in a democracy: "observing and informing, primarily as a service to the public; participating in public life as an independent actor by way of critical comment, advice, advocacy, and expression of opinion; and providing a channel, forum, or platform for extra media voices or sources to reach a self-chosen public."⁴⁵ To accomplish these tasks Christians et al. believe certain requirements must be met:

> The first relies on the public's trust, which in turn depends on the public's perceiving the media as both independent and competent. The second relies primarily on the existence of an efficient and extensive information collection and distribution system, plus an editorial intention to give access to a wide range of sources and views. The third ... arises from journalism's involvement in democratic action and debate, and depends on an active use of press freedom in the context of a healthy public sphere.⁴⁶

Caribbean journalists and the media organizations for which they work have a long way to go before achieving these goals, as many public critics have pointed out. Most of this criticism has questioned Caribbean journalists' competence and independence. Further, there is very little diversity in their coverage and content. Most of the news coverage is focused on urban centers, elite views, political scandal, and crime. Caribbean media provides for limited democratic action and debate. Public criticism is particularly concerned with the sensational coverage of crime, which dominates the public sphere.

Political, economic, and social environments impinge on journalists' ability to advance democracy and their level of skills affects their competence. Compounding these restraints is the fact that information gathering and dissemination is challenging in these societies. Quincy Parker believes media democracy will not exist in these countries "until we have developed a sense of what it is to have a right to information."[47] Parker insists that freedom of information laws alone would not change these societies. He believes it is more important to change the culture of secrecy, especially among the civil service "because the ones who have the real information," according to Parker, "are the senior public servants who see it as their God-given duty to guard against the press getting this information."[48]

Other journalists agree that democracy will only flourish in these societies once they become more open and less secretive. For example, Eddie Carter believes democracy comes with debate and discussion: "I think those *ds* belong together. Because, when you get a consensus of ideas and plans and something that's truly 'we the people,' … that's what we need—we need the 'we the people.' We need to sit here and come up with an environment in which I truly feel that my government is fulfilling the goals that I have for my country. Not goals that a select few sat down and did."[49] Despite his earlier criticism, Carter believes talk shows could help fulfill these goals, explaining:

> I think that the talk show environment has given the average Bahamian an avenue in which to vent. Now, are we using it right? That's another question because I've also become a very strong supporter of "don't just tell me what's wrong, give me a suggestion on how to fix it." I think talk shows [can] do that [provide solutions] as well because then you get some different opinions that may be off the wall, may be wacky, with no chance

of working, but if you get five ideas then ... that may be the way to merge the best of all five and come up with that one great idea.[50]

One area of deficiency in media democracy is investigative journalism. Carter describes the region as a receivership society that sat and waited for the news to come to it. Lacking resources, insight, and drive, and relying mainly on official sources of information, investigative journalists in the Caribbean have been criticized for being too complacent. While accepting some of this criticism, Caribbean journalists pointed to underlying forces that constrained how they practiced their craft. Some journalists believe media agencies or media owners were also to blame for the lack of investigative journalism because they pushed an agenda that demanded that journalists feed a twenty-four-hour news cycle, which left very little time for investigative projects. Others blamed a lack of corporate, listener, and reader maturity. Carter explains:

> If you are a journalist and you investigate a story truly and you find out all these true details ... you can still be snuffed. You can still be told "we're not going to do that." So are we discouraging investigative reporters with this attitude? I think so. Why should I go uncover ... that many layer[s] when I know my editor is not going to want no part of it. I know the owner of my newspaper is scared of me losing sponsors and losing advertisers.[51]

Carter believes journalists must remain vigilant and resist these forms of censorship so as to advance effective public deliberation. If they are to be effective watchdogs in democratic societies, journalists must provide good public information on a variety of issues, and they must make the news comprehensive and proportionate.

Both Freedom House and Reporters Without Borders, non-profit organizations that monitor global press freedom, recognize the region for its high levels of press freedom. However, lack of access to public information and a culture of secrecy constrain the development of a healthy public sphere. Further, structural institutions limit journalists' ability to perform the tasks advocated by Christians et al.

Balancing Sensational Coverage

Holly Edgell, a Belizean journalist and communications professor, noted on her blog on 9 May 2012 that there was a segment of the population in Belize, and throughout the Caribbean, that "anticipated the gore and sensationalism of the latest news headlines with varying degrees of glee." Another segment "follows news and information about law and order and want[s] to see journalists take the sensationalist, invasive approach down several notches."[52] Edgell's comments were made in response to an increase in sensational news coverage in Belize. She cited two cases from Belize that went beyond the bounds of responsible news coverage. The first involved the suicide of a seventeen-year-old girl, the second a missing teenager.

In April 2012, *Amandala* published an article about a teenager who committed suicide with the headline, "She took her life for love!" A photograph showed the seventeen-year-old with a rope around her neck. The newspaper also printed her suicide note. (The original version of the article is no longer available online.) On her blog, Edgell explained the newspaper's defense of its coverage in the following terms: "This is what people want to see; the tragedy of teen suicide is fair game for public consumption."[53] According to Edgell, those who criticized the newspaper's coverage argued that "tragedy is one thing. But why magnify a family's grief and expose this young woman's most intimate feelings? Children need our collective protection."[54]

The second case—that of the missing teenager—was covered by TV News 5. On her blog, Edgell noted that the reporter interviewed the child's mother, "who was emotional but determined to remain in control." After a series of questions, which ended with, "Do you think something bad happened to her?" the mother began to cry. According to Edgell, the station defended its coverage by pointing out that "she [the mother] came to the media for help. She must know they are going to ask her questions. Maybe her emotional plea will lead to finding the child."[55] Edgell wanted to know why the reporter terrified the mother: "Why not simply stick to the facts? They shared the child's photo and the information about when and where she was last seen. There was no need to push a petrified mother to the brink."[56]

Both stories involve sensitive topics; both would be defined as "hard news." However, for Edgell, along with other citizens throughout the region who have made similar critiques about sensational media coverage, what was disturbing was how these stories were covered. "A teen committing suicide could be an opportunity to educate the public on signs and symptoms of depression among young people," Edgell points out. "On the other hand, news media in some countries don't air or publish suicide stories, for reasons ranging from the copycat effect to privacy and sensitivity."[57] The family members of the seventeen-year-old who committed suicide, and many readers, expressed their dismay and outrage by sending letters to the editor; they also voiced their dissent in other media. *Amandala* eventually published an apology. It read:

> Our intent was not to cause further pain and embarrassment to the victim's family, and for this we offer our sincere apologies. Late into the night, we forgot that we are held to a different standard, and treated the story simply as another story, when we should have approached the matter differently.[58]

Edgell admonished journalists to "temper their coverage: balanced storytelling that respects the privacy and allows members of the public to retain their dignity in times of crisis can still be compelling."[59] She believes when it comes to children and youth, journalists should take special care and question what is the right thing to do. "Just because you *can* do something, *should* you? In other words, just because you have access to a photo of a hanging girl, is it appropriate to publish?"[60] Edgell extended this question to include all media: Just because the news media can cater to the segment of the population that feeds on sensationalism, should it? Edgell's angst reveals concerns for media ethics, specifically training journalists in the region on issues of privacy and balancing the public's right to know with the public's need to know.

Achieving comprehensive and proportionate coverage is difficult in the new dispensation of media organizations and journalism. While most owners of news organizations have strongly embraced market-led reforms, journalists throughout the region have not. Journalists believe the negative influence of these reforms on the practice and profession of journalism in the region far outweigh the advantages, which has led to a devaluation of journalism. Some media owners are also concerned about the effects of competition on the content of the media. Ken Gordon, media owner and former journalist, believes the quick changes in the small media markets of the Caribbean have led to lower standards in journalism, particularly in radio, where the increase in media organizations was greatest: "I think there's an absolute crisis, particularly in radio more than anything else. I think it … is having a destructive effect, or impact, on this society. Standards in radio have fallen. I think the role of the media is to influence change and to improve change."[61]

In a crowded market, the need to gain attention becomes a priority. Yet despite the economic logic of gaining attention, many critics feel the media does not have to appeal to the lowest common denominator to get audience attention. If the media is providing fair and balanced coverage of all communities, emphasizing significant hard news stories in combination with significant human interest and investigative stories—stories that reflect the concerns of citizens, balancing facts with fascination—then they could attract and sustain an audience that will continue to read, watch, listen, and engage.

Throughout the region, the "cartographic" nature of journalism has been distorted. Citizens are not getting the type of journalism that advances their participation in democratic societies. Public journalism, or in Roxanne Gibbs's words, "people journalism,"[62] has been pushed aside in favor of journalism that sells. As a result, the media's obligation to society has been reduced to the need to make a profit; in other words, commercial journalism.

When sensationalism becomes the preferred way to present information, then it distorts journalism's mapmaking function. If news is only sensational, then the qualities of enlightenment and enrichment fall by the wayside as entertainment becomes the dominant value. In his book *Scooped! Media Miss Real Story on Crime While Chasing Sex, Sleaze, and Celebrities*, American media scholar David Krajicek discusses the effects of the media's sensational coverage of crime. He concludes that "the media have done an increasingly poor job of developing a balance between what is interesting and what is important. This is the difference between a crime story and crime coverage, between a story about yet another anecdotal crime and one that identifies the anecdote as either representative of a trend or representative of absolutely nothing."[63]

While it is alright for editors to provide news that creates a sensation, meaning, feeling, or reaction, a media diet comprised of only sensationalism makes citizens numb to the world around them—especially the important socioeconomic or sociopolitical realities of their community.[64] In the Caribbean, a region filled with complex, complicated issues that emerged from colonization, journalism should act as a bridge between the governed and the elected governors. Managing editors or media decision-makers have a responsibility to present a balanced diet of news and information to the public. This diet could be informative and entertaining, engaging and educational, interactive and comprehensive. For as Holly Edgell has advised, "it's time to temper guts and gore with balance and context."[65]

Media decision-makers have tremendous power: they decide what media consumers will ultimately consume. In small countries like those of the English-speaking Caribbean, this type of power is very important for effective democratic governance. When it is distorted in any way, it has the ability to weaken democracy, or even destroy it. When sensational coverage becomes the norm, truth, accuracy, relevancy, comprehensiveness, and proportionality are subsumed to market ideals; the public forum is inundated with an abundance of coverage that is meant to titillate rather than educate; the public sphere becomes a marketplace where deliberation takes a backseat to the market-driven logic of selling sensationalism.

Peter Christopher expressed his views on the effects of media owners pushing a market-driven logic on the newsgathering and dissemination process in Trinidad and Tobago using the following examples:

> There are journalists who want to take the newspapers or want to take the TV stations in different directions but the owners and even some of their fellow journalists are so stuck in the mindset that they have to ... [deliver] the paper tomorrow just to get the advertisers' money, that it doesn't change. We've been having meetings in the *Express*, we've been saying that we're going to be more community oriented, we had the investigative desk launch recently, and what has happened? We're still writing the same stories "who got shot in Laventille," "which politician accused this politician of doing what," and "who made this statement" coming out in the newspaper every day simply because oh that's

what they've been doing for the past five, ten years. We've been number one doing this for the past five-to-ten years. Why are we changing? And a lot of the journalists who want to make change are seeing this mundane thing happening and becoming disheartened and leaving the profession.[66]

Christopher contends this trend was bad for both journalism and democracy. He believes the emphasis on making money produces an internal bias in news organizations where advertisers were given preferential treatment because they were bringing in money. According to Christopher, people in advertising were given better resources while those in the newsroom were given few resources to do their jobs. Examples range from a lack of tape recorders, to the use of old computers, to no transportation for journalists to travel.

More problematic for the region is the trend of local newspapers and their online versions becoming advertising billboards. In 2013, a one-week analysis of the front pages of the two largest newspapers in the Bahamas, the *Nassau Tribune* and the *Nassau Guardian*, showed the *Tribune's* front page had 57 percent news stories and 43 percent advertisements. This was similar to the *Guardian*, which had 55 percent news stories and 45 percent advertisements. In addition to the high percentage of advertisements on the papers' front pages, both had placed advertisements in their top banner and just below their mastheads, in the first column near the left margin, and in two-inch banners across the bottom of the front page; indeed, the front page looked more like an advertising supplement than the cover of a national newspaper. Many scholars believe these changes indicate that advertising has become more important than news. This global trend has also been noted in India, where newspapers have also experienced success. In a 2012 article for the *New Yorker*, Ken Auletta noted that many Indian newspapers' circulation and advertising figures were rising, in part because they had dismantled the wall between the editorial and sales departments. Auletta cited the success of the *Times of India* as "a product of their content and unorthodox philosophy." Vineet Jain, the paper's managing director, told Auletta, "we are not in the newspaper business, we are in the advertising business ... if ninety per cent of your revenues come from advertising, you're in the advertising business."[67]

American scholars Robert McChesney and Ben Scott argue strongly against economic pressure in the news industry because they believe increased pressure from advertisers influences the content of the news and colors the credibility of newspapers.[68] According to American researchers, readers trust the media more when there is a clear division between the sales department and the editorial department. When readers trust the information in their newspapers they will read it more and thus advertisers will continue to have an audience for their products. But when readers lose trust in the credibility of the news, when they cannot distinguish between journalistic integrity and commercial pressure, they often discontinue their reliance on newspapers as credible sources of good public information.

Erica Wells, editor of the *Nassau Guardian*, one of the two largest dailies in the Bahamas, believes the whole issue of sensationalism has been blown out of proportion. Wells says there is some merit to sensational coverage, because ultimately the goal is to sell newspapers. But she points out that this must be balanced with responsibility. She also believes this approach is especially important because of the competitive media environment, especially when it comes to the internet. However, Wells admits, this approach has led to a shift in the presentation of news: "The new media environment means more selling to consumers, putting your product out there and getting people's attention. In doing that, I have seen [how] the presentation [of the news] has shifted."[69]

In the English-speaking Caribbean, the normative purpose of news is being subsumed by economic imperatives. However, there is no discourse in the region on the effects of commercialism on media's responsibilities in these democratic societies. In both the United States and the United Kingdom, the influence of advertisers, business managers, and corporate owners of media on journalism has been criticized and debated by scholars and practitioners since the rise of media conglomerates through mergers and acquisitions of multinational companies in the 1980s. News media became big business and the commercial ethos has since eclipsed the public service mission. This trend is now apparent in the Caribbean and has become more pronounced since the Gleaner Company and Radio Jamaica Rediffusion merged at the end of 2015. Comprehensiveness and proportionality have been undermined in the rush to disseminate information quickly into a crowded marketplace. News has become a commodity that is being manipulated for financial gain.

Making the News Comprehensive and Proportionate

Comprehensiveness and proportionality are key principles for discerning significant and important information in Caribbean societies. Not everything is news, and the everyday should not be made into a significant event. In her work *A Small Place*, Kincaid may have been describing the oral nature of these societies; the propensity in oral storytelling is to make the story dramatic to keep the audience's attention. The evolution of this cultural phenomenon has affected newsgathering in the Caribbean. As such, Caribbean journalists should be influenced by their oral societies; their methods of storytelling should reflect this oral tradition. Caribbean journalists' definition of news, of what is newsworthy, should also align with the global understanding that news is timely, interesting, prominent, proximate, controversial, and unusual—but not at the cost of abandoning their own cultural values.

Caribbean journalism should be understood as a blend of American, British, and local values—a hybrid practice. Ewart Skinner identifies this hybrid nature in Trinidad and Tobago's media structure as "a blend of folk and technical media."[70] He sees the endogenous folk system as more relevant to the sociopolitical context of that country because it is historically and culturally driven. He believes this system should be used to transform the external or exogenous technical structure. Skinner's argument is relevant for the contemporary practice of journalism in the Caribbean. Journalists in the region should operate from the cultural nexus of British, American, and indigenous values so that media transformation can "be seen as a triumph of local culture."[71]

Developed countries in North America and Western Europe have set the standards for the practice and the profession of journalism in the developing countries of the English-speaking Caribbean. While journalism in that region is centered on the British model, there is an ongoing shift toward American-style journalism, particularly in those countries closest to the United States. In this sense British and American standards compete, and the clash is producing a number of tensions. The first is among older journalists, most of whom were trained either on the job in their countries or in the United Kingdom and Canada, and younger journalists who were trained in the United States and have been influenced by American-style journalism. These tensions have been exacerbated by the use of new digital technology. Younger journalists, those between the ages of eighteen and thirty-five, are more knowledgeable when it comes to new technology, while older journalists, thirty-five and older, are more aware of the principles and foundations of journalism and its role in democratic societies.

Keeping the news comprehensive and proportionate requires journalists throughout the region to resolve this tension. Their focus should be on helping citizens to navigate their social worlds. This cartographic role helps journalists to understand what they should cover. Kovach and Rosenstiel believe that thinking of journalism as mapmaking "helps us to see that proportionality and comprehensiveness are keys to accuracy."[72] Limited resources forces media professionals to make decisions about what to cover and how to cover it. This coverage should include a fair and balanced mix of the significant and interesting, and it should reflect the diversity of Caribbean communities.

Examining journalism's cartographic function in the Caribbean context reveals a lot about the shortcomings of news coverage in these multicultural societies. One of the most significant is the lack of diversity. The newspaper organizations in the six countries covered in this study continue to target the dominant demographic sought by advertisers: middle class, educated, and majority black elites in Grenada, Jamaica, the Bahamas, and Barbados, black and mixed, or mulatto, in Belize, and black and Indian in Trinidad and Tobago. Likewise, television and radio are segmented into niche markets that reach a working-class audience. Media in the Caribbean is governed by an economic logic; it targets the most desirable audience, the most profitable demographic. This means many communities, and various ethnic groups, are underserved—or not covered at all—by news organizations in the region. This makes it very challenging to provide comprehensive and proportionate coverage. The mapmaking role is thus reduced to what sells.

The second tension is the competition between local and American coverage of the region. The challenge of competing with American news media has been exacerbated by online media. The influence of the United

States, the region's principal trading partner, became more dominant after the Second World War, and especially since the 1980s. This shift continues to create tension in the political, economic, and social spheres. The region's newest economic partner is China. This relationship will no doubt create tensions as well.

The public's rising appetite for American-style journalism has added to the tension. In particular, there has been increased public criticism of Caribbean journalists' inability to conduct investigative journalism along the lines laid out by their counterparts in the United States. Of course, Caribbean journalists, governed by media laws that were created under British colonization, simply cannot practice this style of journalism. These laws should be revised to allow for the merger of British and America practices; only then will Caribbean journalists find the best way to fulfill their obligations to their fellow citizens, who live in hybrid, or creolized, societies. The media systems should reflect the hybrid nature of the lived realities of the people, functioning as the cultural nexus to produce glocal practices (a hybrid combination of local and global).

If these societies are to find effective solutions to their myriad problems they will have to use hybrid frameworks to guide future development. If they are to forge effective democracies, Caribbean societies cannot continue to use archaic laws inherited from colonizers, or apply ideas coming from the United States and the rest of the world without adjusting them to fit their own environments. Bethel's ideas for reinvigorating journalism's sense of public service should be extended to all institutions and systems in the region. The dominant influence of the United States demands an appropriate response. No longer should Caribbean societies allow themselves to feel like victims of cultural domination—British or American. Rather, they should employ a proactive approach. Caribbean citizens would not be encumbered by smallness if they became active participants in the transformation of their societies. By combining the American and British styles with other ideologies and beliefs that have come to them through the movement of people (African, Asian, Indian, Canadian, Latin American), they could create structures, systems, and ideologies that match their realities. Journalism should play a central role in producing these changes.

The clash of British and American ideologies has created a complex set of issues for Caribbean journalists. First, there is the need to build and protect a Caribbean public sphere, and national public spheres within each country, to promote public discourse on national and regional issues. Close proximity to the United States and the diffusion of new technologies like the internet and wireless telecommunication challenge Caribbean journalists' ability to shape their public spheres. Too often public discourse in the region is controlled by the dissemination of information from external sources—CNN, BBC, Reuters, and other sources like Wikileaks. Second, American media inundates the region with values-laden American-style coverage that has increased the public's taste for American media products and practices.[73] As Bahamian journalist Rupert Missick explains, greater access to foreign media puts additional pressure on Caribbean journalists:

> For instance, if they watch cable news [CNN], our laws are such that you cannot say the same things. If a person has been arrested for murder for example, you cannot say anything other than, "the person is assisting police with their investigation," until the person is charged. When they watch US media ... they will see the sort of trial start [in the media] before the actual trial begins. They would ask us, Why can't we say the same thing? as it is obvious according to them. When we explain it [our law] to them, it's still not acceptable enough.[74]

This has altered the way Caribbean people perceive themselves and their region. Although retaining a British past is important for these former colonies, they have also embraced an American consumer culture, which is depleting the moral responsibility of citizens as more and more people privilege material gain over community, equality, liberty, and justice. Hopeton Dunn believes Caribbean cultural production has been stunted by the American influence: "The tendency has been to look towards the United States for trade, investment, communication technology, and content with consequential impact on regional media, lifestyles, and business."[75]

There are mixed feelings among Caribbean journalists about the American influence. Some journalists viewed it negatively because of its impact on indigenous Caribbean thought, belief, and values. Others viewed it as an opportunity to push Caribbean politicians to pass and implement more contemporary media laws, which would allow journalists to have more access to public information and to conduct more liberal coverage of public officials.

In the Bahamas, the country that is closest to the United States, the American influence is pervasive. But while Bahamian journalists question this influence, very little has been done to combat it. Many are particularly upset at the fact that their audience continuously compares local news coverage to the American example. Bahamian journalists believe the comparison is unfair. As Bahamian journalist Tia Rutherford asked, "Should we compare ourselves to the US? Their system is different, their standards are different. They are more open, allowed to do more things."[76] In the Caribbean, the constraints of the media market—legal, social, economic, and political—play a significant role in what journalists cover and how they cover it, even if Caribbean audiences either ignore or are unaware of these controlling factors.

Jessica Robertson, news director of ZNS, the state-controlled public service television and radio network in the Bahamas, believes the audience has to understand the difference:

> I think also what the public has to understand is that things work differently. Take the US, because I think that is the market that most of our audience is familiar with. I don't think the average person realized that there is this thing called the Associated Press ... and they do all the grunt work. They go to these press conferences. They go to these assignments, they get the video and the info and then they put it up on their wires. Then all of these news organizations pull it down from there, that's why when you tune in to all of the networks, you see pretty much the same kind of thing. So that frees them up then to do their special investigative reporting. They are not bogged down by having to go to all of these day-to-day things that we are [required to do] because we don't have that kind of system. We never will, we don't have a market for it. So the requirements are very different from that of our competitors ... in the US and in other big markets. It just works very differently.[77]

The audience's expectations and the region's media systems make it very difficult for Caribbean journalists to provide comprehensiveness and proportionality. But the public's expectations, particularly with regard to investigative journalism, should encourage Caribbean journalists to provide more holistic and balanced coverage of their diverse societies. They could advocate for public understanding of the differences between the media systems of the Caribbean and the United States. The time has come for Caribbean journalists to create a media system that meets the current needs of their societies. Media literacy programs could help them to educate the public; these programs should be designed to empower the audience to comprehend the effects of mediated communication on the individual and society, the process of production in the creation of content and meaning, the legal environment in which media functions, the ethical and moral obligations of media practitioners, and the effective use of mediated communication. But more importantly, emphasis should be placed on creating hybrid media systems. This approach requires a reconfiguration of media laws and regulations, the creation of media training and educational programs, and media literacy programs that help citizens to understand the role of media in the advancement of their societies and the influence of media in their lives. Clinging to British history, values, and beliefs no longer matches the reality on the ground. Yet the goal is not to replace British values and beliefs with American ones, but rather to integrate the two, blending them with indigenous values and beliefs to create systems that better serve the citizens of the English-speaking Caribbean.

Nicki Kelly, a veteran journalist who has worked in the region since the1960s, explains the need for journalists to advocate and push for change so that citizens could demand more accountability from those that govern them:

> [The liberalization of the market] has helped them [Caribbean citizens] in … being more active participants in democracy. The people are changing. We are becoming a little more demanding of what we want from our politicians. I think … this is where … journalists are failing. If you keep informing people, they will then demand certain things of their government and their leaders, and … the more information that you provide people with, the more demanding they are of accountability. The journalists should initiate this in the public … they should demand accountability.[78]

Another challenge that has evolved out of colonial dominance and dependency, one that is also very pervasive throughout the region, is the "foreign is better" attitude, which can be seen in the compensation packages for foreign-born journalists. Kelly believes this undermines the worth of local practitioners: "Even the publishers don't appreciate their staff. ... They also have this terrible thing: it's only good if it's foreign. Let them bring in a foreign journalist; they will pay them the sun, moon, and stars. But, if they have a good local person, they will not pay them what they are worth."[79]

The belief that foreign journalists are superior to locals presents multiple problems. First, it highlights the continual bias in hiring practices, as local journalists do not receive the same respect and salary as their foreign counterparts, a practice carried over from the colonial period. Second, because editors and publishers do not hold local journalists in high esteem, this undermines their value in the eyes of the general public. If the people responsible for publishing the news do not respect local journalists, then why should the people consuming it?

The speed at which technology now allows information to flow into the region exacerbates the "foreign is better" attitude. Information is often already accessible in the United States, the United Kingdom, or other external media markets, which means Caribbean publics with access to technology use it to assess local journalists' efforts.

A third issue is the conflict between the legal systems that govern journalism and the media environment. This is closely related to the issue of external influence, especially the influence of the US, where litigation is a booming industry. The growth of a similarly litigious culture in the Caribbean region has become a major area of concern. Over the last ten years, there has been a significant increase in the number of lawsuits filed against Caribbean journalists, radio and television talk show hosts, and media owners. Steve McKinney describes these lawsuits as a form of control. "We are in close proximity [to the US] and we have the attitude of America," explains McKinney. "So you say you want to sue somebody; even if someone just slights you, you figure that you'll do it."[80] This increase in the number of lawsuits has resulted in increased forms of self-censorship.

Kovach and Rosenstiel acknowledge the limitations of the mapmaking metaphor in the American context: "Cartography is scientific, journalism is not."[81] They also admit that proportionality and comprehensiveness in newsgathering are both "subjective and elusive." However, Kovach and Rosenstiel believe in the importance of nonetheless striving for proportionality and comprehensiveness and see them as key elements to journalism's popularity and health. Caribbean journalists face additional challenges because of the culture of secrecy and silence. However, if Caribbean journalism is to remain valuable and vibrant, journalists throughout the region will have to provide comprehensive and proportionate accounts. Journalism must be valued by Caribbean societies, Caribbean citizens must evaluate the merits of this service within a Caribbean cultural context, and Caribbean citizens must believe that the type of journalism practiced is one that benefits their societies. The key to credibility is the perception that a Caribbean style of journalism is the appropriate one for these cultures. Proportionality and comprehensiveness can gain the public's trust by demonstrating to Caribbean peoples the value of an indigenous style of journalism.

Caribbean Journalism: Relevant and Engaging

Crick, crack...
Once upon a time, was a very good time, the monkey chew tobacco and spit white lime.[1]

—traditional Caribbean folk sayings

Storytelling plays a significant role in Caribbean societies. How you tell the story matters; whether you leave an impression on the audience matters, too. But it also matters that you tell the audience the right story at the right time, since the right story can change people's lives if told in the right way—if it is relevant and engaging. Such stories have changed people's minds, inspired them, or compelled them to act. These two principles are also important to Caribbean storytelling tradition, which is reflected in all aspects of Caribbean cultural life. "Journalism is storytelling with a purpose."[2] It influences our lives through the stories it tells about the world around us. As such, journalism plays a significant role in Caribbean storytelling and social construction because it influences and helps society to cultivate a particular worldview, language, and understanding. According to Kovach and Rosenstiel, "we need news to live our lives, protect ourselves, bond with each other, and identify friends and enemies. That is why we care about the character of news and journalism we get: they influence the quality of our lives, our thoughts and our culture."[3] They believe that writer Thomas Cahill said it best: "You can tell the worldview of a people ... the invisible fears and desires ... in a culture's stories."[4] Journalism provides us with stories that are essential to our sense of self. Unfortunately, for the last twenty years Caribbean journalism has been providing a debased sense of self, one defined by commercialism, violence, and political scandal.

Journalists have a responsibility to explain what is at stake—the larger picture, the long-term effects of issues or topics or events. They have a responsibility to engage with society about what they are learning. The role of journalism is to make both the significant and the small interesting and relevant. This responsibility may seem counterintuitive in a region where storytelling emphasizes the everyday, the small things, but it should not. Kincaid's critique of the region's inability to attend to significant matters, to bring them to light in a deliberate public forum and resolve them in a way that advances these societies, is key. Journalists are responsible for bringing these issues to light; they are responsible for explaining the "so what." Journalists should attend to how, where, and when they engage to produce a richer, more robust discourse on matters that are important. Caribbean people use the art of storytelling to convey important life lessons. Many of these stories are allegorical or analogical in nature and provide moral guidance for life. Perhaps the most popular are the *Anancy* stories.[5] These stories have their roots in traditional African oral storytelling. Journalists should use this form to engage their audience on relevant issues and topics. So often missing from journalists' stories are the connections between the story or event and its impact on Caribbean people's lives.

Journalism should be made up of stories that identify the significant aspects of the social order, where political and economic development is balanced with personal triumphs or tragedies, interesting stories about human beings in various communities throughout a country or region, and the world. This is what Kovach and Rosenstiel refer to as "engagement and relevance, not engagement versus relevance as the two are sides of the same coin."[6] News stories about Caribbean societies should be fun and fascinating, captivating and important. Journalism should not only give people what they want but also what they need: relevant and engaging stories and their connections and consequences on the personal, local, national, regional, and global levels. Most people want both information and storytelling. They want the business section and the cartoons, the front page and sports.

This balancing act, making news both relevant and engaging, is especially important in contemporary Caribbean societies. The commitment to both will provide journalism with the best opportunity to serve democratic ideals in an era in which information is easily accessible, since democracy works best when citizens receive relevant and engaging information. When journalists provide great reports with connections to social, economic, and political injustices or great reports on human triumphs and tragedies, or compelling accounts of human character and dignity, and they do so with a mixture of great narrative, exceptional analysis, and literary flair, they have moved the needle to the middle of this continuum between relevant and engaging to reflect a combination of both good storytelling and good information. They are also doing it to uphold their commitment to citizens to provide them with information they need to understand their world.

Providing information is not journalism's only task. It must provide information that people will engage with—that they will read, watch, listen and respond to. This is an important challenge in a world of twenty-four-seven news cycles, internet blogs, and citizen journalists. If democratic societies are to function for the good of the polity, Caribbean news organizations must present important matters in a way that captures the eyes, ears, and hearts of the citizenry. Otherwise, the truth—the first moral principle for journalism—will become suspect, and citizens will be persuaded to believe whoever can get the fastest and most compelling information to an audience and persuade them that their version is true. In the age of the internet and mobile telephones, this could quickly descend into a race to the bottom, where the most salacious and inaccurate coverage gets our attention and truth and the moral principle behind the democratic values of equality, justice, and liberty gets trashed in the new wasteland of the plentiful. Then, misinformation, disinformation, inaccuracy, distortion, and fallacy would dominate the marketplace of ideas and democratic principles would be undermined. This prospective future—of an Orwellian world of manipulation, inequality, injustice, and plutocracy—would not bode well for journalism and its role in democratic societies.

Challenges to Relevant and Engaging Journalism in the Caribbean

What are the challenges that prohibit journalists from fulfilling this responsibility? According to American and European media scholars Robert Picard, Howard Tumber and Barbie Zelizer, and Henrik Örnebring and Epp Lauk,[7] the long list of constraints that prohibit good journalism includes such things as inexperience, marketplace logic, haste, ignorance, laziness, bias, lack of training, news traditions, cronyism and self-aggrandizement, censorship, fear and intimidation, and low remuneration.

Around the world, there is growing frustration with journalism, and Caribbean practitioners are not exempt. Public criticism has increased over the last ten years as the public service role of journalism has been subsumed by commercial incentives.

On 21 August 2013, Gary Spaulding, a senior writer for the *Jamaica Gleaner*, wrote a story about a Jet Ski accident that caused the death of a six-year-old girl. The heading was "6-Y-O Dies, Sisters Injured After Freak Accident At Beach."[8] The first four paragraphs of the story read:

> What started out as a pleasant holiday trip to a beach in St. Ann over the weekend was suddenly transformed into a nightmare for a 28-year-old father of two when a jet ski raced out of the water on to land and into his children, killing one and leaving another battling for life.
>
> Richard Hyman's six-year-old daughter, Tonoya, was killed by a deadly blow from the jet ski, while yesterday, it remained touch and go for her four-year-old sister, Remonique.
>
> "Jah know, mi feel it! I don't know that there is any word in the dictionary to express my feelings right now," mumbled Hyman as he spoke with *The Gleaner*. "I don't know anything. I am keeping my fingers crossed. … I have to put God in the midst at this time."
>
> Bryanna, a sibling of the two girls and Hyman's stepdaughter, was also hit but sustained minor injuries, including a broken tooth. She was treated and released.[9]

Jamaican writer and media critic Annie Paul criticized the story on her blog under the heading "Demonic Jet Ski Kills 6-Year Old Girl in Jamaica!"[10] According to Paul, the story focused completely on the victims, and not the perpetrator. It did not tell the reader who was driving the Jet Ski, how it ended up on the beach striking the six-year old and her sisters, or even on which beach the incident happened. In other words, the story did not answer basic journalistic questions of who, what, where, when, why, or how. It is neither balanced nor comprehensive. It leaves out relevant information and does not move the reader to feel a sense of "outrage for the loss of life."[11] This story is typical of the type of journalism currently practiced in the Caribbean.

According to media critics, one of the prevailing reasons for this type of coverage is the quality of practicing journalists and the market logic of media owners. The low salaries do not attract or retain high quality, skilled persons. Therefore, the demand for comprehensive, proportional, relevant, and engaging coverage often goes unfulfilled.

A former general manager of CANA described his frustration with this situation:

> You have, a journalist, somebody [who] says she's going to do an assignment, and she gets there late because [of] shortness of staff and she just manages to get a sound bite or something and she's got to run off to go to another one [assignment] and then comes back in to write something up and she gets paid for that. But I know she's actually short-changing the public. ... All you're putting in is these little sound bites, it's never a complete story it's just a little gist of something which is accurate but it is not the whole truth, it's just part of the truth that comes out. ... I think that the main thing that bothers me ... is the charade that the new journalist has to go through and the mere fact that the public doesn't get the true story.[12]

Journalists interviewed for this book believe there are many constraints that limit their ability to function effectively in the public interest. News organizations throughout the region operate in highly competitive media markets with a media logic that focuses on market-driven ideals; to be successful they must sell news as a commodity. In these competitive markets there is a high turnover of journalists as practitioners move from one media house to another in an attempt to find better opportunities. This often leaves newsrooms with inexperienced staff. Understaffed newsrooms place more demands on journalists, and they in turn submit a harried, hastily assembled product that is neither relevant nor engaging.

Harold Hoyte, one of the owners of the *Barbados Nation*, believes that current labor conditions and the type of people who are entering the field do not advance journalism or democracy:

> The biggest challenge that we face is a lack of interest by young people in the profession. I think the cadre of people that we used to have who were attracted to the profession has disappeared. We used to be able to replenish the supply of people interested in the profession, people with a social conscience, people who were prepared to do the necessary training at university or college to equip themselves. ... Now what we have are people who are in it as a stepping stone to move on to more lucrative opportunities. So the biggest gap that has developed over the last several years would be finding people with the commitment [who are] prepared to make the sacrifices, to do the reading, to do the research, to check the record, to check the facts before they commit to writing.
>
> So the quality of journalism has slipped over the last several years, I would say 10 or more years. ... We have seen ... a definite change in the quality of people that we have as a pool from which to draw for human resources. That is, I think, the biggest challenge that we face.[13]

Hoyte concludes that because of current practices, the fundamentals of journalism have been lost. "The question of ensuring that the less fortunate in the society are protected, that the leaders in society are kept honest at all times and so on—there is no passion for that kind of journalism anymore, so that what we have right through the Caribbean almost without exception are people who would just report what they are told in an unquestioning manner."[14] For Hoyte, journalists are simply recipients of press releases who "regurgitate them for presentation and [do] not discern any hidden messages or innuendo from which a more substantial story could emerge. They don't have that keen interest in those things."[15]

Hoyte also notes that while journalists used to strive very hard to practice the best international standards of journalism, there has since been an erosion of standards, partly because of the journalists and partly because of the media owners. Previously, standards were based on the "best newspapers, particularly in the United Kingdom and to a lesser extent, the United States. And those are the standards by which we operated and so we measured our success against those standards."[16] He believes older journalists upheld these standards despite the fact that they were severely hampered by lack of technology, training, and exposure:

> We sought to be able to do things in the finest tradition of journalism. And that meant always checking our facts. We used to be ashamed by errors and by corrections. Our pride stood or fell based on the accuracy of what we wrote. So when I see wrong names in the newspaper and wrong dates and wrong ages and wrong addresses I squirm because it was something we would just not do. And if you did not know you would ask until you were sure or you would double check.[17]

Hoyte's newspaper and media group merged with Caribbean Communications Network in Trinidad in 2005 to form One Caribbean Media, the largest media conglomerate in the region. As a media owner, Hoyte therefore accepts part of the blame for the reduction in journalistic standards:

> I believe that the record will show that in thirty-five or so years that we have at this newspaper ... been able to aggregate profits that are nothing to be ashamed of. [But] I think we could have done with a lower aggregate and preserve the profession ... that is critical to the success of our operation. So I think as owners we have some responsibility to bear.[18]

To restore the necessary professional standards, Hoyte recommends placing more emphasis on training and mentoring.

Barbadian journalist Reudon Eversley provides a similar description of the changes and challenges facing Caribbean journalism. He too believes the quality has changed over the last ten or fifteen years. "When I joined," Eversley remembers, "most people didn't have degrees, didn't have any formal training. But you had good mentoring because there were a lot of senior people in the newsroom."[19] According to Eversley, the new labor conditions came about because a lot of senior journalists left the profession, which means that "today, you have newsrooms that are essentially green. And even though the reporters are supposedly better trained because most of them are graduates of the community college, with associate's in mass communications programs, that has its deficiencies because they do not come to us newsroom ready. We still have to initiate them."[20] For Eversley, there has been a decline in standards in spite of the increase in college degrees.

Eversley provides a similar assessment of the low knowledge level of current journalists and their lack of interest in reading: "You find many young journalists today, they don't read as much as people from my generation. I mean I still read a hell of a lot. A lot of journalists today, they're not … sufficiently curious." As a result, he believes, "the perspective of many journalists today is very narrow, essentially local, domestic, and they do not have that broader perspective that is so necessary when it comes to analyzing and interpreting events and putting them in their true context, especially where economic issues are concerned."[21] Eversley describes the current generation of journalists as "docile, press-release writers" who regurgitate everything: "They don't go out in the field and dig." He points out that the other major shortcoming "has to do with the whole culture of journalism, because you find that media managers tend to focus more on the quantity of stories produced by journalists than the quality."[22] Eversley believes media managers and owners have placed more demands on journalists for quantity instead of quality to feed a twenty-four-seven news cycle and converged platforms. In other words, journalists work for media organizations that expected them to produce content for all of their media platforms—newspaper, radio, television, online, and social media. They are also required to have multiple skills.

Byron Buckley, of the *Gleaner*, explains that, "once the reporters leave journalism school … and get into the media house [they don't continue training]. … Our sense is that continuing education and deliberation is minimal."[23] He believes the Jamaica Press Institute should establish partnerships with other civil organizations to develop the training and research needed to build a professional identity.

Senior practitioners believe that though students are graduating with degrees in journalism and communication, they are coming to the workplace with too many deficiencies. "We don't want to pick on CARIMAC," says Buckley, "but when the kids come from the journalism school, let me put it this way: We find that they are deficient in some rudiments of language, they don't have the capabilities to take down the language, and sometimes just simply [can't do] the writing."[24]

Peter Ames, a radio broadcaster in Trinidad, attributes this problem to society. He describes the poor quality of the voices on the new radio stations and the associated problems of poor grammar and syntax as "a reflection of society. If you don't like society, I suspect you don't like media. And if you like the media, you probably like society. You know, it's a reflection. I cannot see how media can be one thing and society another."[25] This perspective is contrary to the thesis of this book: In hybrid societies, there must be an acceptance of what has been created in these spaces—in other words, there must be room for the use of both dialect and standard English. After all, the Trinbagonian, Jamaican, Bahamian, Belizean, Barbadian, Grenadian, or any other Caribbean dialect, is the lingua franca of these societies.

Throughout the region, many leaders, whether political, economic, and civic, have complained about the quality of the elementary and secondary educational systems. Some journalists in the region are instructed by their employers to write at a fifth-grade level because the region has a high level of functional illiteracy. Some journalists believe this societal problem also appeals to the lowest common denominator. However, Bahamian journalist Rupert Missick, wary of this type of criticism, points out that journalism walks a fine line between what is useful and what sells: "At the end of the day, if nobody picks up your newspaper, nobody is going to read about changes in the judiciary or trade agreements or things like that. A trade agreement headline will not sell your newspaper in the Bahamas. It will not."[26] Further, Missick bemoans the fact that

> when we get our numbers back ... a lot of times we will see that when there was a murder we will sell 25,000 papers or sell out. When we have, for example, "Marvin Pinder elected deputy

leader of the PLP," it drops to like 15,000. "Prime minister says no to CSME," it drops to 10,000. That's just the reality. ... Things that are useful will end up on page 2 and 3 because they have to. Nobody will buy the newspaper [if these are placed on the front page].[27]

Buckley and other editors argue that training must be the focus of media development in the Caribbean. They acknowledge that the landscape has changed because of technological and economic forces. Consequently, they believe journalists will have to be trained from a broad perspective as information brokers. Buckley believes that, despite global fears for the future of journalism, the profession will remain relevant. However, he insists, journalists will have "to learn more and they [will] have to become knowledge experts because all that's being challenged now with communications technologies. New media will have a place but old-type media [will] still have a place—they just need to refine or define [it] a bit better."[28] Journalists in this new environment will have to be multitalented. A photographer will have to shoot still images and broadcast video and in some markets also write, edit, and report the story.

Media's Filtering System

In his article "Contra the Journalism of Complicity," British media scholar Oliver Boyd-Barrett cites Herman and Chomsky's propaganda model, as proposed in their 1988 book *Manufacturing Consent*, as "one of the most challenging, relevant, and profound—if also frequently misunderstood, underestimated, and flawed—critiques of modern journalism."[29] Despite its drawbacks, this model is a useful framework for critical analysis of media systems. Herman and Chomsky propose "that the collection and dissemination of "news" in mainstream media comprises a five-layered filtering process" including: "the corporate interests of news media, the salience of advertising revenue, overweening dependence on "authoritative" voices, the press's fear of retribution from powerful sources, and shared ideological paradigms—that of 'anti-communism' in 1988 now best reinterpreted as unquestioning presumption of the inevitability and virtue of unregulated monopoly capital."[30] This framework is a good model for analyzing journalism in the Caribbean, as well as the filters used to determine what becomes "news" in the region. However, there is an added filter in today's rapidly changing environment: new technology. This raises concerns about the necessity for journalism as a public service. I will address these issues throughout the remainder of this book, but first, I want to apply Herman and Chomsky's framework to the Caribbean. Because of its history of media development, I want to begin with censorship and the press's fear of retribution from powerful sources.

In 2015 the *Columbia Journalism Review* warned that censorship of the press was growing globally as governments applied a number of stealthy strategies to disrupt independent media and shape the type of information that reaches society. Its verdict: "Censorship is flourishing in the information age."[31] This warning is relevant to the Caribbean. In a region with a history of state-controlled broadcasting, censorship has influenced the practice and profession of journalism. Further, the smallness of these countries has increased the overall impact of censorship—so much so that a form of unconscious self-censorship has emerged. Add to this the litigious societies that emerged from the deregulation, liberalization, and privatization of the 1980s, and current warnings of increasing global censorship do not bode well for press freedom in the Caribbean. In a 2011 report on Caribbean press freedom, the International Press Institute noted that the growing number of criminal lawsuits against journalists and media organizations has threatened Caribbean press freedom by contributing to a climate of self-censorship.[32] The following year, 2012, in an effort to change Caribbean media laws, the IPI and the Association of Caribbean Media Workers (ACM) implemented a public campaign to end criminal defamation in the region and advocate for access to information. The IPI and the ACM published a report on the results of the campaign in which they noted the Caribbean was going against global trends, with increased libel prosecutions.[33] The two organizations urged Caribbean leaders to repeal outdated laws that criminally punished defamation. The two-week campaign was held in Barbados, Jamaica, the Dominican Republic, and Trinidad and Tobago. The IPI and the ACM conducted a follow-up campaign in 2013 to advance the goals of the 2012 campaign.

The English-speaking countries of the Caribbean had criminal defamation laws in place that dated back to the mid-nineteenth century, with penalties of at least one year in prison. The IPI noted in its 2013 report that Caribbean countries were still subjected to "a panoply of repressive measures, from jailing and persecution to the widespread scourge of 'insult laws' and criminal defamation, which are sometimes used by the powerful to prevent critical appraisal of their actions and to deprive the public of information about misdeeds."[34]

The IPI/ACM campaigns aimed to abolish criminal laws in the Caribbean that concern defamation, slander, libel, or insult. The campaign encouraged the use of civil laws, bringing the Caribbean in line with international press-freedom standards and the recommendations advanced by regional and international human-rights bodies.[35] The IPI/ACM campaign was ambitious, as it targeted politicians specifically and did not address the underlying dynamics of Caribbean culture. So far, the campaign has had limited success, with three of the six countries featured in this book decriminalizing defamation in 2013.

Caribbean countries emerged from a history of extermination, abduction, and abortion, a violent cutting off from original African and indigenous cultures. This four-hundred-year history has left the region with sociological and psychological effects that are visible today.[36] It has produced complex issues of identity and a set of cultural practices that emerged through force and resistance. Kincaid examined postcolonial Antiguan society and found it lacking in many areas because the people seemed to be willing partners in their own subjugation. Their deference and subservience to the tourist dollar, political and economic elites, and a British past still causes a lot of indignation. Hilary Beckles discusses these issues in his book *Britain's Black Debt*.

Perhaps one of the most debilitating aspects of Caribbean culture is the need for secrecy and silence. This aspect of the culture, discussed in the previous chapter, was inherited from the colonizers and has been compounded with the reverence for authority and the cult of the leader. Secrecy and silence are the norm. Thus, in effect the people of the Caribbean collude with political and economic elites in their own exploitation. Their silence gives consent and allows outdated laws to remain in effect.

Any campaign to effectively change these laws must include the education of the people about the impact of these laws on their democratic and human rights. This should be a central part of Caribbean media literacy programs. Politicians throughout the region are moved by the votes of the people and the power of external agents, and they will only act to make significant changes to institutions and structures in their countries when their power is threatened. As such, it is important for the IPI and the ACM to get input from the people and external stakeholders to affect the kind of change that will produce new laws. Media was only one of the institutions governed by colonial policies and practices. All state agencies and institutions in these countries need to change to create efficiency and effectiveness at all levels of decision- and policymaking. However, to institute this kind of macro-level change is a tall order for these small societies. This would require media and journalism to play a more active role through the production of engaging and relevant stories that make connections and explain consequences. To practice this type of journalism would require better training and mentoring.

While Caribbean journalists believe a free press exists throughout the region, they also believe press freedom is constrained by a lack of freedom of information laws and the presence of archaic defamation laws. As Byron Buckley explains, "[Jamaican] libel laws are antiquated and they are punitive, because you can still arrest a man ... [and] put him in jail for libeling somebody. It's still a criminal offence. We find that ... the bar for libel for public officials is too high. It needs to be lowered."[37] At the time of this interview, Jamaica had not yet changed its defamation laws. These laws prohibited journalists from questioning the reports of public officials who were very sensitive to criticisms raised by the media. Buckley advocated strongly that the requirements for libel and defamation be lowered and believed judges should determine the damages in libel cases rather than a jury. "Right now ... you can earn more [from] libel ... than the six figures in your life earning. We are victims now ... so we feel that it should be rationalized. We feel that it [libel] should be decriminalized. It is not a criminal offence, but a civil one."[38] In November 2013, Jamaica changed its defamation laws and decriminalized libel.

Caribbean journalists concede that a lack of freedom of information laws and restrictive defamation legislation have reinforced self-censorship. David Ellis notes that factors such as smallness, secrecy, and victimization have exacerbated the problem. The size of these markets makes it difficult for journalists to find people who are willing to speak out against anyone prominent or powerful. Ellis questions the impact of these constraints on journalism. "The absence of freedom of information legislation, to what extent does that limit [journalism]?" asks Ellis. "And even if you had freedom of information legislation, as is proposed for Barbados, what is the cultural norm? Will public servants and other people who have information feel that they are in a position ... to give [it] up?"³⁹

Caribbean journalists believe the smallness of their societies, coupled with the nature of local political culture, has stopped a more rigorous press from emerging. According to Reudon Eversley, these factors have played a significant role in creating an environment that limits journalism, especially investigative journalism, in Barbados. "There is a lot of self-censorship," Eversley explains, "because you have some of [the] politicians who are so thin-skinned they threaten you, they threaten to sue you for the slightest thing. ... I mean the defamation laws here are not like in the United States, where once you are a public official it is expected that you would be subjected to the most rigorous scrutiny. Here that's not the case; people talk about their good name."⁴⁰

This type of environment creates a culture of fear and intimidation as potential sources fear repercussions such as job loss or other forms of victimization. As Harold Hoyte puts it, "there are lots of people who are not prepared any longer to express their points of view for fear that it may affect their mortgage or their family. I do not know what has happened to this society because I don't think that it is a problem that is peculiar to journalism."⁴¹ Hoyte believes journalists have not addressed these issues because "we have become a little too materialistic and people are in it to see what they can get out of it, not what they can contribute to this society."⁴² Eversley was more pointed in his description:

> So you hear on one hand that we're free in Barbados, but free to what extent? People are very restrained because Barbados is a country that has been historically ruled by fear from slavery days. People will come to you and will readily provide you with information but they do not want to be quoted. And the responses, when you ask why, they say, "Well I don't want anybody to burn down my house, I don't want anybody to attack me when I'm going home. I don't want to lose my job. I have my children to send to school, I have my mortgage to pay." You hear all of these reasons and underlying all that is fear.⁴³

Journalists throughout the region have a difficult time covering sensitive topics related to politics, religion, and societal issues like homosexuality, incest, and marital rape. Journalists are wary of politicians, civil servants, and other elites suing them and are constrained by cultural expectations to conform. Self-censorship has become a more effective means of control than state-sanctioned laws. Ironically, these restraints have coincided with an increased demand from citizens for more investigative journalism. This demand has been exacerbated by citizen journalism and people's ability to access and disseminate information using new digital technologies, and it has created tensions between journalists and citizens. The dialectical tension between the public's right to know and its need to know has placed journalism in a precarious position. Rupert Missick summed it up this way:

> Now we have a sort of emergence of this desire ... to know more, but at the same time we have government institutions that don't feel that that is the public's business to know. They feel the public should not know, and for no good reason other than the fact that they feel they are a government institution and their business is their business. It is not seen as the public's business.[44]

Journalists in the Caribbean work in small political systems that are centrally controlled, mostly by the prime minister or president. This makes it challenging for journalists to obtain information or provide criticism of a government's performance. Many journalists describe the relationship between government and the press as hostile. Here, Hoyte reveals the kind of political pressure journalists in Barbados face:

> We had from time to time occasional efforts by successive governments to haul us in, but we never had any overt or persistent attempts to control the media. I have had some prime ministers say some awful things about me and my family, about journalists and so on, and make threats.[45]

David Ellis's and Reudon Eversley's comments are even more evocative. For Ellis, the fear of victimization "is a reality in this environment."[46] He describes the fear journalists had for a former prime minister as "palpable." As for Eversley,

I mean, this is a small society and people who take a stand run the risk of being deprived of opportunities. We have a history of this. The best example is probably a guy called Kendal Wickham, who is easily the best journalist this country has produced. He lived in the early part of the last century. His newspaper was a crusading newspaper advocating improved conditions for the working class. He was sued and he had to leave Barbados and go to Grenada to live, where he died. ... I mean, lots of journalists have had to leave. Once you decided to take on the establishment they pursue this policy where you have to starve. I was almost a victim of that in 1999. After I left the *Advocate* I could not find work in Barbados. I applied for jobs and you would have thought ... someone with my seniority, having served as director of news and current affairs at CANA and then editor of the *Advocate*, you would think corporate Barbados would be happy to snap me up to work in corporate communications. People kept me at a distance, as though I had leprosy ... my solution was to leave Barbados.[47]

Gathering information remains a challenge. Karen Herig, editor of the *Nassau Tribune*, believes a freedom of information act would not address the cultural issue of obtaining reliable information because "getting information is a bit of a problem, and the attitude towards journalists in this country ... is secretive, in things that shouldn't have to be."[48] With or without freedom of information laws, journalists throughout the region believe the constraints of culture would continue to impact journalism. Hoyte believes freedom of information acts would not become law, or, if they did, Caribbean governments would not enforce them. "In small societies," he claims, "[freedom of information] is a dangerous piece of legislation, very dangerous. So I understand from government's perspective their reticence to invoke this legislation. But at the same time, society deserves to have access to public information because it is on their behalf that the decisions are being undertaken."[49]

The culture of secrecy creates a problem for journalists because they are dependent on their sources. With no freedom of information laws, the only way to get reliable information on a consistent basis is to use personal contacts, meaning journalists are walking a tightrope: On the one hand, they are trying to present unbiased, objective information, while on the other, they are trying not to alienate their limited number of valuable sources. With politicians and civil servants being so secretive and wary of journalists, gathering information is incredibly challenging.

The lack of access to information and the hostile attitude of political leaders make any type of investigative reporting difficult. Because getting information in these controlled, small environments is difficult, critical information often goes missing in Caribbean reporting. This inhibits the democratic function of media in society.[50] Further, lawsuits are used as a scare tactic to frighten publishers, media owners, and journalists into not publishing or broadcasting news stories. This discourages reporters from digging too deep; even if they find something and are justified in reporting it, the financial cost of a legal battle could be staggering.

Relevance and engagement cannot emerge in an environment where the predominant mode of information gathering is an overdependence on official sources or "authoritative" voices. Caribbean journalists have been criticized for reproducing official press releases or statements, without asking probing questions or following up with additional investigation that might provide in-depth coverage of the story. David Ellis believes journalists prefer these official sources, since they are an easy way to obtain a story. Some journalists defend this practice; they claim their editors do not give them the time to delve deeper or get another angle.

To understand the reasons for the lack of investigative journalism in the region, Ellis and other journalists believe, one has to understand the Caribbean context, as there are several forces within these environments that have to be factored into any analysis of investigative journalism. One of the forces that limits reporters' investigative work is the size of these countries. "What needs to be done is … to look more closely at all the factors and forces that are at work in a country like Barbados that limits people in this way," says Ellis. "For instance, in a small-sized [country] the function [of investigative journalism may be limited]. … So, does that influence the failure to develop stories in the way that we are talking about? It does."[51]

Journalists are also constrained by economic censorship, which has emerged under the pressure of advertisers who often pull or threaten to pull their advertisements as a means of controlling what stories are published in the news. Juan McCartney provides the following example of the influence exerted by advertisers over journalists' work:

> I did a story on how there were rats in a big food store, and a judge tried to close the food store down. This [case] was in the court; this is what people eat! … I did the story for radio, and when I went to do it for print, they told me to drop it! Drop it because we are working on a big ad campaign with them. Drop it! So I did what I was told.[52]

In the Caribbean, advertisers exert a form of control. In these small societies, it is dangerous to offend any advertiser because they would react by pulling their advertising. This is particularly evident in government advertising. Eddie Carter, host of a popular morning radio show in the Bahamas, recalled an incident when an advertiser reacted this way. According to Carter, the advertiser misinterpreted what he said about one of the company's products, a meatless burger that had failed in the market. The advertiser called the station and threatened to pull all of the company's advertisements. Unlike in New York City, where there are millions of advertisers and a more mature marketplace, the small markets of the Caribbean are limited:

> They are still willing to say, "Forget those listeners. I will yank my ads if you don't treat me right." So, we don't have corporate maturity I don't think, and we don't have general listenership maturity. I don't think we're ready to have the honest conversations on air yet about serious issues.[53]

The influence of advertisers works against journalists seeking the truth, as their efforts to publish are often squashed by advertisers. Journalists are in turn discouraged to pursue stories that they know will likely be pulled.

The sum effect is that the journalist is forced to drop the story, but the underlying problem is that the advertiser never directly tells the news agencies to drop these stories in the first place. Editors often tell their reporters to drop stories because they are working on major advertising campaigns, which indicates an indirect level of censorship. Company representatives then contact journalists directly. Essentially, the pressures of advertisers are so great that editors, publishers, talk show hosts and producers, and other decision-makers have developed their own form of self-censorship in order to avoid a loss of revenue.

Government also exerts advertising pressure. For example, in 2008 the Guyanese government withdrew state advertising from one of the country's independent newspapers, the *Stabroek News*. State advertising was restored to the paper after seventeen months, and then withdrawn again in 2010. State advertisements accounted for 15 percent of the paper's advertising revenue. According to IPI 2013 report, the editor, Anand Persaud, believed the government sought to drive the paper out of business.[54]

Related to the economic influence of advertisers is the growing trend of media conglomerates throughout the region. Each of the countries in this book have one or two dominant media conglomerates. Regional conglomerates are also growing. Media scholars like Herbert Schiller, Ben Bagdikian, and Robert McChesney have written extensively on the effects of conglomeration on journalism and democracy.[55] The trend of mergers and acquisitions in the Caribbean may be a good marketing strategy for media owners, but it portends a negative outcome for democratic rule. The recent merger of the Gleaner Company and RJR in Jamaica should set off more warning bells.

The role of corporate interests in news media is particularly troubling in these small societies, where political and economic forces have already silenced a lot of dissent. Yet there is no discourse on the effect of media conglomeration on the small markets of the Caribbean. Further, issues of anti-trust have not been addressed in these markets and may become a challenge as the trend of mergers and acquisitions continues.

The major criticism of corporate ownership is its concern for the bottom line. Corporate owners push news media organizations to make profits. The profit-making approach often results in more concern for what sells. Media scholars in the United States and Western Europe have been concerned with the power of advertisers to influence news content since the rise of mass media. Their arguments are centered on issues such as the rise in sensationalism, homogenization, and immediacy.[56] Caribbean journalists and media scholars echo these concerns. They believe more checks and balances must be created to contain the growth of media conglomerates in the region. Charles Carter, owner of Carter Marketing, believes there should be oversight committees and regulation that "ensures that the democracy you cherish and that you deregulate the old system for, isn't being harmed by what you created in a new system. That has to be a part of it as well—that somebody would say, 'No, we believe in free enterprise but now you are creating monopolies and this should not happen.' "[57] Hopeton Dunn has issued a similar warning. He believes that lack of regulation has been one of the problems in Caribbean countries since these markets opened up. "These private-sector players come in and we do not have a sufficiently developed regulatory structure. And then the consequences of that runaway activity by private interests become a source of complaint."[58] According to Dunn, "regulation has to be part of what the public sector holds on to. Because that is the fountainhead from which public policy is going to flow."[59]

Being relevant and engaging is challenging in a marketplace that is inundated with foreign information and entertainment, especially from the United States, where the effect of so-called "infotainment" on the public interest has grown quite pronounced. The outsized influence of major American television news networks—CNN, Fox, ABC, NBC, CBS, and MSNBC—and wireless companies such as the Associated Press and Reuters makes it extremely difficult for local news programs in the Caribbean to compete. Local and regional television news production has to compete with the production quality of foreign news outlets. Local newspapers are compared to international newspapers. The internet has increased access to foreign content and increased the pressure for local media products to be more like their larger multinational counterparts. As Rupert Missick has noted, "the demands of the public have changed as well too. We are not compared to the *Tribune* of the 1970s or '80s or even the '90s; we are compared to the *New York Times*, the *Washington Post*."[60] But Missick believes this comparison is not fair: "As you can see, we are not seen as an improvement of what was in the past. We are judged on how much of a shortage we are, compared to the big newspapers of the US or the UK, who have far more resources, time, money, and people."[61]

The latest filter, new digital technology, was discussed in previous chapters. It has imposed another level of influence on journalism. In 2000, John Pavlik identified four major areas of influence: how journalists do their work; the content of news; the structure or organization of the newsroom; and the relationships between or among news organizations, journalists and their many publics.[62] These areas of influence are still prevalent today in news organizations around the world. Many scholars and practitioners believe the internet is the most influential technology to come along, as it continues to raise questions about the survival of journalism and its relevance today.

Although overall internet penetration in the Caribbean is moderate to low, there are some countries in the region with high internet penetration (see chapter 3). Despite these variations, journalists in all of the countries discussed in this book have described the rapid changes taking place in the practice of journalism. These changes align with Pavlik's description of the impact of digital technologies on journalism. Journalists and media owners interviewed for this book described both positive and negative impact of new technologies. As David Ellis explains,

> [the internet] has allowed us to be able to multitask, it has put us in a position where we can do research faster, better. It allows us to be able to get our material out [quickly]. The whole question of convergence is a reality and we have to do more. For me, this is the most significant revolution that I have seen in [my] years ... in the profession. It's the biggest thing everywhere. ... But, there is the question of privacy; everybody's privacy is now being intruded upon by the technology that we have—that is the downside.[63]

Ellis's comments sum up the current reactions to the new media environment. The potential for good and harm are present in our ability to send and receive information anywhere, anytime. We celebrate the impact these technologies are having on the common good, but as more people use technology to invade our privacy, our concerns have increased. These issues affect journalists on both the personal and professional level. They face a difficult task; they must respect privacy, but also protect the public interest. Using user-generated content and information in the public domain has taken on new meaning and journalists must weigh carefully the public's right to know against the public's need to know. They must consider the harm and injury this information will cause if they publish it.

Making the News Relevant and Engaging

Media's filtering system influences news content. Corporate interest, advertising revenue, a dependence on "authoritative" voices, and fear of retribution from economic and political elites influences the type of journalism practiced in the Caribbean. Consequently, this filtering process makes it difficult to provide news that is relevant and engaging. Today, the most significant media filter is the marketplace ideals that drive the decision-making process of owners, editors, and journalists. This filtering process has created a number of trends.

First, media organizations' current hiring practices play a key role in the type of news content that is produced. The hiring of very young and inexperienced people negatively impacts the production of relevant and engaging stories. Many of these young journalists do not stay in the field very long. The high turnover of employees means news organizations are constantly training new staff. One constant refrain from senior journalists in the Caribbean is their concern for the inexperience of young journalists. But this is not confined to the Caribbean; it is a global trend as well. As P. Anthony White, a journalist and media owner in the Bahamas, explains:

> I really think that too many of the young journalists are not given enough training before they are sent out. They should have more on-the-job training. They are doing a lot of things wrong. You've got to be able to interpret what is going on. ... Present the facts themselves in a more definitive manner. The biggest thing is that you need to train the young people more intensely.[64]

As White's comments point out, Caribbean journalists need to be trained how to ask the types of questions that would uncover information that citizens need and want, the kind of information that makes connections and identifies consequences. White points out that, though many young journalists are now university educated, they have not developed what Roxanne Gibbs calls "a nose for news." White's critique suggests the need to implement new training approaches that fit both the market and the culture.

Peter Christopher described the Trinbagonian marketplace as a "merry-go-round" in which journalists constantly move from one organization to another in search of higher salaries and better opportunities.

This has created a cadre of young and inexperienced journalists, which has in turn led to increased training costs for employers.

According to the editors and media owners interviewed for this book, this now constitutes one of the biggest challenges to the industry. Many believe that the number of people who used to be attracted to the profession has decreased significantly. Older, more seasoned journalists are characterized as socially conscientious, trained people with on-the-job experience who are prepared to work hard. Younger journalists, on the other hand, are described as inexperienced, untrained, technically skilled people who are using journalism as the stepping stone for their next big career opportunity. Editors and media owners believe that one of the biggest problems to develop over the last ten years has been finding qualified, well-trained individuals who are committed to the profession and prepared to make the necessary sacrifices. Well-read researchers who check the facts before they commit anything to writing are in especially high demand.

Nicki Kelly, a journalist with more than fifty years of experience, surmised that "the main problem is that the young people who are going into the profession don't seem to be interested in what they are doing. They don't even read their own paper. They don't read generally; they're not curious. They don't want to find out things."[65] While the youthful cadets are credited with mastery of new technology, they are criticized for lacking the fundamentals of good journalism.

Media owners and editors believe that the quality of journalism will continue to decrease unless steps are taken to train and mentor young, inexperienced journalists. The challenge of youth and inexperience is intimately connected with education and training. Some journalists received their education at institutions outside of the Caribbean; others were trained within the region, attending the University of the West Indies, at either the Mona or St. Augustine campus (in Jamaica and Trinidad and Tobago, respectively), or one of the other tertiary institutions or trade schools throughout the region. Some of the editors in this study believe there is still a wide gap between academia and industry as graduates often leave school unprepared for the practice of journalism. Others believe alternative models should be created to train journalists to practice their profession more effectively.

Some of the younger journalists interviewed agreed with this assessment of their performance. Others thought the criticism was unfair; they believe that, like many of their senior colleagues, they would also learn on the job and improve their performance through experience. Thea Rutherford, a younger journalist, believes that "in time, perhaps because of our educational background and technological skills, we might become better journalists than previous generations."[66]

But whether they agree or disagree with the criticism of more experienced practitioners, younger journalists believe one area they could improve immediately is self-regulation. They acknowledge the need to raise the level of professionalism in the practice of journalism throughout the region, which in turn, they admit, would improve the level of respect journalists receive in Caribbean societies. They believe the profession and practice of journalism could be advanced throughout the Caribbean with the development or reestablishment of press associations, the creation of press councils or ombudsmen (and women), and the revision and implementation of professional code of ethics. This is the model I advocate. I believe Caribbean countries should invest in this model and create better training programs to ensure the relevance of journalism in the region. The following section provides a framework for a new training model to advance the role of journalism and communication in the region.

A New Training Model

As Stuart Surlin and Walter Soderlund concluded, the region has implemented a "multifaceted" response to the persistent problem of journalistic training. And yet none of these approaches have resolved the problem. The current model of training is ineffective. The region imports foreign consultants to train journalists through workshops and seminars, sends journalists abroad to foreign media organizations and institutes in exchange programs, conducts in-house workshops or enrolls them in local or regional academic programs. But this model is a quick fix to a complex problem. I propose an alternative approach, a hybrid model that involves the creation of journalism institutes in each country to work collaboratively with press or media associations and regional academic programs. This approach would provide a theoretical framework for understanding the role of media and journalism in the Caribbean and improve the standards of the practice through training and mentoring. This model could eliminate the high employee turnover. One of the major outcomes of this model would be the creation of a stand-alone regional media institute, similar to the Poynter Institute in the United States, to advance media research and training throughout the region.

Caribbean journalists, as Byron Buckley suggested, must take ownership of their own profession and create the kinds of programs that would produce journalism that is essential to their cultures and their markets. This hybrid model would begin by developing partnerships among the current entities—professional associations, academic programs, and media institutes. At the time of this writing, some of the countries in the region have begun implementing new training programs run by academic institutes. In Jamaica, CARIMAC began restructuring its programs in 2015 to address some of the deficiencies in the market and develop a new training program for journalists. Jamaica also re-engineered its professional body, the Professional Association of Journalists, to foster professional growth.

The problem of high employee turnover could be addressed through labor unions and professional associations working with media owners to increase wages and improve working conditions. However, associations and institutes should develop professionalism through their mentoring programs, training workshops, and certification programs. Advancing journalism as a profession could increase longevity within the field as more journalists opt for longer careers. Associations and institutes would encourage innovative approaches to the practice of journalism throughout the region. Through these institutes and associations, journalists could learn how to connect more with their audiences.

This approach embraces the theories of hybridity and participatory communication. Journalism institutes could develop media literacy programs throughout the region to help journalists and their audiences understand all aspects of news production and the impact of that production on people's lives. They could develop new models of the five *W*s and the *H* (who, what, when where, why, and how) in response to the coverage of news in their cultural environment. New forms of narrative writing and storytelling could emerge from the collaborations of professional associations and media institutes. They could produce engaging approaches to visual, verbal, and written forms of storytelling that also embrace and integrate citizen and community journalism. All traditional news formats would be open to the creative process as journalists reinvent traditions like the hourglass, Q&A, experiential storytelling, photography, videography, and captioning. The possibilities are endless and journalism in the region has an opportunity to reposition itself in a fast-paced digital world.

Journalists could connect their stories with the people in their communities through the inclusion of people-oriented stories, using the region's oral history and love of storytelling to connect to the allegories and analogies that play an integral role in Caribbean people's lives. The internet could be used to enhance storytelling, using the interactive elements of the internet to engage the audience through participation in storytelling. This model of journalism could advance "narrative in the service for truth."[67]

At the time of this writing, professional journalism associations, if they exist at all, are ineffective throughout much of the region. Professional associations will only flourish if practitioners value them. In these small countries where media conglomerates are growing, professional journalism will be subsumed by the logic of the market unless professional associations, media institutions, and academic programs become strong advocates of civic or public journalism. Civic or public journalism could be advanced through new partnerships among these entities. Since the interviews for this book were conducted, Barbados has revived its professional association, Trinidad and Tobago has started a journalism institute, and, with my assistance, the Bahamas reestablished its professional association. Belize and Grenada also have associations; Belize's is ineffective and Grenada's suffers from political pressures.

Since it began in 2001, the ACM has done a lot to grow the profession but could do more to advance an indigenous training model and improve professional standards. Caribbean journalists should align their professional associations with international media watchdog associations like the International Press Institute, Freedom House, and Reporters Without Borders. They could strengthen these international relationships by building stronger regional ones and educating members of the public about their rights and responsibilities. The effective implementation of media literacy programs could gain the encouragement of citizens, whose support and understanding may lead them to champion their cause all the way to the ballot box. In addition, Caribbean journalists should continue their campaign to get defamation laws decriminalized and freedom of information laws implemented.

This advice is not given lightly. Political, economic, and social controls are deeply embedded in these societies. However, if journalists are to serve the interest of the people and advance democracy, they will have to collaborate not only with external actors like international watchdog groups; they will also have to partner with citizens to improve the practice and the profession. There are many recent examples throughout the region of bloggers and citizen journalists being sued and arrested. In the Bahamas in April 2013, a political activist, Rodney Moncur, was arrested for posting what was deemed by the police "indecent and obscene" images on his Facebook page. He was later released and fined $10,000.[68] Moncur protested his arrest and claimed this was a violation of his right to free speech as a citizen journalist. The response of local journalists to this incident was divided. Some supported Moncur's position, while others believed Moncur's Facebook posts were an attempt to sensationalize the incident and gain public support. The images in question purportedly presented evidence of police brutality. As they become more active disseminators of information, citizen journalists should be included in media-training programs.

Two of the major components of this training model must be media ethics and law. Increased concerns over privacy raise new ethical dilemmas for journalists in the present media environment. Privacy concerns are particularly important in the small communities of the Caribbean because the impact can be profound. For example, in 2015 there were a number of cases where female journalists' privacy was invaded using the phenomenon known as "slut shaming"—currently one of the prime means used to silence female journalists.[69] Other ethical concerns, such as the influence of political and economic elites, fair and accurate reporting in small environments, discrimination, and covering minors, should also be addressed. Caribbean journalists should also know the local, regional, and global laws that guide the gathering and dissemination of information. And it is very important in today's information environment for journalists to understand the legal issues of hacking, data mining, and national security. These issues are important for the practice of all types of journalism, but they are particularly salient for investigative journalism.

This new model for training journalists and advancing communication programs in the region also requires the participation of media owners. Though many owners know the value of training, the competitive nature of the small Caribbean market is dissuasive. Media owner Ken

Gordon and broadcast journalist Peter Ames believe the development of institutes and professional associations would improve the practice of journalism in the region. However, they both acknowledge the reluctance of media owners to participate in the development of training institutes because the phenomenon of "poaching" trained employees is a harsh reality in these small competitive markets. As Ames explains: "One of the difficulties ... is that you will train and I will hire away from you."[70]

In 2011, Trinidad opened its first journalism institute, the Ken Gordon School of Journalism and Communication, though the school, housed in the College of Science, Technology, and Applied Arts of Trinidad and Tobago, is not a stand-alone institution. In 2013, the Bahamas was in the initial stages of discussing the development of a journalism institute. To that end, I presented a proposal to the College of the Bahamas, though the college had not advanced the proposal by the time of this publication. Jamaica has the oldest journalism institute, CARIMAC, but this institute is not a stand-alone institution, and it operates like a school in a university program. Further, according to some Caribbean media scholars, practitioners, and owners, it has not met the needs of the regional, or even local, marketplace. Some of the interviewees complained that its focus is too theoretical and parochial. Hopefully, the region will continue to develop journalism institutes to work in collaboration with professional associations and academic programs as I believe this model is the best one for the region to create the type of journalism that fulfills the needs and wants of its citizens.

This hybrid approach should result in the professionalization of the field and the fulfillment of its members' training needs. This approach should also develop more research and theory on the role of journalism and communication in the region; there is still very little published research in the discipline. Also, research that has been published is not shared across the region. If regional institutes are developed using this hybrid model, this could produce more research as institutes develop partnerships and share resources. As a result, knowledge will be extended beyond the parochial concerns of each country. Partnerships should also be created with the Caribbean diaspora. Creating interconnected institutes, academic programs, and professional associations could begin the process of developing more scholarly work.

The Bahamas began its bachelor of arts program in journalism and communication in 2011. It is in the initial stages of development. At Barbados Community College there is a two-year program that provides associate of arts degrees in journalism and communication. Belize has a similar program and Grenada has an associate degree program at St. George's University. There are also other programs in Jamaica, Trinidad, Guyana, and the US Virgin Islands. But these are all run parochially; there is limited institutional integration and no regional partnerships.

Finally, the region is too dependent on external actors for solutions to its complex problems. If it is to develop its own model of journalism, one that will fit these environments, it will require the development of the discipline of communication to which journalism belongs. This means more emphasis will have to be placed on understanding the role of communication and journalism in the development of these societies. This includes journalists' understanding of their role in the development of democracy in these microstates. The lack of research and scholarship in the Caribbean in general, and in the field of communication and journalism in particular, leaves the region and its practitioners vulnerable to the continued reliance on models and theories that were designed for larger countries like the United Kingdom and the United States.

6

Caribbean Journalism: Maintaining Independence

> Being impartial or neutral is not a core principle of journalism. … [I]mpartiality was never what was meant by objectivity. But if neutrality is not a cornerstone of journalism, what then makes something journalism? … [T]he critical step in pursuing truthfulness and informing citizens is not neutrality but independence.
>
> —Kovach and Rosenstiel,
> *The Elements of Journalism*

To advance the key concepts of democracy—liberty, equality, community, communication, public opinion, popular consent—media must be free from state- and self-censorship, physical and moral pressure, and political prejudice. In *The Elements of Journalism*, Kovach and Rosenstiel insist that "journalists must maintain an independence from those they cover."[1] They believe this applies to all types of journalism, from hard news and opinion, to commentary and criticism, to talk shows, vernacular blogs, and citizen journalism. Nowhere is this more relevant than in the English-speaking Caribbean.

In these small societies, everyone knows everyone else and degrees of separation are difficult to maintain. The concentric circles of influence are more tightly woven, as politicians can sometimes be family members, friends, neighbors, or former colleagues. These politically centralized social systems also make it difficult for journalists to maintain their independence when covering powerful elites; it is hard for them to criticize those they are related to, those with whom they have worked or maintained friendships. However, Caribbean journalists' lack of independence has engendered much public criticism, as public doubts over their professionalism continue to surface.

On 2 May 2013, Wesley Gibbings, the president of the Association of Caribbean Media Workers, wrote on his blog that, while it was important to celebrate the recent decision by the government of Trinidad and Tobago to repeal some aspects of the country's libel and defamation laws, there is still a long way to go in terms of removing the high levels of self-censorship and lack of professionalism among journalists in the region. Gibbings noted that "journalists are rarely kidnapped, injured or killed in the Caribbean, but many of their stories die. Stories are 'killed' by the chilling effect of draconian legal sanction and by small, closed communities, advertisers, and publishers who either do not wish to offend or are concerned about the protection of people and interests with which they are associated."[2]

In a region where journalists blur the lines between journalism and public relations, it is important to make independence an important standard. Journalists admit that some of their colleagues have moonlighted as public relations practitioners; others have left the profession altogether in order to pursue more lucrative jobs in public relations, drawing on their former relationships in the media. In one case, a Bahamian talk show host had a program on the state broadcaster—a nine-to-five job with a government agency—while simultaneously maintaining, a marketing and public relations company. Journalism, as practiced in the Caribbean, is fraught with similar issues. On his blog, Gibbings cites the following areas of concern: "media colleagues badly compromised either by an inability to contain their political enthusiasm or resist the lure of supplementary personal incomes. The Caribbean media is no exception to the growing emboldening of such partisan elements in the press. This does not, at any time, diminish their own claims to freedom but weakens the professional base from which they operate."[3]

Independence is an essential requirement of journalism; it is a key component of the profession's reliability and validity. "It is this independence of spirit and mind, rather than neutrality, that journalists must keep in focus," argue Kovach and Rosenstiel. "Editorialists and opinion journalists ... are not neutral. Their credibility is rooted instead in the same dedication to accuracy, verification, the larger public interest, and a desire to inform that all other journalists subscribe to."[4] Journalists' loyalty should lie with citizens and the truth, not with special interests, politicians, or political parties. Maintaining independence also requires journalists to avoid arrogance, elitism, isolationism, and nihilism. This is the mandate that journalists must follow as they advance concepts such as truth, fairness, balance, accuracy, and transparency.

In his opening address at the 2001 Caribbean Media Conference in Grenada, Keith Mitchell, the country's prime minister, pointed out that some of the difficulty of maintaining a free press comes from journalists themselves, many of whom are influenced by their personal agendas rather than the development of their societies. "Too often," claimed Mitchell, "personal vendettas, coupled with journalistic pride and the tendency of media people to set themselves aside—or above as the case may be—from the general public, result in judgmental journalism."[5] Not only is this approach regrettable, Mitchell told the assembled journalists—it is also "dangerous, as it undermines the trust and interest the community has in your newspaper, magazine or broadcast station. This can impact on your advertising base, as well as your credibility."[6] While Mitchell may have been referring to the media's coverage of politicians, his comments apply to the broader practice of responsible news coverage.

Bahamian journalist Nicki Kelly's critique of journalistic practices echoes Mitchell's perspective on the diminished capacity for independence among journalists in the region:

> I think if they [journalists] united as a body and if they perhaps got some journalists from the rest of the Caribbean to come and talk to them … they can understand what is going on elsewhere and get over this isolationist idea that they have. … They also have to learn to function in a way independently of their publishers. They have an obligation to the company that they work for to produce the work, but they don't have to bind their minds; their minds are not enslaved to these people. They … should free their minds and realize that there is a whole other world out there and, if they want to improve as people and as journalists, they have to understand what is going on out there and they

have to get rid of the ego bit and join together in a mutual effort to improve themselves.⁷

Kelly's comments point to perhaps the most salient issues facing Caribbean journalism: the need for professional organizations to help journalists. Along with other veteran journalists in the region, Kelly hopes professionalism becomes one of the core areas addressed in the immediate future.

According to Omatie Lyder, the purpose of journalism is "to provide citizens with information so that they [can] make important decisions in their lives."⁸ In order to achieve this, journalists throughout the region must maintain independence from both their subjects as well as their sources. Here, Harold Hoyte explains the challenges of maintaining independence from the powerful elites in Barbados:

> We have had our challenges. We have no censorship per se. We have had challenges with the previous government in particular because the then prime minister was pretty aggressive—combative is the word—and as a result, journalists came under his heel from time to time. I think that may have scared some people because of the awesome power of the prime minister in a small society like this. If he says you cannot get a job here, you cannot get a job here and … nobody will dare touch you because they are afraid of that. … I don't think there is censorship but I think they [politicians] are overly sensitive to the role of independent media.⁹

Roxanne Gibbs's description of the constraints faced by investigative journalists aligns with Hoyte's perspective:

> Really it's not that easy [doing investigative journalism]. … It is not that easy simply because in our culture you unearth something, and trust me, the person involved is connected to this body and that body and is president of this body … and because of this it doesn't get very far because of the smallness of our community and our society. … So for people to say, "Oh we don't do enough investigative [journalism]," it is not as easy as it looks; even from where I sit here, it is not as easy as it appears in

terms of us getting the information to make the story solid and that kind of thing.[10]

Bahamian journalist Juan McCartney agrees that the smallness of Caribbean societies plays a significant role in the types of stories chosen and how they are covered. But the problem also extends to access of information, which he believes permeates the private sector as well. According to McCartney, the only way to get information is "to cultivate sources [and] basically pry it out of people."[11] As a result, journalists are often forced to use unconfirmed reports because they cannot verify the available data. McCartney believes that if there was a freedom of information act, it would allow journalists access to personnel records, civil servants would be able to speak on the record, and, when someone runs for public office, journalists would be able to question their record on certain things without fear. In the current environment, McCartney explains, accessing this type of information is extremely difficult, and is often only possible through the influence of powerful individuals:

> If you want records on things like cabinet papers or things that happened in the government, say, thirty years ago, you still can't get that information. There is no way to get it unless someone like the prime minister says "Hey, give them the cabinet paper."[12]

Caribbean journalists believe this kind of dependency makes it difficult for journalists to maintain their independence. They have become so reliant on political elites and civil servants for information that they have created an asymmetrical relationship between the press and the government, which in turn erodes their independence.

Journalists' lack of independence from political elites is particularly noticeable among public broadcasters. In 2008, Larry Smith, formerly on the board of directors of the Broadcasting Corporation of the Bahamas, as well as a media owner and former journalist, wrote on his blog *Bahamas Pundit* that the state broadcasting institution, Zephyr Nassau Sunshine, "has no respect for either advertisers or its audiences. It indulges in a culture of complacency and entitlement that protects a top-heavy management structure and allows employees to wear their politics on their sleeve. And it is governed by laws that let politicians cherry pick the public interest."[13]

In addition to remaining independent from their sources, it is important that journalists and media organizations control their biases if they want the public to believe they are telling the truth. When journalists lack independence, special interests control what the public perceives as the truth, and when special interests groups control public information, democracy is threatened. Examples of this type of control are prevalent throughout the English-speaking Caribbean.

Hoyte believes this lack of independence created one of the major problems with journalism in the contemporary Caribbean: its inability to uphold its responsibilities to democracy. When journalists neglect this responsibility, the public interest is supplanted by the special interests of political and economic elites. The public is thereby manipulated by the official version of the "truth" instead of a more comprehensive and independent understanding of the issues facing society. This is journalism with an agenda—political propaganda disguised as journalism.

In his 2001 address, Keith Mitchell acknowledged that there was too much partisan political coverage; he advised journalists to change this practice. According to Mitchell, media houses and news services throughout the region concentrated primarily on political matters and neglected other vital areas of society. "Indeed," he pointed out, "attention is often focused on politicians more than anyone else in the society. I believe the media has a responsibility to educate and inform—with the same degree of eagerness—on other issues of national and regional importance such as health care, educational reform, financial matters and all other areas of development in the society."[14] Yet while Mitchell's critique of the emphasis placed on political matters in the region is a valid one, journalists should not lose focus of the fact that monitoring politics is a necessary part of ensuring effective governance.

David Ellis believes that as a result of partisan political coverage, neither the individual journalist nor the profession as a whole is respected in the region. He says many people view journalists as tools to be used and manipulated. Ellis cited the 2010 case of the United States of America versus Michael Christopher "Dudus" Coke, and the ensuing extradition incident in Jamaica to point out media manipulation:

> I have spent a considerable amount of the past week monitoring Jamaica's media and the situation there and I must say that it appears that a number of the journalists went out and braved all of the bullets and everything to get their material out. But there is still ... manipulation and ... disinformation, not only coming from those who are powerful, but those who consider themselves to be powerless. ... When it comes to using the media to manipulate, to say this thing happened and that thing happened, they [both politicians and citizens] do that.[15]

The extradition of Dudus, a Jamaican drug lord, to the United States in 2010 caused civil unrest in Tivoli Gardens, a neighborhood in Kingston, Jamaica. Dudus was indicted in the United States for the transshipment of cocaine and marijuana. Many of his supporters in Jamaica fought with local authorities to prevent his extradition. According to international reports, seventy people died. Ellis believes the manipulation of the media in the wake of this incident was evident in every sphere of society; everyone did it, not just the powerful elites. For example, Ellis was particularly upset when a colleague tried to influence his own independence:

> We are vulnerable to manipulation by all types of people, but there is this notion that we are only vulnerable to misuse by people who have power, and that's not true. At every level people try to use us and what they don't want is for us to say so ... to ask them why. ... I have just received a [legal] letter from a colleague in the newspaper [industry] because I said that his story, his interview with the commissioner of the police, smacked of a public relations story. ... My colleague, who is supposed to be in the vanguard of the fight for freedom of expression ... goes to a lawyer to get a letter sent to me on those grounds.[16]

In such a climate, both independence and transparency are affected by the intersection of media regulations and politics.

Media Regulations and Politics

As print and broadcast media have evolved in the English-speaking Caribbean, two separate paths to regulation have come about. While print media has had minimal state intervention and more self-regulation through independent codes of practice, broadcast media has had more state intervention and is regulated through broadcasting acts, commissions, and authorities. In addition, broadcast media is subject to content rules, which do not include quotas for local content, and are subject to laws that govern defamation, obscenity, and violence. At the time of this writing, there were no press complaint commissions or councils, though the creation of such complaint commissions to deal with press complaints had been discussed in Jamaica and Trinidad and Tobago, with stronger advocacy in Jamaica for implementation. Journalists throughout the region are not required to register with professional bodies or state institutions.

Beyond freedom of expression mandates, there are no statutory rules that govern print media. Jamaica, Trinidad and Tobago, and Grenada have established professional associations that have developed their own codes of ethics to measure professional standards. These codes generally provide guidelines for professional conduct with no clear identification of prohibitions for specific content or penalties for infractions. These guidelines are not binding and depend on journalists remaining vigilant of public interest and community standards. This puts the onus for being fair, accurate, and truthful on journalists rather than citizens. Consequently, over the past five years there has been increased public pressure for the creation of press councils or commissions to adjudicate complaints. Press associations in Barbados, the Bahamas, and Belize fluctuate between periods of activation and dysfunction. Their codes of conduct are either outdated or have gone unimplemented.

Until the recent changes in defamation laws in Jamaica, Trinidad and Tobago, and Grenada, journalists there practiced under restrictive media laws governing libel and defamation. These laws threatened the independent practice of journalism in these countries. Journalists complain that these laws, inherited from the British, restrain them from criticizing elected officials and other public figures. Byron Buckley, associate editor of special projects at the *Jamaica Gleaner*, and president of the Press Association of Jamaica (PAJ), believes the libel laws are both antiquated and punitive.

When he was interviewed, in 2009, libel was still a criminal offence in Jamaica. The libel and defamation laws were reformed in Grenada, Jamaica, and Trinidad and Tobago in 2013 to make libel a civil offence. "We were saying, the MAJ [the Media Association of Jamaica] and the PAJ [the Press Association of Jamaica], we're saying that the only thing you should be able to sue for is malice. Anytime you are a public official, we should have some latitude to question your reports and even hint at some things, once we're not set out to maliciously damage you."[17] Both the PAJ and MAJ recommended that public officials adopt a servant approach toward the public. Jamaica's Defamation Act of 2013 replaced the Libel and Slander Act of 1851 and the Defamation Act of 1961.

Unlike the Bill of Rights in the United States, the constitutions of these countries, except for Trinidad and Tobago, do not guarantee freedom of the press. Instead, the constitutions in five of these countries—the Bahamas, Barbados, Belize, Grenada, and Jamaica—enshrine freedom of expression. Trinidad and Tobago's constitution specifically identifies the rights of a free press but has done very little to encourage its freedom of the press; it was thus downgraded by Freedom House for the government's abusive treatment of journalists in 2012.[18] Journalists believe freedom of expression does not provide the constitutional protection they need to challenge restrictive media laws.[19] Media laws criminally punish defamation, which includes libel, seditious libel, contempt of authority, and insult, both of individuals and of the state itself.

Caribbean journalists, print and broadcast, have to prove the information they report is both accurate and true. According to Chantal Raymond, defamation laws in these countries require minimal proof of defamation and legally start from the position that the information is false: "Politicians and civilians have thus taken advantage of the laws by bringing libel suits against journalists and media organizations that are required to defend their statements as truth."[20] Journalists are therefore very cautious about what they write or say. Consequently, a culture of self-censorship has emerged among Caribbean journalists.

Broadcast media has a long history of state control. It began with public service broadcasting modeled on the BBC, and morphed into state-control broadcasting by the 1950s. This created state-controlled information, which favored the governing party, particularly after these countries became independent states. The majority of state-control broadcasting, associated with propaganda, censorship, and control of information, was dismantled by the first decade of the twenty-first century.[21] All of the countries covered in this book, except Barbados, had restructured their state broadcasting systems into public service broadcasting or sold the majority shares in state broadcasting entities to private broadcasters. Broadcasting commissions, authorities, and other regulatory bodies were formed to regulate the new liberal media environments that emerged in these countries in the 1980s. It is in these new media environments that politicians became more vigilant and filed defamation lawsuits for the slightest offence.

Gary Allen, managing director of Radio Jamaica Rediffusion, points out that the regulatory structure in Jamaica, and by extension the greater Caribbean, evolved out of the turbulent 1990s, when the liberalization of markets emerged without careful evaluation of the marketplace:

> I think that the early stages of the regulatory framework that was put in place could probably be described as inadequate at the time and probably not fully thought out. By the time we got to the late 1990s, and even into the turn of the century, we started the discussion about production quality and standards. … I think one of the disappointments is that those discussions took place around the regulator, and so we did not have the regulators actually being so engaged as to direct even discussion, direct thinking, trying to guide policy.[22]

Of the six countries in this book, Jamaica has the most regulated market, followed by Trinidad and Tobago, and Grenada. The Broadcasting Commission of Jamaica (BCJ), established in 1986, monitors and regulates electronic media, broadcast radio, and television. The BCJ implements public policy and law to balance the interests of consumers, the industries, and the creative community. Prior to the creation of the BCJ, the Jamaican Broadcasting Authority monitored broadcast media. It was eventually integrated into the BCJ, which now also receives and investigates complaints and conducts research.

In the mid-2000s, the BCJ forcibly imposed its regulations. During that period, broadcasting companies, particularly television stations, were producing music videos that promoted a cultural phenomenon called "daggering"—an explicit reenactment of sexual acts through dub or reggae dance that predated Miley Cyrus. According to Hopeton Dunn, chairman of the BCJ, there was a major public outcry against this type of content.[23] The commission forced broadcasters to remove this content, and it implemented new standards for broadcasting, which were incorporated into the broadcast license fee agreement. Not everyone agreed with the BCJ's response and some critics accused it of censorship. While the other five countries of the English-speaking Caribbean did not have a standalone broadcasting commission at the time of this research, they had created regulatory bodies, either in the form of a telecommunications or utilities authority, to regulate the electronic media and establish standards for content. However, they should follow Jamaica's lead and create standalone broadcasting commissions to monitor and regulate their electronic industries more effectively.

The license fee agreements, in all of these countries, now require both public and private broadcasters to maintain standards of decency, protect vulnerable groups, advance cultural diversity, present accuracy and fairness in news and current affairs programs, maintain public service obligations, avoid harmful and incendiary material, and protect national security interests. Some critics have accused Caribbean governments of using the license fee to coerce the media. In 2014, international watchdog organizations Freedom House, the International Press Institute, and Reporters Without Borders reported government influence in granting broadcast licenses. These practices were especially evident in Grenada and Guyana. According to the report, "editors of several newspapers [in Guyana] alleged government discrimination in the awarding of radio and television licenses to friends and relatives of former president Bharrat Jagdeo."[24]

Complaints against libel and defamation laws continued. A 2007 Freedom House report accused the government of Grenada of using the threat of libel laws to pressure the media. The report recounted a 2006 incident involving George Worme, editor of *Grenada Today*. According to Freedom House, "Worme—who has clashed with the authorities over libel issues in the past—was detained by police for several hours on March 14 in relation to a possibly libelous article published the previous month. No charges were made against him, but media freedom advocates claimed it was another indication of the ruling New National Party's efforts to limit media criticism."[25] The US State Department reported in June 2006 that

Grenada's prime minister had won the libel case he had brought against the editor of the newspaper; the editor was ordered to pay approximately US$37,000. Freedom House later reported that there were several occasions when members of the government publicly reprimanded the print media for running critical articles. Indeed, the 2014 report from Freedom House, the International Press Institute, and Reporters Without Borders highlighted the increased number of complaints from Caribbean politicians against media for critical articles or broadcasts.

International and regional organizations have voiced their objections to political influence in the media. In the 1990s, in an effort to reduce political interference, encourage openness and transparency in governance, and advance human rights throughout the region, the United Nations, the World Bank, and the International Press Institute urged Caribbean governments to pass freedom of information legislation to close the gap between government and civil society.[26] The IPI's 2013 report on Trinidad and Tobago noted criminal defamation laws were an "insult to democracy." The report quoted a 2005 joint declaration by the special rapporteurs of the Organization of American States (OAS) and the African Commission on Human and Peoples' Rights (ACHPR): "In democratic societies, the activities of public officials must be open to public scrutiny. Criminal defamation laws intimidate individuals from exposing wrongdoing by public officials and such laws are therefore incompatible with freedom of expression."[27]

Belize began its progress towards transparency with the creation of a freedom of information law in 1994. However, the law was not implemented until 2000; by then, it was considered "too broad in its definition of private and public information."[28] Though it was revised in 2000, it was never implemented. Media scholars, practitioners, and analysts still criticize the Belizean government and its agencies for not implementing the law. Jamaica passed an access to information law in 2002; it became effective in 2004. Jamaica's law allows greater access to public information, but journalists do not receive information efficiently. The Gleaner Company recorded its continued battle with lawsuits and access to information in its 2013 and 2014 annual reports. While it believed the new laws improved the practice, it also claimed that "they do not go far enough in better enabling media to tackle the corruption prevalent in our society."[29]

The passage of the new laws represented a step in the right direction, but it took almost ten years for politicians and civil servants to implement their requirements. The Bahamas passed its freedom of information law in 2012 but it did not formally enact it. Barbados and Grenada have not passed similar laws. Trinidad and Tobago, too, passed a freedom of information act in 2001 but did not enact it. The implementation, scope, and types of exemptions in these acts leave critics like Venkat Iyer and Toby Mendel questioning their effectiveness in advancing openness, accountability, and transparency among Caribbean governments.[30] Most troubling for these societies is the fact that the Official Secrets Act remains law. A holdover from colonization, this law makes it an offence to disclose official information or breach official trust. This means people working in the civil service who disclose information could be prosecuted. Many Caribbean journalists feel the Official Secrets Act negates any freedom of information law.

Barbadian journalist Reudon Eversley points out that the Barbadian government had promised to bring freedom of information legislation but were still drafting the legal framework of the bill in 2010. Eversley did not believe the act would be passed; at the time of the publication of this book, Barbados still had not implemented it. Even with the passage of a freedom of information act, some journalists believed they would still be constrained. As Eversley points out, "we have a lot of old laws, too, like the Official Secrets Act, a lot of old colonial laws that are still on the statute books that can be used effectively against you. But libel is the biggest challenge because people will sue you for anything. ... People sue for the slightest thing, especially, politicians."[31]

Senior journalists believe politicians have taken advantage of the inexperience of young journalists to instill a new level of fear and intimidation. For example, in March 2012 the prime minster of Grenada was blamed for the dismissal of Rawle Titus, a news reporter for the *Grenada Advocate*. An article published in the *Grenada Advocate* on March 9, 2012, prompted Titus's dismissal. In that article "Titus reported that the prime minister had selected the ruling National Democratic Congress's candidates for the next general election without consulting with the party's leaders."[32] Later, other media also carried reports that supported this claim. The prime minister's press secretary, Richard Simon, requested a retraction and an apology from the *Grenada Advocate*. Shortly thereafter

Titus received notice that his contract with the *Advocate* would be terminated.³³ At that time, Reporters Without Borders called on the government of Grenada "to provide a frank explanation of a matter liable to endanger media independence."³⁴ This incident is not the only example of threat and intimidation. The prime minister or president, and the ruling party in these small states, wields a lot of power. In 2013, a young reporter in Grenada recounted the threats made towards her by the prime minister. The owner of her media company, a close friend of the prime minister, conveyed the threats.³⁵ Her name is omitted here because of concerns of repercussions.

According to Reporters Without Borders, Jamaica was ranked thirteenth on the list of global press freedom in 2012—the highest of any Caribbean country. The same year, Freedom House described Trinidad and Tobago's democracy as "flawed." Freedom House also described the Bahamas, Barbados, Belize, and Grenada as having a "moderately" free press.³⁶

In 2011, Wesley Gibbings, president of the ACM, claimed restrictive laws prohibited journalists from protecting and advancing democracy throughout the region. He identified the challenges to press freedom and freedom of expression in Caribbean countries as "a complex mix of direct and insidious phenomena that include overt state hostility towards media organizations, a heritage of restrictive legislative environments, control of media content by commercial and special interest groups, corrosive effects of systemic self-censorship, and general public apathy."³⁷ Two years later, Gibbings acknowledged that the current blend of media regulations and commercial interests did not bode well for the future of democracy in these countries.³⁸

Caribbean journalism continues to operate under the influence of archaic British laws. Journalists in the Caribbean strongly believe these laws must be changed and new ones implemented if they are to function more independently. Although they believe freedom of speech and a free press are not absent from the region, they admit scarcity of freedom of information laws and a culture of secrecy prohibits journalists from performing their duties independently. While it appears some governments are changing their laws, others are reacting to the digital environment with the application of restrictive new laws. Grenada's enactment of new electronic media laws in 2013 seemed counterintuitive to its recent announcement to decriminalize defamation. Despite protest from Caribbean journalists, the

IPI, and private citizens, Grenada did not repeal its new electronic media law and the fear remains that other governments throughout the region may adopt similar legislation.

Maintaining Independence in Small Caribbean Societies

Despite the enactment of freedom of information laws in eight of the English-speaking Caribbean countries—Antigua and Barbuda, Belize, Bermuda, the Cayman Islands, Guyana, Jamaica, St. Vincent and the Grenadines, and Trinidad and Tobago—and the recent decriminalization of defamation in Grenada, Jamaica, and Trinidad and Tobago, the secretive practices inherited from British colonial administrators continue to permeate all aspects of Caribbean life. Thus, Caribbean journalists find it difficult to obtain information that is in the public interest. Some journalists have had to resort to cultivating a small network of reliable sources, but in small societies these sources often do not have the same level of anonymity as they do in large countries, and this impedes free expression.

In these small, secretive societies, media systems are plagued by partisan politics, which presents itself in a variety of ways and influences the performance of journalists. This concept has been referred to in the literature as political clientelism. In their article "Political Clientelism and the Media: Southern Europe and Latin America in Comparative Perspective," Daniel Hallin and Stylianos Papathanassopoulos argue that political clientelism plays a significant role in media performance. They define clientelism as "a pattern of social organization in which access to social resources is controlled by patrons and delivered to clients in exchange for deference and various kinds of support."[39] They examine how this concept presents itself in the media systems of four southern European countries—Greece, Italy, Spain, and Portugal—and three Latin American countries—Brazil, Columbia, and Mexico. The concept of political clientelism is not new; it is present throughout all political systems. However, Hallin and Papathanassopoulos argue that it is particularly useful in the case of the news media because "the ideals of neutral professionalism based on Anglo-American media history are widely accepted by journalists around the world, even where the actual practice of journalism departs radically from them. The concept of clientelism is useful in media analysis, in part precisely because it illuminates normative issues of media performance in a democratic system."[40]

The challenge of maintaining neutrality and independence, or in journalistic parlance, objectivity, is much more difficult in small states, where there is a heightened awareness or need to maintain unity and a collaborative atmosphere; in such an environment, managing boundaries is challenging. Many of the journalists interviewed for this book spoke of the realities of practicing in small communities and the challenge of responding to relational expectations, including the expectation of covering family and friends. Social cohesion is valued. Bahamian journalist Thea Rutherford alluded to this in her description of the working conditions in her country. "I think it is really difficult to practice in a small country," she explains, "because everybody knows everybody, and it's probably the same problems that the police have [with regard to crime]." Rutherford believes "that is the biggest challenge to our responsibilities, because our responsibility is to be reasonably objective. The responsibility is, ideally, that nobody should be out of bounds to cover. The reality is, however, when you look at a small community, there are going to be limits."[41]

How should journalists cover their relatives and friends in small countries? How do they maintain credibility while covering public officials or prominent members of society when they are related to them? Journalists in small towns in the United States and Great Britain have also raised these questions. Their professional associations, the Society of Professional Journalists (SPJ) in the United States and the National Union of Journalists (NUJ) in Britain do not address these questions directly. The SPJ admonishes journalists to "act independently. Journalists should be free of obligation to any interests other than the public's right to know."[42] The SPJ's code of ethics details how journalists should do this, but it fails to address the question of close relationships. The NUJ is less detailed in its code of conduct but implies that journalists should avoid conflicts of interest. The current codes of ethics of professional associations in the Caribbean do not address these issues. Like the SPJ, they provide guidance on conflict of interests and disclosure but do not specifically address the issue of covering close relationships, especially in small communities.

Caribbean journalists have been criticized for lack of independence from those whom they cover. The perception that journalists are biased in their coverage of political elites was most prevalent among broadcast journalists, many of whom had been accused of being government propagandists. This perception persists. In terms of professionalism, ethics, and independence, journalists struggle to maintain a professional distance from those they cover.

As Claude Robinson explained, "the major role of these broadcasting systems in the 1960s and 1970s was public education, cultural enrichment, national identity, or a sense of 'nation-ness.'"[43] But these systems lacked independence, editorial autonomy, and financial stability, and they were not accountable to the public. In her 2007 study, Cinzia Padovani noted most of these systems were starved of public funds and relied heavily on commercial advertising. Most were in debt by the beginning of the 1990s.[44]

Many scholars, like Monroe Price and Marc Raboy,[45] and Indrajit Banerjee and Kalinga Seneviratne,[46] believe these systems were operated as state-run institutions with direct dominance or interference from ruling political elites. As a result of political and economic constraints, these systems were not able to effectively promote public service values, editorial independence, quality programs, and democratic and accountable systems of administration.[47] However, having dominated their markets for decades, they did make important contributions, providing some of the region's rich cultural heritage in terms of music, drama, and the arts.

Government influence in broadcasting remains a concern throughout the region. Broadcast journalists who work for state-owned radio and television stations are often accused of political clientelism. Further, because of the size of these markets, private broadcasters also favor one political party over another. Broadcast licensing is controlled by the state and favoritism is sometimes evident in the provision of licenses. Partisan relations are also evident in newspaper ownership and, historically, favoritism in print journalism's coverage of political parties was perceived as highly partisan. In Belize, Grenada, and Guyana, with their history of party ownership of major newspapers, partisan political coverage is highly visible.

Hallin and Papathanassopoulos focus on five major characteristics of political clientelism evident in the performance of media systems included in their study: "low levels of newspaper circulation, a tradition of advocacy reporting, instrumentalization of privately-owned media, politicization of public broadcasting and broadcast regulation, and limited development of journalism as an autonomous profession."⁴⁸ These characteristics are also present in Caribbean media systems—except, whereas the European and Latin American examples show low levels of newspaper circulation, the Caribbean varied, from high circulation in Trinidad and Tobago and Jamaica, to medium circulation in the Bahamas and Barbados, to low in Belize and Grenada.

Throughout the Caribbean, particularly in wake of the liberalization of the 1990s, "there was a strong tendency for media to be controlled by private interests with political alliances and ambitions who sought to use media properties for political ends."⁴⁹ In some countries, these relationships were very visible as media companies with known political affiliations openly supported their party, often times the governing party. Some media houses have an adversarial relationship with political parties. These partisan relationships were strongest in Antigua, Belize, Grenada, and Guyana, but they were also present in the others. Caribbean countries have a history of politicizing public broadcasting. As such, journalistic autonomy was limited throughout the region.

Political pressure can take the form of commercial action. For example, the withdrawal of state advertising from *CaymanNet News*, in the Cayman Islands in 2004, was in response to politically unfavorable journalism, as was the withholding of state advertising from the *Stabroek News* in 2009. The concentration of media ownership, particularly by conglomerates, could also diminish independence. Wesley Gibbings laments the fact that "low professional standards, defective media institutions, adverse political circumstances, and uncompromising commercial interests conspire severally and collectively to create conditions that militate against the free press in the Caribbean."⁵⁰

The conclusions of Hallin and Papathanassopoulos's study, when applied to the Caribbean context, are amplified by the size of these markets. Hallin and Papathanassopoulos believe journalism in the Caribbean is "not strongly developed as an autonomous institution, differentiated from other institutions—the family business, the political clique, the party—with a distinctive set of professional values and practices."⁵¹ Although Jamaica is a stand-alone example for advancing professionalization, I concur with Hallin and Papathanassopoulos. There is limited professionalization, evident in the limited development of institutions of journalistic self-regulation. Professional associations are important in a region where authoritarianism, clientelism, and secrecy are strongly embedded in local cultures. Professionalization could lift the integrity of journalism and bring about more media autonomy throughout the region.

According to Hallin and Papathanassopoulos, the region emerged from an early form of clientelism, "a dyadic one based on relations of dependence,"[52] which was replaced with the "complex pyramidal clientelism"[53] evident today. The latter form emerged as "national political institutions developed, including political parties and centralized administration, and combined with clientelistic relations to create a more complex form of clientelism."[54]

The new form of clientelism has led many people to criticize the structure and quality of journalism. The main concerns are the lack of professionalism, media bias, poor quality reporting, lack of autonomy, and journalists' lack of knowledge of their environments and social histories. These deficiencies are noticeable in these small societies and have led to a diminished respect for journalists. However, during the independence movement and immediately after independence, journalists were praised for their contributions to the development of these countries. This was the period when developmental journalism was the dominant model.

In interviews conducted for this book, journalists described the emergence of a hostile relationship between the media and politicians; many recounted incidents of direct intimidation. In particular, Guyana provides one of the most notorious examples of press intimidation. According to the IPI's 2013 country report, the relationship between the government and the press, although somewhat improved since the replacement of former president Bharrat Jagdeo, remains hostile. During his tenure, President Jagdeo referred to journalists as "carrion crows" and "vultures," and he compared certain Guyanese media professionals to their Rwandan counterparts, some of which were accused of instigating the 1994 genocide.[55] President Jagdeo also banned Gordon Moseley, a reporter for *Capitol News* and the president of the Guyana Press Association, from the office of the president. Verbal assaults on the press are common throughout the region and many politicians use the term "opposition press" to describe media who oppose the government. Incidents of physical violence have been reported as well. In 2012, for example, the IPI condemned the beating of *Kaieteur News* reporter Freddie Kissoon. In an earlier incident in 2010, according to the IPI's 2013 report, a bucket of human waste was thrown in Kissoon's face. Kissoon is a well-known critic of the People's Progressive Party.[56] In

2012 in Antigua and Barbuda, the investigative news website *Caribarena* reported serious allegations of intimidation. According to the IPI, "*Caribarena's* editors reported incidents of violence, and fear for their safety led the editors to remove bylines."[57] The editors also reported that their homes had been broken into, that stones were frequently thrown at their cars, and they claimed that "the government has pressured private advertisers not to cooperate with *Caribarena*."[58] They believed they had been targeted with this harassment campaign because of their reporting on sensitive issues.

According to other reports, Caribbean politicians have employed intimidation tactics, such as sending security officers to press conferences, having ghostwriters send letters to the editors of local newspapers containing vicious verbal attacks to editors of local newspapers, selective advertising, enforcing national security laws, controlling attendance at press conferences, and ignoring, obfuscating, or delaying information requests.[59] The relationship between government and the press in the Caribbean has become hostile and mistrustful. To diffuse the growing tension, in 2014 the IPI recommended increased dialogue between public officials and journalists to enhance the government's understanding of the media's role in democracy.

In conjunction with the negative climate, there is a high level of bias and clientelism among media owners and politicians. Several journalists claimed that they were pressured to report from a particular political standpoint, and some editors altered copy "to supply a particular bent."[60]

The dominant sentiment among journalists interviewed for this book is that they are not respected. Anthony Forbes, a former journalist who was employed at the time of research with the Bahamas Information Services, noted that while there were more journalists with university degrees, "we haven't had the same level of the quality of news reporters. They aren't as aggressive in going after the real good stories as opposed to just sensational stuff."[61] Harold Hoyte recalled his encounters with ministers of government and prime ministers at press conferences, "where they dare not slip because we were onto them. Now you watch a press conference, and the questions are very patronizing and people are very polite and so on. There are no follow-up questions they are just token questions, a token question here and a token question there."[62] Hoyte believes that to some extent there is also manipulation of the media—for example, when "governments try to handpick people [at press conferences]. ... So people who may ask unsettling questions are unwelcomed."[63]

That the public and other key stakeholders do not care about the work they do or understand the many challenges and constraints within which they work has a demoralizing effect on journalists. This lack of empathy and support does not inspire them to produce the kind of work that many of their critics demand. The Barbadian journalist Reudon Eversley and the Bahamian journalist Ava Turnquest both believe that public criticism and public apathy towards journalism has had a negative effect on their performance. As Turnquest explains, "we need the public's feedback. When I do a story on a significant issue I want that feedback from the public. That's what motivates me to do what I do. When the public doesn't provide that feedback it seems to me that they don't really care about these issues."[64] Likewise, Eversley complains that people do not understand how news is produced, the conditions journalists work under, or other constraints that impact journalism. "You have a lot of self-appointed experts on journalism who call for investigative journalism but they are not sufficiently appreciative of the underlying factors that hinder it. Nor will they be bold enough to mount a lobby. They expect you to go out there and fight for them but they don't want to fight for you."[65]

Some Caribbean journalists also believe that independence is culturally specific. For instance, Omatie Lyder, editor of the *Trinidad Express*, provides an example of gift-giving in the Caribbean context:

> We also have to keep in mind that our culture is different and there are things that you would [not do]. I'll give you an example. The banks would send us carnival T-shirts. The banks would never do that in the US so you'd never be put in that position. But do you make a big deal out of it and send them back? You know five credit union T-shirts? When they are not expecting [or] they are not perceiving it as a gift. It is just something they do for their customers anyway. They don't expect that a journalist is going to end up on their side. They don't expect it and to actually send a T-shirt back would just insult someone you have forged a decent relationship with, a decent working repertoire. So there are those things we have to keep in mind.[66]

Although Lyder believed these types of activities were not interpreted as opportunities to influence or manipulate journalists, these gifts could influence journalists indirectly and an unconscious bias toward the gift-giving individual or organization could emerge.

Another cultural practice is "envelope journalism," which happens when journalists receive payment for attending press conferences and other events. In the Caribbean, media scholars and professional associations are aware of these forms of influence, but they have not taken a hardline against them.

So, the questions arise, How do journalists practice independence in such an environment? How do they develop a professional identity while balancing overlapping relationships? Journalists' observations underscore the difficulties of accomplishing this goal under the current working conditions. Reudon Eversley believes these small, authoritarian societies make it extremely challenging to practice effective journalism. He provides an example of how difficult it is to investigate or cover sensitive topics like race relations in the Caribbean. When he worked as an editor for the *Barbados Advocate*, he created a special assignments desk to explore some of the issues that plague Barbadian society. Eversley noted they were forced to drop a story on race relations because of economic and political pressures:

> I mean, we always knew in Barbados ... [that] we have our own unofficial system of apartheid. Whites, it's only now that you're seeing a bit of integration. But when I was a boy growing up there was no mixing. I went to an old grammar school where white boys sat in my class and we would talk during the week but on Friday afternoon that relationship came to an end.
>
> So we wanted to look at what it meant to be white in Barbados. Because there are a number of issues—like, for example, unemployment. Unemployment is not a white issue in Barbados; unemployment is a black issue. Most white guys who are at school will tell you they don't have to study; education is not that important to them because they control the economy and when they come out they will get a job. They find it easier to get access to bank loans to start businesses that people like myself [blacks] the banks will give us hell.

> So we wanted to look at what it meant because ... for example, in St. John's, a parish here, we have a community of what we call "ecky-beckies," they're poor whites. They came here as ... virtual slaves from Ireland, indentured servants. They were expelled by Oliver Cromwell, but they have retained their identity and they're among some of the most racists people you could come across because they refer to people like myself as niggers.
>
> So we wanted to explore some of these issues and my manager called me one day and told me we had to end it because certain powerful elements in this country were accusing me of trying to stir up racial strife, when basically it was my view that the black community was entitled to know what was the experience of whites. They know what our experience is, they see us on the front page with crime and what not, they know of our struggles. Why we don't know about their privileged living? So you're not going to have any real investigative journalism in this country. It would be for someone from the United States or from England to come in and dig it up, where they don't give a hell what happens here. But if you have to live in this community, this community has a way of getting back at you and punishing you in the area where it hurts most—in your pocket.[67]

Eversley's description of race relations clearly speaks to the continued issues of race in these postcolonial societies. But it also points to society's need to maintain a sense of group cohesion. As collectivist societies, Caribbean countries value group harmony, which sometimes was maintained through submission to the social order. There are few public discussions of race, sexism, ethnic relations, or same-sex relations as they exist in these countries, and when they are discussed it is either in the context of a response to incidents like the accusation of radio stations inciting racial discrimination in the 2002 Trinidad elections, the work of international and local NGOs, or the academic discourse on race and sexual orientation within the Caribbean intellectual community. Race relations in the Caribbean are anchored in the past—both the recent past, just prior to independence, and the colonial past under the mercantile system of slavery and exploitation. Caribbean journalists are prohibited from frank discussions of race and sexual orientation. Homophobia is also deeply embedded in these societies. Senior journalists, those who have lived and worked before, during, and after independence, discuss the continued challenges of covering black-white relations. Many can provide examples of the racism they experienced when they were first hired. For example, as Ken Gordon noted, in the 1940s a radio station ran an advertisement for an announcer which read, "Announcer needed. Only white need apply."[68]

These political, economic, social, and cultural constraints undermine the principle of independence, but more importantly, they cheat the public and betray the truth. When the biases of political, social, and economic elites and media owners align on questions of censorship and social cohesion, important issues like ethnic identity, race relations, gender bias, and sexual orientation remain hidden from public scrutiny. This represents an egregious breach of the public's trust and a compromise of Caribbean journalists' ability to report fairly and accurately. Worst of all, there are no mechanisms of oversight to police these types of biases.

"Independence of mind" is further eroded by the increase in radio punditry. The initial impact of these shows on political elites was tremendous. But, the initial euphoria and increase in power was subverted. Many talk show hosts embrace their celebrity status and try to maintain audience share by trafficking in opinion, speculation, and misinformation. Like their American counterparts, they see themselves as the new information elites. Many exuded the star syndrome.

Critics accuse journalists and talk show hosts of paying more attention to their stardom than their role as newsgatherers. Some of the journalists interviewed agree that the issues of arrogance, egoism, and elitism are affecting the quality of journalism. This phenomenon has led to accusations of bias and unfair coverage as journalists are accused of spending more time advancing their status in society than upholding the principles that guide the practice and profession of journalism. Rupert Missick, a young Bahamian journalist, believed that instead of fueling their egos, journalists should be more concerned about understanding complex and complicated issues like the CSME and EPA (Economic Partnership Agreement). He admitted that journalists, during the time of the debates over the CSME and EPA, did not have the background to understand them and so they did not know how to explain how these issues would impact their audience on an individual and collective level. He acknowledged his own lack of training and described how a senior journalist explained to him how he had to write so that the audience understood the CSME or EPA. Missick confessed he did not know how to write that way. "How do you write that?" he queried. "I can barely understand it, and I can't listen to it for more than two minutes without losing interest. How does a reporter who is not an economic expert, how does he dumb it down or make it simpler to educate somebody fully about what it is?"[69] Missick believes that citizens only want to know how to stop these agreements because the journalists only provided them with one side of the story. They do not understand the benefits, nor, according to Missick, do they care to understand them. The coverage of these agreements has not been comprehensive, proportionate, relevant, or engaging. As a result, a lot of misinformation, disinformation, and fear has been circulated. Missick acknowledges that during these debates some journalists took an elitist approach to their audience, believing the audience was not smart enough to understand these agreements. He believes journalists' weak coverage of these two agreements was related to elitism, a lack of resources to meet the expectations of the population, a lack of access to information, and a lack of knowledge, time, and training.

Elitist attitudes and the phenomenon of the celebrity journalist do not engender independent journalism. Although journalists are troubled by the emerging phenomenon of the "star," they are equally relieved that the impact of this phenomenon has not reached the same levels as the United States or Britain. Journalists in the region, unlike their American and European counterparts, do not yet command significant remuneration for speaking engagements, lectures, or book deals, but some have obtained significant rewards from political and economic elites in exchange for favorable coverage. Some journalists have moonlighted in public relations, while others have created their own private media or communication firm while working as a journalist for other media. These conflicts of interest are important and are the purview of professional associations.

While independence is a valuable principle to uphold, it should not preclude journalists from presenting a voice in their stories, which is not the same as being biased. They should use a voice that excites the reader, listener, or viewer, but they should remain balanced, accurate, and fair. They should not confuse fact with opinion. Speculation and bias should not replace facts. While there are journalists and journalism scholars who would argue fiercely for objectivity as the holy grail of journalism, no journalist can truly be objective as the human condition has inherent biases based on background, personality, values, and beliefs. Despite the acknowledgement that true objectivity is impossible to practice in the field, some journalists still strive to achieve this. Dan Gillmor, author of *We the Media*, rejects the notion of objectivity, and in his essay "The End of Objectivity (Version 0.91)," he advocates that journalists drop the word objectivity and replace it with thoroughness, accuracy, fairness, and transparency. "We are human," he writes. "We have biases and backgrounds and a variety of conflicts that we bring to our jobs every day."[70]

The majority of the journalists interviewed agreed that there is a need for independence and the application of objectivity through the verification of facts in the pursuit of truth. However, journalists also acknowledged the challenges of upholding this principle.

Professional Associations

Professional associations are synergistic groups of people who come together to further their career and enhance their profession. They setup guidelines for ethical conduct and best practices. It is unfortunate in a region that has such rich intersecting histories and cultures that journalism has not developed as a professional, lifelong career. Further, the size of the markets, political and economic control of the market, media organizations, and educational institutions do not facilitate the development of a journalistic culture that is vital to the growth and development of democracy. As a result, it is difficult for young people entering the field to see themselves in lifelong careers.

In order to build a professional culture, media owners, policymakers, media scholars, and journalists will have to decide on the role journalism plays in the development of these societies and provide the training and opportunities for journalists to develop lifelong careers and a professional identity. Caribbean journalists believe that throughout the region journalism has not yet developed into a professional career. Creating a professional culture would advance this goal. Professionalism would also benefit the reputations, morale, and success of journalists. To have the greatest impact the goals of professional associations should be specific, measurable, attainable, relevant, and timely. A clear plan of action should be created to achieve these goals.

This call to action is extremely important at a time when journalists will be expected to make sense of the overwhelming amount of information citizens receive every day. If they are not held accountable to citizens for what they write and present, how are they any different from the propagandist? The level of criticism regarding the quality of Caribbean journalism should motivate journalists to improve the quality of their work. To this end, the most important contributions of professional associations are a code of ethics that clearly articulates how journalists should practice, as well as the mechanisms of accountability.

Brent Dean and Peter Christopher, two younger journalists, viewed the lack of professional careers in journalism as a multifaceted problem with media owners, political leaders, educational institutions, and journalists themselves sharing the responsibility for the haphazard development of journalism throughout the region. Journalism is perceived as a short-term employment opportunity that can propel journalists into better careers in public relations, law, or politics. In Dean's opinion, journalists do not join professional associations because they do not have a stake in journalism. Rather, "for there to [even] be an association, you have to have people who have something at stake. If people are just passing through, they are not going to risk anything … [to] create a very active association or union. They are just going to keep their jobs, not get in any trouble, and go home on time."[71] He believes that treating journalism as career or profession, along with the resources that go with such status, could improve the value of professional organizations, "but media owners will have to play a big role in this. Once people are making very little and they don't think they can stay they will go. I think that's … the main reason why we don't have associations, unions or such."[72]

Christopher also believes journalists are not being very responsible or accountable. "There should be some kind of accountability. You also have to be mindful of what danger you can put the public in, what effects your writing has on the public because there are a lot of stories that are written that end up putting members of the public in danger, they cause innocent people their jobs."[73]

Christopher is perturbed because many journalists do not check their facts; others use unattributed sources and rumors with very little substantiation. In Trinidad and Tobago, he explains, "newspapers are full of errors. We like to sensationalize stories. We like to fabricate stories. We don't get all the facts. We overlook many things. *X* newspaper is supporting this party, this political side. There is no objectivity in the media. That's the common criticism."[74] He cites the example of journalists reporting the rumors of a human trafficking story as fact instead of investigating the rumors to get to the truth:

> What happened last week or two weeks ago with the whole fiasco with the multi containers on the port where these young journalists were so thirsty to break this media story [that they] went out and reported [that] this container full of children was found in the port and this is something that is continuously happening. Everywhere I go … I will always encounter somebody who says that the media in Trinidad never gets the story right. It's because a lot of the reporters … don't double check what they're hearing or they just take the first thing they hear and say, "hey, this is the story. I'm gonna write it as this." And as such, the credibility of the media in Trinidad has suffered a lot.[75]

For Christopher, this incident underscores how far the standards have fallen. He believes a lot of these weaknesses could be attributed to youth, inexperience, and lack of training: "Because a lot of journalists who are currently in the media are very young, they don't have the full approach to journalism and the quality [that is needed]."[76] As such, Christopher noted, the quality is not very high. "Some of these senior journalists who are still around would try to tell us 'hey you could look at what the BBC does or read … one of the English newspapers and see how they approach different stories.'"[77] However, the younger journalists did not follow through. The problem was also exacerbated because "some of the editors who are in place now are these same young journalists who came up without guidance, and they are just doing what they heard from before and not really getting it right. So there is a lack of guidance."[78]

Christopher is disheartened by the ineffectiveness of the professional association in Trinidad and Tobago. "I don't consider it very effective," he explains. "I was nagged into joining. They're going to have a meeting on Saturday, which I probably will not attend because I have been very disheartened by how they have approached previous media affairs. They normally adopt a wait-and-see policy on most things, so I've not been impressed by their operations."[79]

Professional organization is one of the key elements for the advancement of journalism throughout the Caribbean. Jamaica provides a good case study for the region. Jamaica's professional organizations, the Press Association of Jamaica and the Media Association of Jamaica, have attempted to professionalize journalism and standardize its practice. Both organizations have articulated the principles and guidelines for the practice and profession. The annual distribution of professional awards has helped to standardize and enhance the value of the profession as well.

To actualize their role as independent monitors of power, journalists in the Caribbean should first define what independence means to them and identify the standards of independence they want to uphold. They should also determine how they would implement these standards. Improving the profession would also require the creation of codes of conduct for national, regional and international practices as the emphasis of coverage shifts to the need for glocal perspectives; this means understanding the local and the global. Professional associations should also work with academic programs and institutes throughout the region to improve the quality of education and training. Further, as a result of increased criticism, press councils or a formal oversight structure should be established to create a system that handles media complaints.

7

The Future of Caribbean Journalism

Although the future of journalism in the United States, Europe, Canada, and Australia is still in question, the debate continues to receive a lot of attention from academics, practitioners, media owners, and citizens in these countries. This has not been the case in the Caribbean. However, it is not that there is denial about the changes taking place in the media industries or in the practice, but rather that the changes are taking place in a different milieu. Caribbean journalism does not have the same academic or professional history. Caribbean media owners attribute the slow pace of change to cultural differences and lower internet penetration, which is changing rapidly in some countries and more slowly in others. In general, newspaper readership, television news consumption, and radio listenership is still relatively high. People in the Caribbean still love the news and integrate it into their everyday lived experience through oral storytelling. This factor lies at the heart of media consumption in the region, which, at the time of this research, was still mostly done offline.

The lack of debate on the future of journalism in the region does not mean practitioners and media owners are unaware of the global debate; a few attempts have been made to discuss the issues of change with the aid of international and regional organizations such as the Commonwealth Broadcasting Association, the Caribbean Broadcasting Union, and the Association of Caribbean Media Workers.[1] The low level of professionalism, coupled with a lack of communication scholarship, also inhibits robust debate in the region. This has resulted in elongated silences, and consequently, the changes that are taking place in journalism within these countries seem to be of little import. The global discussion centers on issues of the survival of a profit-making model of journalism, the need to innovate, the relevance of journalism in twenty-first-century democracies, and queries of who is a journalist in an era when anyone with the technology can gather and disseminate information whenever and however they choose. Media owners and practitioners in the Caribbean acknowledge the increase in citizen blogging and other social-media activity, and admit that these activities circumvent traditional channels of communication. They also believe bloggers serve a useful purpose in these secretive societies, where freedom of information is either ignore or does not exist. However, there has been little discourse on the impact of citizen journalism. Further, journalists in the region still believe they hold the public's trust in terms of the credibility of their information.

Beyond the increase in citizens' ability to gather and disseminate information, technology has also provided journalists with the opportunity to access information more efficiently and effectively from online sources. Media environments operate in a twenty-four-hour information cycle that has placed more demands on a journalist's time and skills. Investigative journalism, moreover, is constrained by the political, social, and economic environment, which makes it difficult to develop effective and consistent investigations. While citizens are demanding more investigative journalism, the current dictates of the media environment limits journalists' ability to meet this demand. Cultural constraints—a culture of secrecy and silence, limited sources in small societies, a lack of access to information, and fear of intimidation and victimization—have also disrupted the gathering of information. Other constraints include low levels of professionalization and inconsistent training. Until these are removed, investigative journalism will continue to be limited and sporadic.

The future of journalism in the small developing countries of the Caribbean may seem more certain than journalism as practiced in developed countries. In spite of this optimistic forecast, the future trajectory should be one that uses a variety of methods to produce not a single type of journalism but rather a hybrid approach to the practice. Multi-skilled journalists are the way of the future, in the Caribbean and globally. Currently, and even more so in the future, journalists must cultivate a variety of skills, as more will be expected of them. Editors and media owners stress this need, with some admitting they have trimmed their number of employees and may do so again in the future as more of their activities move online. More engagement with the audience or consumers will also drive the demand for more highly trained and specialized journalists. Beyond the need to know how to write or speak effectively, journalists will be required to know all aspects of the production process and become effective interpreters in an era of information overload, misinformation, and disinformation. Their cartographic skills will be in high demand.

Journalists of the future will also have to form strategic partnerships with citizens in the process of gathering and disseminating information. More will be required of citizens, particularly those that have become involved in this process. In the current media environment, such people are not viewed as direct competitors, but as more of them become accurate and reliable sources of information, they will impact traditional news sources, syphoning audiences in the process. The blogosphere, along with Twitter, Facebook, YouTube, WhatsApp and other platforms, may become more legitimate sources. For cultures that thrive on rumor and innuendo, that make small things significant and significant things small, this trend may represent a dangerous shift as more misinformation and disinformation enter the public sphere masquerading as the truth. Despite the litigious nature of Caribbean societies, these activities will grow unless regulations are applied to the online environment. Some Caribbean governments have already initiated new laws to monitor online activities, though many critics view the imposition of such laws as a threat to free speech and democracy.

Journalists are concerned about the increase in online activity and the use of social media. Erica Wells, editor of the *Nassau Guardian*, describes the impact of online information on the future of journalism and democracy as troubling. "It's these anonymous bloggers who I think ... are doing a lot of damage [to journalism]. I think there is no level of responsibility or accountability and they are not held, obviously, to the same standards that we are being held to. I think most people dismiss it but I think some people take that stuff very seriously."[2] Wells believes there has to be a way to enforce some sort of standard for bloggers. "It's one thing if you have a blog name ... [then] there is a certain level of responsibility. But if you don't identify yourself ... you are being irresponsible ... you are libeling people and damaging people's reputations and lives. That is a very serious thing. It needs to be addressed."[3]

This warning is echoed in the growing concerns over incivility, both on- and offline. In a recent essay on the future of journalism, Robert Picard affirms that "journalism belongs to society."[4] This claim has taken on new meaning in an audience-driven world where concern for feedback has grown significantly over the last twenty years. Digital technologies have broken down traditional barriers between journalists and their audience, as ordinary citizens invade cyberspace with their feedback, comments, analyses, reports, photographs and videos. While theorists like Robert Picard, Cass Sunstein, and John Merrill see this as a benefit for democracy others, like Nicholas Carr, Andrew Keen, Zizi Papacharissi, and Edward Shils, emphasize the costs of digital technology. In the midst of this avalanche of information, there is growing concern for privacy and the lack of civility in cyberspace as people become more obnoxious and uncivil in their responses to each other and present inaccurate, unfair, untruthful, and specious information.

Despite these dire warnings, libertarian proponents believe the increase in citizen participation in the dissemination of information can aid in advancing Caribbean democracies from autocratic systems with power centralized in the hands of a few, to a more open and direct participatory system. Encouraging more citizen participation in the gathering and disseminating of news could also improve one of the fundamental principles of journalism—that of giving voice to the voiceless. Many global media organizations understand the importance of this new dynamic in the flow of information and are embracing and encouraging citizens' participation. Richard Sambrook, director of the news division at the BBC, acknowledged the crucial role of citizen participation during the 2005 London subway bombing when he claimed that "the quantity and quality of the public's contributions moved them beyond novelty, tokenism or the exceptional and raises major implications that we are still working through."[5] Citizen participation also played an important role in the gathering and dissemination of information in the 2013 Boston Marathon attack, and the mass migration of people fleeing war-torn Syria for refuge in Europe in 2015.

In this new environment, Caribbean news organizations should follow the path of their global counterparts and develop partnerships with citizens to cover and present issues and events. These partnerships could be more fruitful and helpful in small societies where resources are limited, especially in rural areas where the use of digital technology is low and the needs of local populations are underserved by traditional media. This revised version of community or public journalism would extend the global journalist-citizen partnership model, not only during times of crisis, but also during regular news cycles. Consequently, rural or underserved areas of society would receive more coverage that specifically addresses their social, economic, and political needs. News organizations would have to develop special initiatives or projects to drive this activity, but such an approach would provide journalism with an opportunity to explore ways it could better serve local and global communities while simultaneously involving the public in the production of news.

Public involvement would result in more citizens producing news without the aid of traditional media, which in turn would change the dynamics of the production and distribution of information. Such a shift could result in a change of news values as citizens determine what information is important to them. This could be good for democracy, as more community issues and concerns would be covered from the audience's perspective. On the negative side, this increase could lead to more misinformation, disinformation, and propaganda. However, these concerns could be addressed through media literacy programs.

Journalism's traditional reliance on advertising for economic stability is no longer viable, but a new economic model has yet to emerge. According to the Pew Center, the best online news sites have limited ability to produce content; their future reportorial capacity will depend on finding a revenue model that could sustain it. The projections for online advertising do not look promising. The 2013 Pew Report indicated old and new media would face the same dilemma—finding a revenue source to sustain their future. The report also predicted more alliances between old and new media and the spread of citizen journalism, but many practitioners, media owners, and citizens are unclear about how these new partnerships would work.

These issues remain undefined; there are no rules for what is acceptable and what is not. However, the new approaches that have emerged in the United States, Europe, and other parts of the world provide lessons for the Caribbean, where the diffusion of technology still lags behind other regions. Caribbean countries should identify global best practices and adapt them to fit the needs of their markets. One of the latest shifts to occur is the collapse of the dichotomy between old and new media, with many industry experts now using the broad term "media" to characterize all mediated communication. The collapse of this false dichotomy is producing renewed optimism for the future.

At the time of this research, the countries of the English-speaking Caribbean were adapting their economic model to stay viable. However, the Gleaner Company was perhaps the most aggressive in its marketing approach. Like the *New York Times*, the *Gleaner* instituted a partial pay wall, limiting unsubscribed readers to fifteen free articles. The Gleaner Company and other news organizations in the Bahamas, Barbados, Belize, Grenada, and Trinidad and Tobago also continue to use a number of strategies that integrate an older advertising model with new marketing strategies to capitalize on the most profitable target audience—the middle class and the diaspora.

The Role of Journalism in Twenty-First-Century Caribbean Societies

Journalism in the twenty-first century should be executed with the values of accuracy, fairness, balance, objectivity, sense-making, independence, providing a public forum, monitoring the powerful, relevance, comprehensiveness, proportionality, and engagement while being loyal to both citizens and the truth. News partnerships with citizens would increase the diversity of opinion in the public sphere. As Kovach and Rosenstiel argue,

> where once the [journalist's] role was simply providing information as a tool of self-governance, it now becomes a role to provide citizens with the tools they need to extract knowledge for themselves from the undifferentiated flood of rumor, propaganda, gossip, fact, assertion, and allegation the communications system now produces. Thus the journalist must not only make sense of the world but also make sense of the flood of information as it is being delivered to citizens.[6]

Both authors believe this new role should be driven by the need for verification, transparency, and accountability. This approach could create a new type of citizen journalist, one who, like the traditional journalist, has a responsibility to uphold the fundamental principles of journalism. Based on the emerging role of citizen journalists, Kovach and Rosenstiel outlined the rights and responsibilities of citizens in an information-driven world.

Although valuable, Kovach and Rosenstiel's thesis refers to the United States, a large country rich in resources. In the small countries of the English-speaking Caribbean, where the dynamics of producing news are different, the journalist's role must also include advocacy and radicalism. While many of the ideals of the profession extolled by American and European scholars are relevant to the standards and values of news, the role of Caribbean journalists must be more dynamic; not only should they embrace and encourage citizen participation, but they should also advocate on behalf of citizens and embrace journalism's ability to affect radical change in these "authoritarian-leaning systems." In a region where internet penetration is still moderate to low and a cultural history of secrecy and silence prevails, journalists should push citizens to become more responsible political participants, nationally, regionally and globally. Journalists will have to become both educators and activists.

Keith Mitchell believes the role of the press is different in smaller states than in larger ones since it plays an important part in regional development. Owen Arthur, former prime minister of Barbados, reaffirmed this role in June 2013 during a public lecture at The Bahamas at 40 Conference. Both Mitchell and Arthur believed regional integration was intrinsically connected to regional development, which they claimed would only become a reality if journalists and media played an active role. Mitchell explained "that the successful attainment of both depends, to a large extent, on how effectively the free press functions."[7]

Mitchell acknowledged the internet and information communication technologies (ICTs) were changing the way media practitioners operated, but he warned that journalists should not let these changes diminish their responsibility with respect to presenting correct and reliable reports and images to the public. Mitchell, like Erica Wells, believed "the plethora of information or, in some cases disinformation, on the internet, and the ease with which anyone can establish a website for whatever purpose, places even greater pressures on the mainstream media houses to ensure accuracy and responsibility in carrying out reporting duties and structuring program memes and special features."[8] In this new environment, he explained, the press must play a strong role in educating and informing people about the information available on the internet.

Ultimately, the goal is to ensure that the new form of citizen journalism leads to the dissemination of good public information that helps create an informed democracy. This goal requires Caribbean journalists to understand their role in democracy and teach it to the citizens with whom they will partner to produce the news of the future. This type of citizen journalism requires an understanding of market-driven demands and the centralized position of governments, the two most powerful forces in these societies. As such, journalists and citizens must understand their responsibilities as participants in a monitorial democracy.

In addition to the changing role of journalism, one of the most daunting challenges in the region is the need for freedom of information laws that work. The history of secret deals, covert decision-making, and hidden records of the public's business hinders the effective practice of journalism in the Caribbean. How can journalists monitor powerful political elites if they cannot gain access to public records? How can they provide citizens with the truth about their government's decision-making if they do not have access to meetings where national affairs are decided? How can they advance democracy if they are sued or threatened for exposing corruption and wrongful behavior?

The hierarchal structures in these countries allow prime ministers or presidents to have so much power. It is therefore a daunting task for journalists to criticize their leaders publicly for their decisions or behavior. Societal structures make it difficult for journalists in the Caribbean to uphold Western ideals of journalism, such as building democracy and being a strong advocate, making sure that information is disseminated accurately and fairly, and ensuring that government and business functions without exploiting the masses. And yet these ideals often elude Caribbean journalists.

Journalism should evolve in the Caribbean so that it becomes a more effective pillar of society. Currently, the profession is subject to too many constraints. This has impelled Harold Hoyte to forecast a pessimistic future for journalism and democracy in the region. "I don't want to sound despairing … [but I fear that] that what we have could get worse, that democracy could be very seriously challenged. That governments resort to strong-arm tactics that people's views are suppressed, that people rebel and that that cycle starts all over again."[9] He advocates for a free, vibrant, and independent media to build a thriving democracy.

Hoyte believes the dreamlike transitions that took place in the region during the independence movements of the 1960s and 1970s provided a false sense of security for Caribbean countries because they did not experience the rampant corruption and greed that assailed many of the countries in Africa and South America, plunging them into years of turmoil and exploitation. He wonders if the region is on the cusp of this type of experience. "Are we opening [the same] opportunities for opportunistic leaders?" he asks.[10] He believes that the only way to abort this path is to train journalists throughout the region so that they are equipped to report on corruption and injustice. To accomplish this goal requires a training model that helps journalists to advance their role in safeguarding democracy. As Byron Buckley explained, "we have a university here, in Jamaica and elsewhere … [but while] they teach the tools of journalism, they do not sensitize journalists enough to their role. So we have people here who have gone through tertiary education but who do not have a refined perspective of our social history, who are unable to tie the freedoms that we want with the rights that the media must have."[11]

Wendall Jones, owner of Jones Communications in the Bahamas, has a similar perspective. "There are people practicing today who do not know their own history, who do not know world history. For example, reporters in my newsroom did not know what the Basilica is or their own type of government. They should know these things but they don't read and they are not interested."[12] Hoyte believes the problem is also systemic, as this phenomenon is not only prevalent among journalists but also among young people in media management who, he claims, understand neither the social history of the media nor its traditional role. Nonetheless, as he points out

> They are running media companies, they are running news departments, they are running advertising departments and they could be running it so badly with these same attitudes because they don't bring that understanding, that grasp of the essentials that make us who we are as a pillar of democracy, they do not have it. … And when I talk to young people out there they're like, What does this have to do with me getting my next story?

> ... Their appreciation of their role is eschewed, completely eschewed. So we have some work to do.¹³

Younger journalists recognize the need for training, but they have a different perspective. For example, Juan McCartney believes the errors or mistakes that young journalists make are not new; he advocates that younger journalists should learn from their older colleagues through mentoring programs. He also believes older journalists could learn from younger ones, many of whom have more experience with new technology. McCartney agrees there is a need for training. "I think we are kind of behind the times as far as what a lot of journalists actually do out there in the wider world, as opposed to what happens in the Bahamas. I think the Caribbean world is about ten years behind as to what happens in the rest of the world so there is a lot of catching up."¹⁴

Veteran radio broadcaster Peter Ames believes competitive media markets challenge the journalist's role. He views Trinidad and Tobago's marketplace as oversaturated, with thirty-seven radio stations, and predicts more acquisitions and mergers. The 2015 merger of the Gleaner Company and RJR in Jamaica has created another media conglomerate. This trend raises more questions about the role and responsibility of media in democracy.

According to Ken Gordon, if this trend continues Caribbean media will come under more pressure as the economic pie is divided and some people are forced out of the media industry altogether. However, he also predicts that global changes will have less economic impact than some predict. "Within the next five to ten years, I don't see too much change. I think the direction has been relatively settled. I do accept there is a threat, but it's potentially there from the internet. How far that will go, we'd have to see. As of now, I would tend to feel that we may well find the cultural wars here may continue."¹⁵ But, he explained, "we may well find that we won't have the same extensive impact on circulation that you've had abroad, but that is in the hands of the gods."¹⁶

Despite global predictions of journalism's demise, journalists, editors, and media owners throughout the Caribbean feel that the profession will continue to exist. But the future of journalism in the Caribbean is far from secure. To change this trajectory, there has to be a shift in how journalism is practiced and how journalists are trained and educated. Colonial ideologies should no longer be used to advance democratic societies that serve the needs of hybrid cultures; rather journalism and communication should be used to fulfill the needs of these hybrid societies. Yet while the influence of American culture is pervasive throughout the region, American models, ideas, or theories of how journalism and communication should function in democratic societies must be adapted to a Caribbean context. These are hybrid societies that need a hybrid model to guide the understanding and practice of journalism. Hopeton Dunn believes hybridization is the way forward in terms of increasing local production at all levels. As he puts it, "while hybridization is not unique to the Caribbean, the Caribbean provides a whole new way of refashioning it to our benefit."[17] It is this refashioning that journalism must do for the benefit of these societies.

Keith Mitchell believes media houses in small island states like those of the Caribbean are often closer to the community than media in developed countries like the United States and the United Kingdom. As a result, Mitchell believes, people in the Caribbean generally feel more connected to their local media than their counterparts in the metropolitan centers of larger countries. "This is evident in the letters to the editors, the response to radio and television talk shows, as well as the instances of people who feel comfortable walking into a local media house with information, a complaint or, in some cases, gossip and slander, and expect this to be published or aired."[18]

For Mitchell, this close relationship should lead to more community journalism, since "there is great scope for the media to take advantage of this sense of closeness that Caribbean people feel towards their local media outlets."[19] Mitchell's perspective aligns with ancient Greek philosophers Plato's, Aristotle's, and eighteenth-century philosopher Rousseau's belief that smaller states have more effective democracies, as citizens know each other and are therefore more likely to support and protect each other. These philosophers believed the governance of small populations is more likely to be effective because policies and programs can be more easily adjusted to work effectively. When applied to the field of journalism and communication, this philosophical perspective is prescient. It also aligns with my previous recommendations for a new type of community journalism, one that not only takes advantage of Mitchell's ideas, but that also uses new technology to develop new perspectives on the role of communication and journalism in the advancement of the region's democracies.

This perspective aligns with the participatory model of communication as advanced by communication and development scholars and practitioners. The participatory paradigm has been promoted by Jan Servaes, Paolo Freire, John Friedmann, Srinivas Melkote, Thomas Jacobson, and Paolo Mefalopulos,[20] as the best model for development since it embraces multiple perspectives and advocates for community involvement in identifying and solving social problems. This model presents Caribbean journalism with an opportunity to embrace a new way to practice journalism in the region and advance professional development and democratic ideals.

Paradigm Shift: Advocates, Radicals, and Citizens

Journalism in the Caribbean must embrace a hybrid model by taking various elements from global practices and melding them with local ones to create a model that helps to refashion these societies. A hybrid model of journalism that is open and flexible, objective and subjective, participatory and cartographic would provide a framework for the further development of the practice and profession. It should include the best elements of the American and British models, as these two systems have had the greatest influence on world systems. The hybrid model, or models, should take account of the cultural context of each country, as these values will play a significant role in future practice.

As Dick Hebdige purports,[21] Caribbean journalism has to "cut 'n' mix"—that is, take the elements of journalism as they are currently practiced, reshape it within a Caribbean milieu, and advocate on behalf of citizens and communities to force social, political, and economic change. As with the musical heritage of soca, calypso, reggae, and junkanoo, journalism in the region must "cut 'n' mix" to find solutions for current realities like crime, corruption, poverty, illiteracy, domestic violence, incest, and rape.

Hybrid Journalism: The Backyard Approach

Hybridity is neither new nor unique to the region; all Caribbean cultures or societies are hybrid. However, the region has emerged with a complex set of worldviews, values, and practices that sustain the ambivalence and contradictions that permeate these societies. The Caribbean is a third space, fashioned out of Old- and New-World ideologies. In such a space, old ideas have been refashioned into cultural artifacts to create an identity called "Caribbean." These artifacts include calypso, soca, reggae, junkanoo, and oral storytelling. Other cultural symbols can be found in food, language, and physicality.

In this fusion of ideas, Caribbean people should use a multiplicity of approaches to solve their problems and pursue opportunities; they should not hold fast to colonial legacies and ideologies that are no longer useful in these societies. Does it really matter if it is British or American spelling or grammar as long as it is correct spelling or grammar? The correct form should be the barometer, not British versus American. That should never have been the battle. Do we dare to accept a paper from a student that mixes British and American grammar or spelling? These cultures have been transformed, but traditional ideas and archaic institutions have them clinging to standards and values that were never fashioned for them in the first place.

Caribbean countries are experiencing a paradigm shift. Globalization is transforming these societies and their cultures. New opportunities and challenges are emerging from new technologies. As these societies shift their focus to the global marketplace, they are creating goods and services for world consumers. Through these transactions, Caribbean ideologies are changing as globalization replaces the dogma of cultural imperialism. These global interactions are creating new hybrid entities that are evolving into something different than their postcolonial identities. Caribbean storytelling, the storytelling of journalism with a purpose, must lead the way, identifying these stories and refashioning new identities that help Caribbean societies to reposition themselves from their ambiguous, invisible space and deconstruct their cultural subordination.

To do this effectively, journalism must create a framework (or frameworks) to guide the profession and practice. If not, these transitions may happen chaotically and the economic windfall brought about by current development in the cultural industries, and from which Caribbean countries hope to benefit, may come at a great cost. In his book *Hybridity: The Cultural Logic of Globalization*,[22] Marwan Kraidy offers a critical, wide-ranging analysis of the extensive reach of hybridity across the globe and explores new concepts such as "critical transculturalism" and its role in the formation of cultural identity. Kraidy examines the intermingling of people and media from different cultures through hybridity. In so doing, he builds an argument for understanding the importance of the dynamics of communication, uneven power relationships, political economy, and cultural hybridity. Kraidy develops the framework of transculturalism to study global cultural mixture; "transculturalism uses hybridity as its core concept and also provides a practical method for examining how media and communication work in international contexts."[23] This is the proposition of this book.

Kraidy acknowledges that hybridity is a risky concept. "It comes without guarantees. Rather than a single idea or unitary concept, hybridity is an association of ideas, concepts, and themes that at once reinforce and contradict each other."[24] Contradictions are a core part of Caribbean identities. Kraidy believes hybridity "challenges fixed categories and the reliance of empirical research on stable classifications."[25] It is for these reasons that journalism in the region cannot strictly follow the normative classifications of American or British journalism. There should be no fixed categories for practicing journalism—only the appropriate categories for current societal needs. Hence, I recommend a hybrid form of journalism that practices and embraces both objective and subjective forms of journalism, utilizes the monitorial, radical, and advocacy roles, and has at its core community journalism.

Journalists in the Caribbean should combine the radical, advocacy, and monitorial roles and advance community journalism by producing coverage that emphasizes localized practices. That is, journalists should produce not a single type of journalism but multiple types: journalism that incorporates the local and the global in new formations of glocalism.

Radical Journalism

Christians et al. contend that "the radical role of media and journalism insists on the absolute equality and freedom of all members of a democratic society in a completely uncompromising way. It ensures that no form of injustice is tolerated. The radical democratic commitment works for the continual elimination of concentrations of social power to enable every person to participate equally in all societal decisions."[26] These ideals are also extolled by philosophers who point to small states' ability to achieve direct democracy. Caribbean journalists would be required to instigate changes such as new voting procedures, constitutional reforms, and changes in the structure of social institutions. This relates to Nicolette Bethel's proposition concerning the need to change government institutions and agencies throughout the region.

The radical role goes beyond the monitorial role, which "takes a given power structure for granted and provides the systematic information needed to make such social configurations work. In other words, maintain the status quo."[27] The radical role, by contrast, "recognizes that power holders impede the flow of information and that it is necessary to change the system of public communication so that less powerful groups can get the information they need."[28] Further, because citizens are now disseminating information via internet and social media, they could assume many of the monitorial duties of journalism, leaving professional journalists to provide depth and understanding through investigation and analysis.

The goal of radical journalism is to undermine and disrupt or dismantle the underlying political-economic power structure in society that reproduces the hegemony that "privileges the interests of a few over those of the majority."[29] This role seems most appropriate for Caribbean societies caught between an authoritarian worldview and global influences. These "authoritarian-leaning" systems, mostly present in government, politics, religion, economics, and culture, leave democracy stranded between the forces of colonial tradition and globalization. There are too many important and significant issues that go unaddressed or unchallenged in these societies. According to the UN, the World Bank, the IMF, and other international organizations, there are too many social crises in these countries that impede the development of human capital, from escalating levels of crime, corruption, incest, rape, sexual and domestic violence, to illiteracy and poverty.

Caribbean journalists have a more urgent responsibility than their Western counterparts, and they should not claim that the radical and advocacy roles go against standards of objectivity and neutrality. The

Caribbean context demands a different approach, one that radically empowers citizens through the practice of alternative forms of journalism. These include: community journalism, community media, alternative media, and citizen journalism, which collectively could be called hybrid journalism, or what I refer to colloquially as "backyard journalism." The backyard is an intimate cultural space in Caribbean communities where cultures blend and innovations emerge through storytelling and play. It is a hybrid space, a third space that has the power to relocate relationships of power.

Caribbean journalists should use this space to empower ordinary people to expose the concentration of power—political, economic, and social—to public opinion, especially undemocratic practices in the region. Yes, this means journalists in the Caribbean will have to persuade and mobilize public opinion to elicit "public action toward the redistribution of power. Such consciousness-raising regarding power structures requires media that are more participatory and dialogical than the conventional media."[30] The backyards of Caribbean communities would become alternative spaces for storytelling with a purpose. In a region with high levels of corruption, backyard journalism could expose not only abuses of power but also the causes and consequences of power's concentration, and help the public to seek avenues of action for its redistribution. It is through backyard journalism that Caribbean societies could close the gap between the privileged and the unprivileged, the rich and the poor. Backyard journalism, a combination of radical, advocacy, and community journalism, moves beyond the paradigm of improving the system; it is revolutionary and requires active participation on the part of journalists and citizens alike.

The digital age could propel backyard journalism to new heights as alternative media organizations and independent citizens make more use of technology to disseminate their ideas and opinions. But there are no standards for citizen journalism; this is especially troubling for a profession founded on the principal of truth-telling. While the world has seen, and will continue to see, technology aid social movements like the Arab Spring, Occupy Wall Street, and various anti-globalization movements, there are some limitations to this type of activity. Mainly, the power to inform mass audiences is limited, so far. However, the potential power of independent voices in the form of weblogs, video blogs, and independent media provides exciting opportunities for the bettering of democracy. From YouTube, Wikipedia, Wikileaks, Khan Academy, and other open-source technologies, to online magazines and blogs, alternative forms of communication are creating a paradigm shift not only in journalism but also in education and literacy, and they are providing new channels for radical thought and action. Journalists in the Caribbean should integrate this digital activity into all forms of journalism but especially radical, advocacy, and community journalism. These three types of journalism should work together to reposition the region away from rigid colonial traditions and overconsumption of American and European ideas and products.

Of course, radical journalism has a lot of critics. Key issues for those who object to the use of the radical role include legitimacy and accountability. Many critics view it as "unsettling and subversive."[31] As Christians et al. note, "radical journalists oppose this description; they consider their approach to be highly legitimate. While there are times when the radical role accepts no accountability to society at large or the state, this only happens when radical journalism is reacting to extreme abuses of power."[32] Christians et al. point out that, "conceptually, the radical role is a reaction to hegemonic power." Indeed, "such radicalism is unthinkable in the absence of the dominant power structures at which it is directed. Therefore, radical actors cannot totally delink themselves from the rest of society; an accountability relationship between the source and the target of radicalism always remains."[33] This type of journalism may be problematic for Caribbean leaders who believe journalists are too judgmental of public figures. But journalists are supposed to judge public officials, as long as it is without malice and in the public interest. Radical journalism is appropriate when it fulfills its obligation to society fairly, accurately, and responsibly.

Elites will challenge this type of journalism. However, journalists can counter with professional organizations and institutions. Further, the radical role will not always be dominant. There will be times when the radical role must give way to the advocacy and community roles.

Advocacy Journalism

Advocacy journalism has a bad rap. Some of its staunchest critics, such as David Lyon and Thomas Hanitzsch,[34] are concerned with its seeming disregard for values like objectivity, neutrality, and detachment. David

Loyn, one of the strongest defenders of objective and impartial journalism, boots advocacy journalism to the domain of public relations.[35] But journalism as practiced in the United States and Europe is not objective or impartial; indeed, all journalism advocates for something in the name of truth. The type of journalism that advocates for change is no different than that which exposes corruption or monitors the powerful, and it too must follow the principles of accurate and impartial news coverage. "Good journalism is responsible journalism."[36] Good reporting that gets rid of or reduces illiteracy, corruption, domestic violence, incest, and disease is responsible journalism. Wilhelm Kempf argues that advocacy journalism should answer the questions "What is the problem?" and "How can it be resolved?"[37] Some time ago, Johan Galtung demanded that journalists become active participants by "playing a part in the complex 'cat's cradle' that makes up a conflict."[38] Kempf writes that peace journalism's (a form of advocacy journalism) role is not to be at the table negotiating, say, a peace treaty, but rather bringing the participants to the table in the first place. Advocacy journalists play an active role in identifying problems and solutions. Thus it should be approached as a two-step process of identification and solution. For identification, there is a need for objective, accurate, balanced, and distanced coverage.[39] The purpose is to make the public aware of the problems and how they impact them individually and collectively. For solution, "advocacy journalism seeks ways to bring all participants of the problems together to actively find ways to solve the problems."[40] Using this approach, advocacy journalism could be balanced, accurate, fair, and independent, "thus avoiding the trap of propaganda and public relations."[41] But to practice this approach effectively, journalists need knowledge, competency, and skills that go beyond traditional journalistic training and enable them to avoid factual inaccuracies.[42]

According to Robert Niles, a former editor of the *Online Journalism Review* (published by the University of Southern California's Annenberg School of Journalism), "when 'objective' journalism decays into a cowardly neutrality between truth and lies, we need advocacy journalism to lift our profession—and the community leaders we cover—back to credibility."[43] Niles thinks too many critics see advocacy as an "antonym for objectivity," when it is not. He explains that "objectivity is the goal of accounting for our own biases when observing external reality so that our report accurately reflects that reality. By reporting objectively, the goal is that you be able to produce an observation that others, observing the same reality, can reproduce."[44]

Niles strongly believes there is nothing about objectivity that prohibits journalists from advocating on behalf of their communities; "in reality, journalists advocate for their stories every day."[45] For Niles, the problem some journalists have with advocacy is not the concept itself, but rather "those who put advocacy ahead of the truth instead of behind it, where it belongs. Objectivity is a means to an end—that end being truthful reporting. And if truthful reporting leads to an obvious conclusion, a reporter and publication cheat their readers if they pull back and don't follow their reporting to that conclusion, and fail to advocate for their community reading it—and acting on it."[46] For Niles, "our disdain for propagandists should not turn us against advocacy, but instead embolden us to be more aggressive advocates for the truth."[47]

Practicing radical and advocacy journalism does not mean journalism falls prey to propaganda, and nor am I proposing that traditional roles and news values be abandoned. What I am recommending for journalists in the Caribbean is a hybrid approach to journalism, one that uses all of the tools to create new ways of doing and being. Radical and advocacy journalism should be practiced with the principles espoused in the previous chapters. However, if journalism is to remain relevant in these small countries, radical and advocacy journalism must move to the forefront of the practice and journalism must embrace the participative communication paradigm, one that involves community journalism.

Community Journalism

Taken literally, community journalism, also known as civic or public journalism, is often defined as journalism about communities, for communities, by communities, whether local, national, global, or digital. The main goals of community journalism are "increased diversity, greater depth and context of news coverage,"[48] and increased understanding of the communities that media serves. Christians et al. believe community is "a very receptive site" for journalism's radical and advocacy roles, as "most radical media are created or supported by a community—geographic or interest-based."[49] Community is also at the heart of the participatory model of communication and development. Media scholars Nico Carpentier, Rico

Lie, and Jan Servaes identify four approaches to community media that provide a framework for understanding how community media should work to advance the interests of community members: "1) media serving community, 2) community media as alternative to mainstream media, 3) community media as part of civil society, and 4) community media as 'rhizome' embedded in flexible social movements."[50]

In the first approach, media is used to serve the community. The relationship between media and community is symmetrical and topics should be chosen by the community to meet their needs and interests. This approach aligns with participatory models of communication and development where two-way communication defines the relationship between media and community through participation of community members in the production and dissemination process. "Members of the community have access to media when they want to for whatever purpose—education, information, or entertainment."[51] In this way community media validates and empowers the community.

The second approach, "community media as alternative to mainstream media, is based on a distinction between mainstream and alternative media. Alternative media are seen as a supplement to mainstream media."[52] Carpentier, Lie, and Servaes caution against interpreting alternative media as being in a negative relationship with mainstream media as, "the contingency of this concept should be emphasized: what is considered 'alternative' at a certain point in time could be defined as mainstream at another point in time."[53] From the community perspective, alternative media could take several forms: "small-scale and oriented towards specific communities (e.g. disadvantaged groups); independent from state and market; horizontally structured, allowing for the facilitation of audience access and participation within the frame of democratization and multiplicity; and carriers of non-dominant (possibly counter-hegemonic) discourses and representations, stressing the importance of self-representation."[54] Consequently, community media as alternative media can show that a third way of media organization is possible.

Carpentier, Lie, and Servaes believe that "by defining community media in this way, it can be considered the "third voice" between state media and private commercial media." This approach underscores the important role civil society plays in the "democratic imagination."[55]

In the fourth approach, community media as rhizome, Carpentier, Lie, and Servaes propose a more radical use for media. By combining Gilles Deleuze and Felix Guattari's theory of the rhizome[56] with the relational approach of community media as alternative media, these scholars see community media as a practice which "ceaselessly establishes connections between semiotic chains, organizations of power and circumstances relative to the arts, sciences and social struggles."[57] Further, "in the case of community media, these connections apply not only to the pivotal role community media (can) play in civil society, but also to the linkages community media (and other civil organizations) can establish with (segments of) the state and the market, without losing their proper identity."[58]

The rhizome approach also emphasizes the importance of civil society. In this sense it contrasts with the third approach in that "the main emphasis for describing the importance of community media is not their role as part of the public sphere but the catalyzing role they can play by functioning as the crossroads where people from different types of movements and struggles meet and collaborate."[59] As a result, "community media not only functions as an instrument that gives voice to a group of people for a specific issue; it is also a catalyzator."[60] Community media, therefore, can function as the core of the backyard paradigm as it integrates communication and culture for storytelling with a purpose.

Using these four approaches, community media can accommodate radical, advocacy, and other types of journalism. The main goals of this blended approach are greater civic participation, wider access, and more media diversity. When these goals are accomplished, community journalism fulfills its radical and advocacy role and moves us closer to the ideals of the democratic process.

Keith Mitchell's idea of community journalism also aligns with Carpentier, Lie, and Servaes's concept of community media. Mitchell believes community journalism provides an opportunity for Caribbean media to participate in the improvement of society by forcing communities or citizens to be active participants in solving their own problems. For, as Mitchell explains, community journalism "provides an opportunity for social workers, teachers, police officers, parents, politicians and others in the community to express their views and make suggestions as to how the problem can be overcome."[61] The shift to community journalism, says Mitchell, "challenges the traditional role of the media as impartial observer.

... By investigating and reporting on an issue such as truancy, the media is actually facilitating the search for a solution. In other words ... you, as members of the media, become participants in the improvement of the education system."[62] He believes "such coverage provides the balance that the public needs on an important and very real issue in their lives, and one that has enormous impact on societal development as a whole."[63]

Community journalism should be placed at the core of the backyard paradigm, as it would complement the close relationship that already exists between citizens and the media and assist Caribbean societies in transforming themselves into independent democratic states.

The Future

This final chapter attempts to advance theories of hybridity. Melding radical journalism, advocacy journalism, and community journalism under the umbrella of glocal journalism provides a local perspective for global practices. The proposal for a hybrid practice of journalism, one that places community journalism, radical journalism, and advocacy journalism at the core of the practice allows for the continued practice of monitorial or watchdog journalism.

There are many structural constraints that shape and limit the work of journalists throughout the region (and the world): "pressure of deadlines, a chronic lack of space, limited budgets, censorship and disinformation, editorial expectations, the needs of the public, the laws of the market, and cultural expectations."[64] These constraints play a significant role in the practice and profession and can only be reduced through the collective will of media owners, media practitioners, and citizens.

The lack of professionalization in Caribbean journalism is still prevalent despite the fact that there are more journalists with degrees working both independently and as part of established media institutions. This remains one of the biggest challenges in the region.

While the lack of professionalization, especially in small states, is nothing new, Caribbean journalists will have to become more professional if they want to see journalism play a more meaningful role in their societies. Journalists throughout the region will have to police themselves in order to raise the standards of the practice. This must become a priority as global advances and new technology encroach on issues of sovereignty and the proper dissemination of good public information. Criticism from both the public and political elites, could be diminished through media literacy campaigns designed to educate the public and politicians on media's role in democratic societies. Journalism and media institutes should create and advance these programs and partner with various stakeholders to implement them.

Caribbean journalists have an opportunity to create a more sustainable form of journalism for the twenty-first century, one that meets the evolving needs of their societies. It is my hope that they will follow-through on these recommended actions. But beyond the limitations outlined in this book, journalists in the Caribbean also have an opportunity to rethink how journalism is practiced. Journalism in the region has to explore and advance new ways of producing content and distributing it. Journalists should take advantage of the region's love of oral storytelling and its close relationship with media houses to create new styles of storytelling. Websites could be used more engagingly to include video stories from the community, thereby creating new forums for oral storytelling and advancing the story function of news. This approach will require journalists to create new, innovative work cultures. They could work in conjunction with history departments and historical societies to preserve many of the region's stories and drive more engagement with the audience. This approach would also provide an opportunity for journalism to be more relevant to the communities it serves, providing more comprehensive and proportional coverage of local issues.

Educational programs and institutes should play a pivotal role in this process. Journalism educators will have to rethink how they teach their craft. They will have to equip students, journalists, and citizens with the right skills and mindsets for the evolving media landscape. We are in the midst of a renaissance in information production and distribution, and the next ten years will bring more changes than any of us could anticipate. These changes will happen more quickly. They will bring more disruptions and we must be prepared to respond to them. The need for credible journalistic knowledge and wisdom is greater than ever, but we must keep in mind that with great opportunity comes great responsibility. As exciting as the future seems for innovative storytelling, journalists must rebuild society's trust in their profession and restore rational thinking at a time when information flows twenty-four-seven—from public and private organizations, to governments and individuals.

Having more opinions and ideas in the public forum does not necessarily mean a better democracy. Better democracy comes about through active involvement and engagement of all citizens in the pursuit of liberty, equality, justice, and truth. Everyone must understand the need to adhere to the principles of truth telling, fact checking, and using credible sources. Democracy requires all citizens to be responsible, accountable, and transparent when introducing information into the public sphere. The future of journalism in the region and the world could be better than the past, but everyone must ensure that journalism continues to play a significant role in the democratic project.

Notes

PREFACE

1. Howard Tumber and Barbie Zelizer, "Editorial: Special 10th Anniversary Issue—The Future of Journalism," *Journalism* 10, no. 3 (2009): 277–279.
2. Ibid.
3. The Caribbean has a rich intellectual tradition bookmarked by the works of Diana Lebacs, Frank Martinus Arion, Albert Helman, Boeli van Leeuwen, Cynthia McLeod (Dutch); C. L. R. James, Wilson Harris, Jan Carew, Joan Armatrading, Lloyd Best, V. S. Naipaul, Derek Walcott, Kamau Brathwaite, Edward Brathwaite, Eric Williams, George Lamming, Stuart Hall, Franklin W. Knight, Arthur Lewis, Walter Rodney, Samuel Selvon, Clive Thomas (English); René Depestre, Anténor Firmin, Edouard Glissant, Jacques Stefan Alexis, Leon Damas, Frantz Fanon, Gisèle Pineau, Aimé Césaire, Félix Morisseau-Leroy (French); and Alejo Carpentier, Juan Bosch, Roberto Fernández Retamar, Nicolás Guillén, Pedro Mir, Manuel Moreno Fraginals, Frank Moya Pons (Spanish).
4. http://mona.uwi.carimac.com/about-us (accessed 25 June 2013).
5. Ibid.
6. Hopeton Dunn, interview by author, 6 June 2015.
7. Mikhail Bakhtin, *The Dialogical Imagination: Four Essays* (Austin: University of Texas Press, 1981), xix–xx.
8. Ibid.
9. Homi Bhabha, *The Location of Culture* (London: Routledge, 1994).
10. John Hutnyk, "Hybridity," *Ethnic and Racial Studies* 28, no. 1 (2005): 80.
11. Jamaica Kincaid, *A Small Place* (New York: Farrar, Straus and Giroux, 1988).
12. Dick Hebdige, *Cut 'N' Mix: Culture, Identity and Caribbean Music* (London: Methuen, 1987).
13. Paul Gilroy, *The Black Atlantic: Modernity and Double Consciousness* (Cambridge, MA: Harvard University Press, 1993), xi.
14. Ibid., ix.
15. Rosario Ferré, *Maldito Amor* (New York: Vintage Español, 1998) and Rosario Ferré, ed., *Sobre el Amor y la Política. El Coloquio de las Perras* (Rio Piedras: Editorial Cultural, 1990); Maryse Condé, "Chercher nos vérités" in *Penser la créolité*, Maryse Condé

and Madeleine Cottenet-Hage, eds., (Paris: Karthala, 1995), 305–310; Maryse Condé, *I, Tituba, Black Witch of Salem* (New York: Ballantine Books, 1994); Maryse Condé, "Order, Disorder, Freedom, and the West Indian Writer," *Yale French Studies* 83, no. 2 (1993): 121–135; Toni Morrison, *The Bluest Eye* (New York: Plume, 1994); Toni Morrison, "Memory, Creation, and Writing," *Thought* 59, no. 235 (1984): 385–390; Toni Morrison, "*The Site of Memory*," in *Inventing the Truth: The Art and Craft of Memoir*, William Zinsser, ed. (Boston: Houghton Mifflin, 1995), 103–124.

16 Rex Nettleford, *Caribbean Cultural Identity: The Case of Jamaica* (Los Angeles: Center for Afro-American Studies and UCLA Latin American Center Publications, 1979).

17 Josef Raab and Martin Butler, "Introduction: Cultural Hybridity in the Americas," in *Hybrid Americas: Contacts, Contrasts, and Confluences in New World Literatures and Cultures*, Josef Raab and Martin Butler, eds. (Tempe: Bilingual Press, 2008), 2–3.

18 Ibid.

19 Marwan Kraidy, *Hybridity: the Cultural Logic of Globalization* (Philadelphia: Temple University, 2005), vi.

20 Ibid.

21 Stuart Hall, "Cultural Identity and Diaspora," in *Colonial Discourse & Postcolonial Theory: A Reader*, Patrick Williams and Laura Chirsman, eds. (New York: Columbia University Press, 1994); Stuart Hall, "Identity: Community, Culture, Difference," in *Identity: Community, Culture, Difference*, Jonathan Rutherford, ed. (London: Lawrence & Wishart, 1990); Derek Walcott, "The Caribbean: Culture or Mimicry?" *Journal of Interamerican Studies and World Affairs* 16, no. 1 (1974); Derek Walcott, *What the Twilight Says: An Overture* (New York: Farrar, Straus and Giroux, 1998); Paul Gilroy, *The Black Atlantic: Modernity and Double Consciousness* (Cambridge, MA: Harvard University Press, 1993).

22 Tumber and Zelizer, "The Future of Journalism," 277.

23 Bonnie Brennen, "The Future of Journalism," *Journalism* 10, no. 3 (2009): 301.

24 Juliette Storr, "The disintegration of the state model in the English speaking Caribbean: Restructuring and redefining public service broadcasting," *International Communication Gazette* 73, no. 7 (2011): 555.

25 Hilary Beckles, *Britain's Black Debt: Reparations for Caribbean Slavery and Native Genocide* (Kingston, Jamaica: University of the West Indies Press, 2013).

26 Eric Williams, *Capitalism and Slavery* (Raleigh: University of North Carolina Press, 1944).

27 Hilary Beckles, *Britain's Black Debt: Reparations for Caribbean Slavery and Native Genocide*, 15.

28 Manuel Puppis, "Media Regulations in Small States," *International Communication Gazette*, 71 (2009): 7–17; Manuel Puppis, Leen d'Haenens, Thomas Steinmaurer, and Matthias Künzler, "The European and Global Dimension: Taking Small Media Systems Research to the Next Level," *International Communication Gazette*, 71 (2009): 105–112

29 Örnebring and Lauk, "Does Size Matter?" "Journalistic Values and Working Conditions in Small Countries," (paper presented at ECREA conference, Hamburg, Germany, 12–15 October 2010).

1 | JOURNALISM AND MEDIA IN THE CARIBBEAN

1. See Clifford Christians et al., *Normative Theories of the Media: Journalism in Democratic Societies* (Chicago: University of Illinois Press, 2009).
2. See Marc Raboy, "Public Service Broadcasting in the Context of Globalization," in *Public Service Broadcasting: The Challenge of the Twenty-First Century*, Dave Atkinson and Marc Raboy, eds. (Paris: UNESCO Publishing, 1997), 77–90; Marc Raboy, "The World Summit on the Information Society and its Legacy for Global Governance," *International Communication Gazette* 66 (2004): 225–232; Robert McChesney, *Rich Media, Poor Democracy: Communication Politics in Dubious Times* (New York: New Press, 1999); Robert McChesney and Jon Nichols, *The Death and Life of American Journalism: The Media Revolution that Will Begin the World Again* (Philadelphia: Nation Books, 2010).
3. Ian Bremmer, *The End of the Free Market: Who Wins the War Between States and Corporations?* (New York: Portfolio/Penguin, 2010); and Daron Acemoglu and James Robinson, "Is State Capitalism Winning?" at http://www.project-syndicate.org/commentary/why-china-s-growth-model-will-fail-by-daron-acemoglu-and-james-a--robinson (accessed 2 September 2012).
4. Acemoglu and Robinson, "Is State Capitalism Winning?"
5. Ibid.
6. James Fallows, *Looking at the Sun: The Rise of the New East Asian Economic and Political System* (New York: Pantheon Books, 1994); Alice Amsden, *The Rise of The Rest: The Challenges to the West from Late-Industrializing Economies* (Oxford: Oxford University Press, 2001); and Aldo Musacchio, and Sergio Lazzarini, "Leviathan in Business: Varieties of State Capitalism and Their Implications for Economic Performance," http://www.hbs.edu/faculty/Publication%20Files/12-108.pdf (accessed 3 November 2012).
7. Most of the English-speaking countries of the Caribbean became independent states in the 1960s and 1970s, with Jamaica and Trinidad and Tobago becoming the first independent states in 1962.
8. Fragano Ledgister, "Democracy the Caribbean: Post-Colonial Experience," http://www.academia.edu/428522/Democracy_in_the_Caribbean_Post-Colonial_Experience (accessed 14 September 2013).
9. Ibid., 5.
10. Ibid.,16.
11. "Final Report on the 2013 IPI Advocacy Mission to the Caribbean: Focus on Criminal Defamation, International Press Institute," http://ipi.freemedia.at/fileadmin/resources/application/Caribbean_Mission_Report_2013.pdf, 26 (accessed 12 March 2014).
12. Mitchell Stephens, *A History of News* (Oxford: Oxford University Press, 2007). By the seventeenth century, printed weeklies appeared throughout most European countries.
13. Howard Pactor, *Colonial British Caribbean Newspapers: A Bibliography and Directory* (New York: Greenwood Press, 1990).
14. John Lent, *Third World Mass Media and their Search for Modernity* (Lewisburg: Bucknell University Press, 1977) and *Mass Communications in the Caribbean* (Iowa City: Iowa State University Press, 1990).

15 Stuart Surlin and Walter Soderlund, eds., *Mass Media in the Caribbean* (New York: Gordon and Breach, 1990).
16 See Pactor, *Colonial British Caribbean Newspapers*, x–xiii, for a description of these colonies once they lost their economic value (through the decline and eventual extinction of the cotton industry and the decline of the sugar industry).
17 Hopeton Dunn, "The Politics of the Media in the English-Speaking Caribbean," in *Who Owns the Media? Global Trends and Local Resistance*, Pradip Thomas and Zaharom Nain, eds. (London: Zed Books, 2004), 75.
18 Mark Alleyne, "Mass Media in Barbados," in *Mass Media in the Caribbean*, Stuart Surlin and Walter Soderlund, eds. (New York: Gordon and Breach, 1990), 58.
19 Ewart Skinner, "Mass Media in Trinidad and Tobago," in *Mass Media in the Caribbean*, Stuart Surlin and Walter Soderlund, eds. (New York: Gordon and Breach, 1990), 41.
20 "Ideas and Opinions," http://amandala.com.bz/news/ideas-opinions-2/ (accessed 11 October 2012).
21 Anne Sutherland, *The Making of Belize: Globalization in the Margins* (Westport, CT: Bergin & Garvey, 1998), 178.
22 Yvette Stuart, "The Two Bahamian Dailies: A Study of International News Flow," *International Communication Bulletin*, 36 (2001): 3–4.
23 Pactor, *Colonial British Caribbean Newspapers*, x.
24 Ibid.
25 BNA CO 9647/1: "Superintendent Salter's Memorandum to Colonial Secretary Jarrett, October 27, 1936."
26 Juliette Storr, "Changes and Challenges: A History of the Development of Broadcasting in The Commonwealth of The Bahamas, 1930–1980" (PhD diss., University of Ohio, 2000), 324.
27 Harold Lasswell, "The Structure and Function of Communication in Modern Society," in *The Communication of Ideas*, L. Byron, ed. (New York: Harper & Row, 1948).
28 Charles Wright, *Mass Communication: A Sociological Perspective* (New York: Random House, 1959).
29 Storr, "Changes and Challenges," 324.
30 Ibid.
31 Christians et al., *Normative Theories of the Media*, 31.
32 Michael Schudson, "News and Democratic Society: Past, Present and Future," *Hedgehog Review* (2009): 17–18, http://www.iasc-culture.org/eNews/2009_10/Schudson_LO.pdf (accessed 1 August 2012); Silvio Waisbord, "Democracy, Journalism, and Latin America Populism," *Journalism* 14 (2013): 501–521.
33 Christians et al., *Normative Theories of the Media*, 31.
34 Ibid., 127.
35 Ibid., 31.
36 Ibid., 127.
37 Schudson, "News and Democratic Society," 17–18.
38 Ibid.
39 Christians et al., *Normative Theories of the Media*, 127.
40 Ibid.
41 Storr, "Changes and Challenges," 324–325. Television broadcasting began in the 1960s, with Jamaica beginning the first television service in 1962.

42 Ibid., 324–325.
43 Ibid., 325.
44 Ibid.
45 Two dominant media systems emerged in the world—the British and the American. Almost all others evolved from these two models. The British evolved with a public service ethos as the core of it system until the 1970s; the American evolved with commercialism at its core and added a public service element in the 1960s. The BBC came into existence by Royal Charter in 1927. According to Charles Curran, the charter provided "genuine freedom for the BBC—particularly for its governors, who could do what they thought was in the best interest of broadcasting and the nation." John Reith, the first Director General of the BBC, also contributed to the development of the public service ethos. The BBC developed the social responsibility theory of media and continued to view the medium as a valuable public service even after it included commercialism. The 1947 US Hutchins Commission on the freedom of the press recommended five requirements for a free and responsible press: The media should provide a truthful, comprehensive and intelligent account of the day's events in a context, which gives them meaning; the media should serve as a forum for the exchange of comment and criticism; the media should project a representative picture of the constituent groups in the society; the media should present and clarify the goals and values of the society; the media should provide full access to the intelligence of the day. See Charles Curran, *A Seamless Robe* (London: Collins, 1979), 37.
46 Fred Siebert, Theodore Peterson, and Wilbur Schramm, *Four Theories of the Press* (Illinois: University of Illinois Press, 1956). In this work Siebert, Peterson, and Schramm devised four major theories to explain the function of the world's media: the authoritarian theory describes all forms of communications under the control of the governing elite or authorities or influential bureaucrats; the libertarian theory arose from the works of Milton, Locke, Mill, and Jefferson, who advocate freedom from authority, control, or censorship. It also supports the ideas of individualism, natural rights, and a free marketplace of ideas, which helps discover the truth; the social responsibility theory advocates free press and no censorship but acknowledges media has obligations to the public and professional responsibilities; and the Soviet communist theory, an expanded version of the old authoritarian theory, where government has total control of the media for the benefit of the people.
47 See John Merrill and Ralph Lowenstein, *Media, Messages and Men: New Perspectives in Communication* (New York: Longman, 1979), and Jennifer Ostini and Anthony Fung, "Beyond the four theories of the press: A new model of national media systems," *Mass Communication & Society* 5, no. 1 (2002): 41–56.
48 Ostini and Fung, "Beyond the four theories of the press," 41.
49 Surlin and Soderlund, *Mass Media in the Caribbean*, 3.
50 Ibid., 5.
51 Ibid.
52 Ibid.
53 Humphrey Regis, ed., *Culture and Mass Communication in the Caribbean* (Gainesville: University Press of Florida, 2001), 3–13. Regis believes both frameworks of cultural domination, importation/exportation and reexportation, are complementary rather

than oppositional. "The importation/exportation framework is for studying (mass communication and) the domination that involves those aspects of culture that are developed in one society, are exported to another, and then engender change in the latter. But the reexportation framework is for studying (mass communication and) aspects of culture developed in one society and changed by another with the change adopted by the originator." (12–13).

54. Bill Kovach and Tom Rosenstiel, *The Elements of Journalism: What Newspeople Should Know and the Public Should Expect* (New York: Crown Publishers, 2007), 189.
55. George Kennedy and Daryl Moen, *What is Good Journalism? How Reporters and Editors Are Saving America's Way of Life* (Columbia: University of Missouri Press, 2007), 1.
56. Kennedy and Moen, *What is Good Journalism?*, 1.
57. Pew Research Center's Project for Excellence in Journalism, http://www.journalism.org/resources/principles/, 1/ (accessed 14 August 2012).
58. Ibid.
59. Ibid.
60. Ibid.
61. Tosheena Robinson Blair, interview by author, 27 June 2008.
62. Nicki Kelly, interview by author, 26 June 2008.
63. Karen Herig, interview by author, 30 June 2008.
64. Press Association of Jamaica, http://pressassociationjamaica.org/code-of-practice-revised/ (accessed 10 June 2012).
65. Eric Smith, interview by author, 25 May 2010.
66. David Ellis, interview by author, 27 May 2010.
67. Harold Hoyte, interview by author, 25 May 2010.
68. Omatie Lyder, interview by author, 13 March 2009.
69. Peter Christopher, interview by author, 12 March 2009.
70. Ibid.
71. Holly Edgell, http://hollyedgell.wordpress.com/2012/05/09/journalism-in-belize-its-time-to-temper-guts-and-gore-with-balance-and-context/ (accessed 1 November 2012).
72. Ibid.
73. Ibid.
74. See Christians et al., *Normative Theories of the Media*, for a discussion of the role of contemporary journalists in democratic societies.
75. Kovach and Rosenstiel, *The Elements of Journalism*, 208.
76. Ibid., 209.
77. Ibid., 187.
78. Ibid., 188.
79. Ibid., 189.
80. Ibid.
81. Ibid.
82. Ibid.
83. Ibid., 118.
84. Ibid., 116.
85. Ibid., 140.
86. Ibid.

2 | PRACTICING JOURNALISM IN SMALL PLACES

1. See Alberto Alesina and Enrico Spolaore, *The Size of Nations* (Cambridge, MA: MIT Press 2003) and Alberto Alesina, Enrico Spolaore, and Romain Wacziarg, "Trade, Growth and the Size of Countries," in *Handbook of Economic Growth*, Philippe Aghion and Steven Durlauf, eds. (Amsterdam: North Holland, 2004).
2. See Alesina and Spolaore, *The Size of Nations*, 3–4.
3. See Aristotle's *Politics*, trans. Benjamin Jowett (London: Forgotten Books, 2012) and Jean Jacques Rousseau's *The Government of Poland,* trans. Willmoore Kendall (Indianapolis: Hackett Publishing, 1985).
4. Portions of this section were first published as "The disintegration of the state model in the English speaking Caribbean: Restructuring and redefining public service broadcasting," *International Communication Gazette* 73, no. 7 (2011): 553–572.
5. Jamaica Kincaid, *A Small Place*.
6. In the essay "The Dialogical Imagination," Mikhail Bahktin describes the discourse of a novel as the construction of a diversity of styles and voices into a structured artistic text. Heteroglossia is the term used by Bahktin to describe discourse, "a multi-perspective assemblage of speech, words, and expressions that come from a variety of voices, styles and references."
7. Kincaid, *A Small Place*, 56.
8. "A Small Place: Important Quotations." www.sparknotes.com/lit/smallplace/quotes.html
9. Lino Briguglio, "Small Island States and Their Economic Vulnerabilities," *World Development* 23 (1995): 1615–1632.
10. Lino Briguglio and Eliawony Kisanga, eds., *Vulnerability and Resilience of Small States* (Msida: Commonwealth Secretariat and Islands and Small States Institute of the University of Malta, 2004).
11. Manuel Puppis, "Media Regulations in Small States," *International Communication Gazette* 71, no. 1–2 (2009): 7–17.
12. Ibid., 8.
13. UNDP Report 2004, "Supporting Public Service Broadcasting, Learning from Bosnia and Herzegovina's Experience," http://www.undp.org/content/dam/aplaws/publication/en/publications/democratic-governance/oslo-governance-center/ogc-fellowship-papers/supporting-public-service-broadcasting-learning-from-bosnia-and-herzegovinas-experience/PublicServiceBroadcasting.pdf, 15–19.
14. Benjamin Page, *Who Deliberates? Mass Media in Modern Democracy* (Chicago: University of Chicago Press, 1996); Robert Dahl, *On Democracy* (Cambridge, MA: Harvard University Press, 2000); Jürgen Habermas, *The Theory of Communicative Action* (Boston: Beacon Press, 1984); Jürgen Habermas, *The Structural Transformation of the Public Sphere* (Cambridge, MA: MIT Press, 1989).
15. See analyses of power in society by Karl Marx, *Collected Works* (New York and London: International Publishers, 1975); Louis Althusser, "Sur la Dialectique Matérialiste (De l'inégalité des origines)," *La Pensée* 110 (1963): 5–46; Stuart Hall, *Policing the Crisis: Mugging, the State, and Law and Order* (London: MacMillan, 1978); Antonio Gramsci, *Selections from the Prison Notebook*, trans. and ed. Quintin Hoare and Goffrey Nowell

Smith (London: Lawrence and Wishart, 1971); and Michel Foucault, *The Order of Things*, trans. Alan Sheridan (New York: Vintage, 1966).

16   See Benjamin Barber, Friedrich Hayek, and Joseph Schumpeter's work in *Theories of Democracy: A Reader*, Ronald Terchek and Thomas Conte, eds. (Lanham: Rowan and Littlefield, 2001).

17   Robert Dahl, *On Democracy*; Jürgen Habermas, *The Structural Transformation of the Public Sphere*; John Keane, *The Life and Death of Democracy* (New York: Simon & Schuster, 2009); and Benjamin Barber, *Strong Democracy: Participatory Politics for a New Age* (Berkeley: University of California Press, 2003).

18   Aukse Balčytienė and Halliki Harro-Loit, "How to Preserve Journalism?" (Paper presented at "Comparing Media Systems: West Meets East," Wroclaw, 23–25 April 2007); Ben Bagdikian, *The New Media Monopoly* (Boston: Beacon Press, 2004); James Carey, "Where Journalism Education Went Wrong," http://www.mtsu.edu/~masscomm/seig96/carey/carey.htm (accessed 30 October 2011); McChesney and Nichols, *The Death and Life of American Journalism*; Herbert Schiller, *Communication and Cultural Domination* (New York: M.E. Sharpe, 1976) and *Culture, Inc.: The Corporate Takeover of Public Expression* (Oxford: Oxford University Press, 1991), and Michael Schudson, *Why Democracies Need an Unlovable Press* (Cambridge: Polity Press, 2008).

19   John Keane, "Journalism and Democracy Across Borders," in *The Press, The Institutions of American Democracy*, Geneva Overholser and Kathleen Hall Jamieson, eds. (Oxford: Oxford University Press, 2005), 92–114.

20   Ibid., 93.

21   Alleyne, "Mass Media in Barbados."

22   Norman Girvan, "Societies at Risk? The Caribbean and Global Change," http://www.unesco.org/most/girvan.htm (accessed 12 August 2015).

23   Keith Nurse, "The Creative Sector in CARICOM: Economic and Trade Policy Dimensions," https://www.monroecollege.edu/uploadedFiles/_Site_Assets/PDF/concept_paper_creative_sector.pdf (accessed 12 August 2015).

24   Portions of this section were first published as "The disintegration of the state model in the English speaking Caribbean: Restructuring and redefining public service broadcasting," *International Communication Gazette* 73, no. 7 (2011): 553–572.

25   Örnebring and Lauk, "Does Size Matter."

26   Ibid.

27   Puppis, "Media Regulations in Small States," 7–17; Puppis et al., 105–112.

28   Werner Meier and Josef Trappel, "Small States in the Shadow of Giants," *Dynamics of Media Politics: Broadcast and Electronic Media in Western Europe*, Karen Siune and Wolfgang Truetzschler, eds. (London: Sage, 1992): 129–142.

29   Peter Humphreys, *Mass Media and Media Policy in Western Europe* (Manchester: Manchester University Press, 1996).

30   Gabriele Siegert, "The Role of Small Countries in Media Competition in Europe," in *Media Economics in Europe*, Jürgen Heinrich and Gerd Kopper, eds. (Berlin: Vistas, 2006), 191–210.

31   Puppis, "Media Regulations in Small States," 7–17.

32   Örnebring and Lauk, "Does Size Matter?" 3.

33 Norman Girvan, "Notes for a Retrospective on the Theory of Plantation Economy of Lloyd Best and Kari Polanyi Levitt," in *Caribbean Economies and Global Restructuring*, Marie Derne and Keith Nurse, eds. (Kingston, Jamaica: Ian Randle Publishers, 2002), 17–24.
34 Puppis, "Media Regulations in Small States," 10.
35 Ibid.
36 Ibid.
37 Ibid.
38 Jean-Claude Burgelman and Caroline Pauwels, "Audiovisual Policy and Cultural Identity in Small European States: The Challenge of a Unified Market," *Media, Culture and Society* 14 (1992): 169–83.
39 See Aggrey Brown, "Caribbean Cultures and Mass Communication Technology: Reexamining the Cultural Dependency Thesis," in *Globalization, Communications, and Caribbean Identity*, Hopeton Dunn, ed. (Kingston, Jamaica: Ian Randle Publishers, 1995), 40–54; Lynette Lashley, "Television and the Americanization of the Trinbagonian Youth," in *Globalization, Communications, and Caribbean Identity*, Hopeton Dunn, ed., 83–97; and Juliette Storr, "Cultural Proximity, Asymmetrical Interdependence and a New NWICO: A Case Study of Bahamian Television 1977–1997," *International Communication Bulletin*, 43 (2008): 11–24.
40 Portions of this section were first published as "The disintegration of the state model in the English speaking Caribbean: Restructuring and redefining public service broadcasting," *International Communication Gazette* 73, no. 7 (2011): 553–572.
41 See Girvan, "Notes for a Retrospective," 17–18.
42 See Sandra Ball-Rokeach and Melvin DeFleur, "A Dependency Model or Mass Media Effects," *Communication Research* 3 (1976): 3–21. Like uses and gratification theory, media dependency theory predicts our dependence on media to meet our needs and wants though, according to Ball-Rokeach and DeFleur, dependence is not always equally distributed among the various types of media. The more dependent we are on media to fulfil this role, the more important media becomes to us. Media dependency theory shares a relationship with agenda setting theory; when media becomes the most important source of information, it sets the agenda.
43 See MacBride's report "Many Voices One World: Towards a New More Just and More Efficient Information and Communication Order," http://unesdoc.unesco.org/images/0004/000400/040066eb.pdf, (accessed 8 July 2013) and Ulla Carlsson's report "The Rise and Fall of NWICO—and Then? From a Vision of International Regulation to a Reality of Multilevel Governance," http://www.nordicom.gu.se/sites/default/files/kapitel-pdf/32_031-068.pdf (accessed 8 July 2013).
44 See Joseph Straubhaar, "Beyond Media Imperialism: Asymmetrical Interdependence and Cultural Proximity," *Critical Studies in Mass Communication* 8 (1991): 39–59; Antoni Pastina and Joseph Straubhaar, "Multiple Proximities Between Television Genres and Audiences," *International Communication Gazette* 67 (2005): 271–288.
45 Puppis, "Media Regulations in Small States."
46 Thomas Steinmaurer, "Diversity Through Delay? The Austrian Case," *International Communication Gazette* 71 (2009): 77–87.
47 Puppis, "Media Regulations in Small States," 11.

48   Ibid.
49   Meier and Trappel, "Small States in the Shadow of Giants," 129–142.
50   Puppis, "Media Regulations in Small States," 7–17.
51   Dunn, "The Politics of the Media," 69–95.
52   Stuart, "The Two Bahamian Dailies," 1–16.
53   Skinner, "Mass Media in Trinidad and Tobago," 44.
54   Puppis, "Media Regulations in Small States," 7–17.
55   Siegert, "The Role of Small Countries"; Josef Trappel, "Born Losers or Flexible Adjustment? The Media Policy Dilemma of Small States," *European Journal of Communication* 6 (1991): 355–371.
56   Dunn, "The Politics of the Media," 69–95.
57   Robert Martin, "Broadcasting and the Struggle of Cultural Autonomy in Canada," in *Globalization, Communications, and Caribbean Identity*, Hopeton Dunn, ed. (Kingston, Jamaica: Ian Randle Publishers, 1995), 135–162.
58   Brown, "Caribbean Cultures and Mass Communication Technology," 40–54.
59   Keith Nurse, "The Creative Sector in CARICOM," https://www.monroecollege.edu/uploadedFiles/_Site_Assets/PDF/concept_paper_creative_sector.pdf (accessed 12 August 2015).
60   Burgelman and Pauwels, "Audiovisual Policy and Cultural Identity," 169–183.
61   Paul Ashley, "New Media, Journalism and Democracy in the Caribbean Symposium, (Kingston, Jamaica, 18–19 July 2011)," http://www.youtube.com/watch?v=wkz4_JRur6I (accessed 3 January 2014).
62   Mark Beckford, "New Media, Journalism and Democracy in the Caribbean Symposium (Kingston, Jamaica, 18–19 July 2011)," http://www.youtube.com/watch?v=wkz4_JRur6I (accessed 3 January 2014).
63   "The Caribbean Free Trade Association," http://www.caricom.org/jsp/community/carifta.jsp?menu=community (accessed 17 October 2015). According to CARICOM, Antigua and Barbuda, Barbados, Guyana, and Trinidad and Tobago founded CARIFTA (the Caribbean Free Trade Association) on 15 December 1965 with the signing of the Dickerson Bay Agreement. Dominica, Grenada, St. Kitts-Nevis-Anguilla, St. Lucia, St. Vincent and the Grenadines, Montserrat and Jamaica joined in 1968, and Belize in 1971. "These countries had recently become independent and CARIFTA was formed to unite their economies and give them more presence internationally. CARIFTA became CARICOM in 1973."
64   Other organizations that helped the development of Caribbean media systems included the Canadian Broadcasting Corporation and the Commonwealth Broadcasting Association. The idea for the Commonwealth Broadcasting Association evolved from a conference of public service broadcasters in London in 1945. In 1974 the CBA was formally ratified and brought together former and current territories of the British government that had national public service broadcasting to assist each other through training and shared resources. Membership was extended to commercial broadcasters in 1995. The name was changed in the 2000s to the Public Media Alliance to accommodate changing media environments. The Alliance provides "knowledge exchange, advocacy, research, training and support for content development for public media worldwide." See http://publicmediaalliance.org (accessed 11March 2016).

65 Aggrey Brown, "The Caribbean—A Chance for Community Media to Develop," http://www.waccglobal.org/en/19981-communication-issues-in-the-caribbean/896-__The-Caribbean---a-chance-for-community-media-to-develop-.html (accessed 2 June 2012).
66 Aggrey Brown, "Towards Regionalization of New Communication Services in the CARICOM: A Technological Free-for-all," *Canadian Journal of Communication* 20 (1995): 3.
67 Ibid.
68 Patrick Prendergast, interview by author, 2 June 2009.
69 Ibid.
70 Hopeton Dunn, interview by author, 6 June 5, 2015.
71 Patrick Prendergast, interview by author, 2 June 2009.
72 Ibid.
73 Former general manager of CANA, interview by author, 26 May 2010. (The subject requested anonymity.)
74 Marlene Cuthbert, "The Caribbean News Agency: Third World Model," *Journalism Monographs*, 71 (1981): 1.
75 Former general manager of CANA, interview by author, 26 May 2010.
76 Ibid.
77 Norman Girvan, "Is ALBA a New Model of Integration? Reflections on the CARICOM Experience," http://www.normangirvan.info/wp-content/uploads/2011/09/girvan-alba-and-caricom-lmet-revised2.pdf (accessed 17 March 2012).
78 Norman Girvan, "ALBA, PETROCARIBE and CARICOM: Issues in a New Dynamic," in *CARICOM: Policy Options for International Engagement*, Kenneth Hall and Myrtle Chuck-A-Sang, eds. (Kingston, Jamaica: Ian Randle Publishers, 2010), 218–234.
79 Norman Girvan, "Is ALBA a New Model of Integration?" 3.
80 Ibid., 3.
81 Havelock Brewster and Clive Thomas, *The Dynamics of West Indian Economic Integration* (Mona: Institute of Social and Economic Research, 1967).
82 Mesquita Moreira, Mauricio Mendoza, and Eduardo Mendoza, "Regional Integration: What Is in It for CARICOM?" *Economia* (2007): 97–142.
83 Girvan, "Is ALBA a New Model of Integration?" 3.
84 Ibid.
85 Reciprocal trade and investment liberalization is applied to partners of highly unequal size and levels of development.
86 Wendall Jones, interview by author, 11 June 2008.
87 Nicki Kelly, interview by author, 26 June 2008.
88 Beate Josephi, "Journalism in the Global Age," *International Communication Gazette* 67 (2005): 575–590.
89 Daniel Hallin and Paolo Mancini, *Comparing Media Systems* (Cambridge: Cambridge University Press, 2004).
90 Ibid., 277.
91 Ibid., 295.
92 Ibid.
93 Habermas, *The Structural Transformation of the Public Sphere*; Benedict Anderson, *Imagined Communities: Reflections on the Origin and Spread of Nationalism* (New York: Verso Books, 1983).

94 Stig Hjavard, "News Media and the Globalisation of the Public Sphere," in *News in a Globalized Society*, Stig Hjavard, ed. (Gothenburg: Nordicom, 2001).
95 Peter Dahlgren, "The Public Sphere and the Net: Structure, Space, and Communication," in *Mediated Politics: Communication in the Future of Democracy*, W. Lance Bennett and Robert M. Entman, eds. (Cambridge: Cambridge University Press, 2001), 35–55; Ari Heinonen, "Reconsidering 'Journalism' for Journalism Research," (paper presented at "Journalism Research in an Era of Globalization," Erfurt, 3–4 July 2004); Klaus Bruhn Jensen, "Why Virtuality Can Be Good for Democracy," in *News in a Globalized Society*, Stig Hjavard, ed. (Gothenburg: Nordicom, 2001), 93–112.
96 Heinonen, "Reconsidering 'Journalism.'"
97 Dane Claussen, "If Even Journalism Professors Don't Know What Journalism Is, Then All Really Is Lost," *Journalism & Mass Communication Educator*, 67 (2012): 329–330.
98 Denis Weaver, "U.S. Journalism in the 21st Century—What Future?" *Journalism* 10 (2009): 396–397.
99 World Press Freedom Index, "Biggest Rises and Falls in the 2014 World Press Freedom Index," https://rsf.org/index2014/en-index2014.php (accessed 14 March 2014).
100 "United States press freedom ranking drops sharply, report says," http://www.foxnews.com/politics/2014/02/18/united-states-press-freedom-ranking-drops-sharply-report-says/.

3 | CARIBBEAN JOURNALISM'S MEDIA ECONOMY

1 "Caribbean journalism's media economy: Advancing democracy and the common good?" *International Communication Gazette* 76, no. 2 (2014): 177–196.
2 Immanuel Wallerstein, *The Modern World System: Capitalist Agriculture and the Origins of the European World Economy in the Sixteenth Century* (New York: Academic Press, 1974).
3 Aukse Balčytienė, *Mass Media and Journalism in Lithuania: Changes, Development and Journalism Culture* (Berlin: Vistas, 2006).
4 Rick Edmonds, "The State of the News Media 2009: An Annual Report on American Journalism," Pew Project for Excellence in Journalism, http://www.stateofthenewsmedia.org/2009/narrative_newspapers_intro.php?media=4 (accessed 19 July 2010).
5 See McChesney and Nichols, *The Death and Life of American Journalism*, Raboy, "Public Service Broadcasting," 77–90, and Marc Raboy, "Dreaming in Technicolor: the Future of PSB in a World Beyond Broadcasting," *Convergence*, 14 (2008): 361–365.
6 See John Pavlik, "A Sea-change in Journalism: Convergence, Journalists, Their Audiences and Sources," *Convergence* 10, no.3 (2004): 21–29; Chris Atton, "Why Alternative Journalism Matters," *Journalism* 10, no. 3 (2009): 283–285; Jan Servaes, "We Are All Journalists Now!" *Journalism* 10, no. 3 (2009): 371–374; Brian McNair, "Journalism in the 21st Century—Evolution, Not Extinction," *Journalism* 10, no. 3 (2009): 347–349; Vincent Mosco, "The Future of Journalism," *Journalism* 10, no. 3 (2009): 350–352; Bonnie Brennen, "The Future of Journalism," *Journalism* 10, no. 3 (2009): 300–302; and Tumber and Zelizer, "The Future of Journalism," *Journalism* 10, no. 3 (2009): 277–279.

7   "State of the News Media 2010," Pew Research Center's Project for Excellence in Journalism, http://stateofthemedia.org/files/2011/05/2010_execsummary.pdf (accessed 17 February 2011).
8   Ibid. "The Pew Research Center is an American non-profit think tank that prides itself on providing nonpartisan information that informs the public about issues, attitudes and trends shaping the United States and the world. The Center conducts public opinion polls, demographic research, media content analysis, and other empirical social science research. It is a subsidiary of the Pew Charitable Trusts."
9   Ibid.
10 Ibid.
11 "The State of the News media 2012," Pew Research Center's Project for Excellence in Journalism, http://www.pewresearch.org/2012/03/19/state-of-the-news-media-2012/ (accessed 10 April 2013).
12 Ibid.
13 Ibid.
14 Ibid.
15 Ibid.
16 "Facebook's Worldwide Ad Revenues Will Pass $5 Billion This Year," http://www.emarketer.com/Article/Facebooks-Worldwide-Ad-Revenues-Will-Pass-5-Billion-This-Year/1008858 (accessed 15 November 2013).
17 European Publishers Council, *Global Media Trends Book 2012–2013*, http://epceurope.eu/wp-content/uploads/2012/09/EPC_ExecSum_press.pdf (accessed 14 March 2014).
18 Ibid., 3.
19 Ibid.
20 Ibid., 5.
21 Ibid. MAGNA GLOBAL is the strategic global media unit of IPG Media Brands, who are associated with giant media brands through the MAGNA Consortium, such as A&E Networks, AOL, Cablevision, Clear Channel Media and Entertainment, ESPN, and Tribune.
22 Bob Franklin, "The Future of Newspapers: A Comparative Assessment," http://orca.cf.ac.uk/18315/1/bsc_3_-03-09_-_paper_2a_-_prof_bob_franklin_-_cardiff_university.pdf (accessed 14 August 2011).
23 Ibid.
24 Ibid.
25 Ibid.
26 Juliette Storr, "The Disintegration of the State Model in the English-Speaking Caribbean: Restructuring and Redefining Public Service Broadcasting," *International Communication Gazette*, 73 (2011): 553–572.
27 Bob Franklin, "The Future of Newspapers."
28 Omatie Lyder, interview by author, 13 March 2009.
29 "Jamaica Gleaner, Caribbean's Oldest Newspaper Profits Plummets," http://www.siliconcaribe.com/2009/06/15/jamaica-gleanercaribbean's-oldest-newspaper-profits-plummets-vows-to-focus-on-increased-market-share-online/ (accessed 18 February 2011).
30 Ibid.

31   Jamaica's news industries have also been affected by the country's long-term economic struggles, which date to the 1980s and the decline in the bauxite industry.
32   Hopeton Dunn, interview by author, 8 June 2009.
33   Jamaica signed a four-year agreement with the IMF to reduce its debt-to-GDP ratio and obtain IMF support. Multilateral loans were cut off in 2012 following the breakdown of Jamaica's previous IMF agreement. Jamaica's history of debt continues to hinder its economic growth.
34   John Busterna and Robert Picard, *Joint Operating Agreements: The Newspaper Preservation Act and its Application* (New York: Ablex Publishing, 1993).
35   Robert Picard, "Natural Death, Euthanasia, and Suicide: The Demise of Joint Operating Agreements," *Journal of Media Business Studies*, 4 (2007): 41–64.
36   As quoted in Lisa Benjamin and Catherine LeGrand, "Sound and Fury: Newspaper Coverage of the Marital Rape Debate in New Providence," *The International Journal of Bahamian Studies* 18 (2012): 16–35.
37   *One Caribbean Media 2012 Annual Report*, http://www.onecaribbeanmedia.net (accessed 15 July 2013).
38   *One Caribbean Media 2013 Annual Report*, http://www.onecaribbeanmedia.net (accessed 18 March 2014). The Pew Research Center media formula was applied to indicate the growth in newspaper revenues.
39   http://www.barbadosadvocate.com (accessed 17 June 2012).
40   http://www.onecaribbeanmedia.net/wp-content/uploads/2013/09/OCM-Annual-Report-2014-FULL-PDF.pdf (accessed 10 August 2014). Barbados's economic crisis is highlighted in this report.
41   Ibid.
42   http://www.onecaribbeanmedia.net (accessed 3 May 2013).
43   Ibid.
44   The Gleaner Company's 2008–2013 annual reports are available at http://old.jamaica-gleaner.com/gleaner/about/.
45   RJR's 2011 annual report is available at http://rjrgroup.com/sites/default/files/documents/Radio%20Jamaica%20Ltd%20Annual%20Report%202011.pdf.
46   See http://jamaica-gleaner.com/rjrgleanermerger.
47   Ibid.
48   Omar Oliveira, "Mass Media in Belize", in *Mass Media in the Caribbean*, Stuart Sarlin and Walter Soderlund, eds. (New York: Gordon and Breach, 1990) 115–128.
49   "Most Widely Read Newspaper," http://www.belgrafix.com/gtoday/2007news/Jan/Jan13/Most-widely-read-newspaper.htm (accessed 21 July 2012).
50   Laurie Lambert, "The Revolution and its Discontents: Grenadian Newspapers and Attempts to Shape Public Opinion during Political Transition," *The Round Table: The Commonwealth Journal of International Affairs* 102 (2013): 143–153.
51   Ibid.
52   Ibid.
53   Hopeton Dunn, interview by author, 8 June 2009.
54   See Herbert Schiller, *Mass Communication and American Empire* (New York: Westview Press, 1992); Bagdikian, *The New Media Monopoly*; and Robert McChesney, *Rich Media, Poor Democracy*.

55 Norman Solomon, "Coverage of Media Mergers: Does it Provide a Window into the Future of Journalism?" http://www.nieman.harvard.edu/reports/article/101938/Coverage-of-Media-Mergers.aspx (accessed 23 September 2013).
56 Ibid.
57 Ibid.
58 Hopeton Dunn, interview by author, 8 June 2009.
59 Charles Carter, interview by author, 13 June 2008.
60 Ibid.
61 Paul Gillin, "Surprise! Researchers See Industry Growth," http://newspaperdeathwatch.com/surprise-researchers-see-industry-growth/ (accessed 24 January 2014).
62 "World Press Trends: Increasing Audience Engagement is Future for News Media," http://www.wan-ifra.org/press-releases/2013/06/02/world-press-trends-increasing-audience-engagement-is-future-for-news-media (accessed 15 February 2014).
63 Ibid.
64 See summary of "World Press Trends Report 2014," http://www.wan-ifra.org/reports/2014/10/07/world-press-trends-report-2014 (accessed 25 August 2015).
65 Paco Nunez, interview by author, 25 February 2013.
66 See Edward Brathwaite, "African Presence in Caribbean Literature," *Daedalus*, 103 (1974): 73–109, and Orlando Patterson, "Rethinking Black History," *Harvard Educational Review*, 41 (1971): 297–315.
67 Paolo Guenzi and Ottavia Pelloni, "The Impact of Interpersonal Relationships on Customer Satisfaction and Loyalty to the Service Provider," *International Journal of Service Industry Management*, 15 (2004): 365–384.
68 The author conducted a survey of the media in the Bahamas in 2013. She interviewed eight editors, publishers, and media owners on four of the major islands of the Bahamas in February and March 2013.
69 Lime is a colloquial expression in Trinidad and Tobago which refers to the way people gather to hang out and talk about events and other things.
70 Omatie Lyder, interview by author, 13 March 2009.
71 Ken Gordon, interview by author, 14 March 2009.
72 Economic Commission for Latin America and the Caribbean, "Population Ageing in the Caribbean: An Inventory of Policies, Programmes and Future Challenges," http://www.cepal.org/celade/noticias/paginas/8/14928/lccarg772.pdf (accessed 17 May 2012).
73 Ibid., 4.
74 Roxanne Gibbs, interview by author, 26 May 2010.
75 "Internet World Statistics," http://www.internetworldstats.com/carib.htm (accessed 25 August 2014).
76 Ibid.
77 Andrea Polanco, journalist at GBTV News 5, Belize, "New Media, Journalism and Democracy," Jamaica 18–19 2011, https://www.youtube.com/watch?v=wkz4_JRur6I (accessed 3 August 2013).
78 Gunn Enli, "Redefining Public Service Broadcasting Multi-platform Participation," *Convergence*, 14 (2008): 105–120.
79 Erica Wells, interview by author, 2 July 2008.
80 Juan McCartney, interview by author, 2 July 2013.

81 Karyl Walker, online news content editor at the *Jamaica Observer*, panelist at the "New Media, Journalism, and Democracy" symposium held in Jamaica, 18–19 July 2011.
82 See Jay Rosen, "The People Formerly Known as the Audience," http://archive.pressthink.org/2006/06/27/ppl_frmr.html (accessed 15 October 2015), and Mark Deuze, "The People Formerly Known as the Employers," *Journalism* 10, no.3 (2009): 315–318.
83 Ibid.
84 David Ellis and Reudon Eversley, interview by author, 26 and 27 May 2010.
85 Ken Gordon, interview by author, 14 March 2009.
86 Peter Christopher, interview by author, 12 March 2009.
87 Roxanne Gibbs, interview by author, 26 May 2010.
88 Brent Dean, interviewed by author, 27 June 2008.
89 Ibid.
90 Paul Ashley, political commentator and lawyer, panelist at the "New Media, Journalism and Democracy" symposium held in Jamaica, 18–19 July 2011.
91 Mark Beckford, online editor the *Jamaica Gleaner*, panelist at the "New Media, Journalism and Democracy" symposium held in Jamaica, 18–19 July 2011.
92 Karen Madden James, Caribbean journalist, member of the audience at the "New Media, Journalism and Democracy" symposium held in Jamaica, 18–19 July 2011.
93 Manuel Velasquez et al., "The Common Good," *Issues in Ethics* 5, no. 1 (1992).
94 See Christians et al., *Normative Theories of the Media*.
95 Ibid., 67.
96 Ibid., 68.
97 Ibid.
98 Ibid., 68–69.

Table 1 Source Information
http://amandala.com.bz/news/
http://www.barbadosadvocate.com
http://www.barbadostoday.bb
http://belizenews.com
http://www.belizetimes.bz
http://www.broadcastingcommission.org
http://www.caribbean-radio.com
http://www.caribbeannewsnow.com/grenada.php
http://www.caribbeannews.com/radio.html
"Country Report on the State of the Media in Saint Lucia for the period 2012 to 2014," http://www.masl.lc/content/country-report-state-media-saint-lucia-period-2012-2014
https://freedomhouse.org/reports
http://www.freemedia.at
http://firstmonday.org/htbin/cgiwrap/bin/ojs/index.php/fm/rt/printerFriendly/1369/1288
https://gerardbest.wordpress.com/2013/08/23/an-overview-of-the-trinidad-and-tobago-media-landscape/
http://www.grenadaadvocate.com

http://www.thegrenadainformer.com
http://www.guardian.co.tt
"Internet World Statistics," http://www.internetworldstats.com/carib.htm
http://jamaica-gleaner.com
http://www.jamaicaobserver.com
Lambert, Laurie. "The Revolution and its Discontents: Grenadian Newspapers and Attempts to Shape Public Opinion during Political Transition," *The Round Table: The Commonwealth Journal of International Affairs* 102 (2013): 143–153
"Most Widely Read Newspaper," http://www.belgrafix.com/gtoday/2007news/Jan/Jan13/Most-widely-read-newspaper.htm
http://www.thenassauguardian.com
http://www.nationnews.com
http://www.newsday.co.tt
http://thenewtoday.gd/category/local-news/#gsc.tab=0
http://www.ntrc.gd
http://www.onlinenewspapers.com/belize.htm
http://www.onlinenewspapers.com/grenada.htm
Personal interviews.
http://www.puc.bz
https://tatt.org.tt
http://www.telecoms.gov.bb/website/
http://www.tribune242.com
http://www.trinidadexpress.com
http://www.urcabahamas.bs
http://wesleygibbings.blogspot.com

Table 2 Source Information
http://amandala.com.bz/news/
http://www.barbadosadvocate.com
http://www.barbadostoday.bb
http://belizenews.com
http://www.belizetimes.bz
Benjamin, Lisa and Catherine LeGrand, "Sound and Fury: Newspaper Coverage of the Marital Rape Debate in New Providence," *The International Journal of Bahamian Studies* 18 (2012): 16–35.
http://www.caribbeannewsnow.com/grenada.php
https://gerardbest.wordpress.com/2013/08/23/an-overview-of-the-trinidad-and-tobago-media-landscape/
The Gleaner Company's 2008–2013 annual reports are available at http://old.jamaica-gleaner.com/gleaner/about/.
http://www.grenadaadvocate.com
http://www.thegrenadainformer.com
http://www.guardian.co.tt
http://jamaica-gleaner.com
http://jamaica-gleaner.com/rjrgleanermerger

http://www.jamaicaobserver.com
http://www.thenassauguardian.com
http://www.nationnews.com
http://www.newsday.co.tt
http://thenewtoday.gd/category/local-news/#gsc.tab=0
http://www.onecaribbeanmedia.net
One Caribbean Media 2012 Annual Report, http://www.onecaribbeanmedia.net (accessed 15 July 2013).
One Caribbean Media 2013 Annual Report, http://www.onecaribbeanmedia.net (accessed 18 March 2014). The Pew Research Center media formula was applied to indicate the growth in newspaper revenues.
http://www.onecaribbeanmedia.net/wp-content/uploads/2013/09/OCM-Annual-Report-2014-FULL-PDF.pdf
http://www.onlinenewspapers.com/belize.htm
http://www.onlinenewspapers.com/grenada.htm
Riley, Ingrid. "Jamaica Gleaner, Caribbean's Oldest Newspaper Profits Plummets," http://www.siliconcaribe.com/2009/06/15/jamaica-gleanercaribbean's-oldest-newspaper-profits-plummets-vows-to-focus-on-increased-market-share-online/ (accessed 18 February 2011).
RJR's 2011 annual report http://rjrgroup.com/sites/default/files/documents/Radio%20Jamaica%20Ltd%20Annual%20Report%202011.pdf
http://www.tribune242.com
http://www.trinidadexpress.com

4 | CARIBBEAN JOURNALISM: COMPREHENSIVE AND PROPORTIONATE

1 "A Small Place: Important quotations."
2 Perhaps one of the best expressions of this mode of storytelling, of weaving the significant into the everyday, is exemplified by Caribbean calypso music. Calypso began in Trinidad and Tobago as a form of protest against British rule. It has since spread throughout the region and has become a popular genre that utilizes a variety of styles to deliver potent messages—double entendre, puns, satire, wit, humor, blatant lyrics, and caustic language. Some scholars have argued (Hinds, 2010; Lashley, 2001; Regis, 1998) that calypso is a more potent vehicle for social and political commentary than other channels of communication. In the region, calypsonians are highly respected and regarded as agents of change. According to David Hinds, the calypsonian plays the role of a messenger who "simultaneously teaches, defines, affirms, reports, interprets, attacks, scolds, and condemns." (See citation below.) The calypsonian as storyteller and agent of change is part of the oral tradition of the region. Calypsonians as change agents provide a contradictory narrative to Kincaid's argument of making the small things big and the big things small. Calypso music and Caribbean people contest the everyday, the "small things," and the significant. Hinds identifies the calypsonian as a potent messenger who ridicules and criticizes the power structures of society, especially the political. See David Hinds, "A Mailman to make Government Understand: The Calypsonian (Chalkdust) as Political Opposition in the Caribbean," http://www.

music.ucsb.edu/projects/musicandpolitics/archive/2010-2/hinds.pdf. See also Lynette Lashley, "The Calypso as 'Political Football' in Trinidad and Tobago: The Status of Contemporary Political Commentary" (paper presented at 26th annual Caribbean Studies Association conference, St. Maarten, Netherlands Antilles), and Louis Regis, *The Political Calypso: True Opposition in Trinidad and Tobago* (Gainesville: University Press of Florida, 1998). Finally, see Gordon Rohlehr, *Calypso and Society in Pre-Independence Trinidad* (Port of Spain: G Rohlehr, 1990) and "The Calypsonian as Artist: Freedom and Responsibility," *Small Axe Number 9* 5, no. 1 (2001): 1–26. Rohlehr describes political calypso as a "popular newspaper" with the calypsonian playing the role of editor and reporter. He believes the calypsonian personifies the voice of the man in the street as he "narrates through song the highs and lows of lived reality." But he also believes the calypso, political commentary or otherwise, is the "ambivalence of hero-worship," as politicians and economic elites share personal bonds with many calypsonians in these small societies that results in continual reverence. (David Hinds, "A Mailman to make Government understand.") This ambivalence sometimes undermines the power of the calypsonian.

3   See Geert Hofstede, *Culture's Consequences: International Differences in Work-related Values* (Beverly Hills: Sage, 1980), and Edward Hall, *The Silent Language* (New York: Fawcett Publication, 1959).
4   See Edward Hall, *The Silent Language*. New York: Fawcett, 1959.
5   Kincaid, *A Small Place*, 53.
6   Ibid.
7   Kovach and Rosenstiel, *Elements of Journalism*, 208.
8   Nicolette Bethel, interview by author, 25 June 2008.
9   Ibid.
10 Ibid.
11 Juan McCartney, interview by author, 24 June 2008.
12 "Nottages Should Sue the Guardian & Tribune for Libel," http://www.bahamaspress.com/2008/04/12/the-nottages-should-sue-the-guardian-tribue-and-punch-for-libel/ (accessed 17 August 2013).
13 Juan McCartney, interview by author, 24 June 2008.
14 See the UNICEF reports, "Child Sexual Abuse in the Eastern Caribbean" (2008); "Violence Against Children in the Caribbean Region Regional Assessment" (2006); "Breaking the Silence: A Multi-sectoral Approach to Preventing and Addressing Child Sexual Abuse in Trinidad and Tobago" (2012); *The World Bank Study on Caribbean Youth Development, Issues and Policy Directions* (Washington, DC: The World Bank, 2003); and the *World Report on Violence and Health* (Geneva: WHO, 2002).
15 See Michael Schudson, "What Public Journalism Knows About Journalism but Does Not Know About the Public," in *The Idea of Public Journalism*, Theodore L. Glasser, ed. (New York: Guilford, 1999), 118–135.
16 Christians et al., *Normative Theories of the Media*, 30.
17 www.Dictionary.com
18 Ibid., 31.
19 Kovach and Rosenstiel, *Elements of Journalism*.
20 Quincy Parker, interview by author, 11 June 2008.

21 Steve McKinney, interview by author, 11 June 2008.
22 David Ellis, interview by author, 27 May 2010.
23 Steve McKinney, interview by author, 11 June 2008.
24 Krissy Love, interviewed by author, 12 June 2008.
25 Ibid.
26 Freedom House, "Freedom of the Press 2013—Belize," http://www.refworld.org/docid/51e7d0c28.html (accessed 17 July 2013).
27 Freedom House, "Freedom of the Press 2013—Guyana," http://www.refworld.org/docid/5229988514.html (accessed 5 September 2013).
28 "Country Report on the State of the Media in Saint Lucia for the period 2012 to 2014," http://www.masl.lc/content/country-report-state-media-saint-lucia-period-2012-2014 (accessed 6 September 2014).
29 Ibid.
30 Graeme Turner, "Politics, radio and journalism in Australia: The influence of 'talkback,'" *Journalism* 10, no. 4 (2009): 411.
31 Graeme Turner, *Ordinary People and the Media: The Demotic Turn* (London: Sage, 2010). Turner describes the demotic voice as a discourse of the people that differs from populism in that it does not necessarily involve an explicit political or social agenda and will have more than one voice. "The demotic is unruly, contingent and potentially cacophonous" (117). He defines the "demotic turn" as an increase in the visibility of ordinary people through media content and thus increasing their "celebrity" status. Turner believes this is producing new ways of constructing identity in the digital storytelling movement.
32 Richard Hoggart, *The Uses of Literacy* (Harmondsworth: Penguin, 1958).
33 Graeme Turner, "Politics, radio and journalism in Australia: The influence of 'talkback,'" 420.
34 Graeme Turner, *Ordinary People and the Media: The Demotic Turn*, 119.
35 Ibid.
36 Eddie Carter, interview by author, 10 June 2008.
37 Peter Christopher, interview by author, 12 March 2009.
38 Ibid.
39 Nicolette Bethel, interview by author, 25 June 2008.
40 Ibid.
41 Christians et al., *Normative Theories of the Media*, 179.
42 Ibid.
43 Ibid.
44 Ibid.
45 Ibid., 116.
46 Ibid.
47 Quincy Parker, interview by author, 11 June 2008.
48 Ibid.
49 Eddie Carter interview, 10 June 2008.
50 Ibid.
51 Ibid.

52 Holly Edgell, "Journalism in Belize: It's Time to Temper Guts and Gore with Balance and Context," http://hollyedgell.wordpress.com/2012/05/09/journalism-in-belize-its-time-to-temper-guts-and-gore-with-balance-and-context/ (accessed 12 March 2013).
53 Ibid.
54 Ibid.
55 Ibid.
56 Ibid.
57 Ibid.
58 Ibid.
59 Ibid.
60 Ibid.
61 Ken Gordon, interview by author, 14 March 2009.
62 Roxanne Gibbs, interview by author, 26 May 2010.
63 David Krajicek, *Scooped! Media Miss Real Story on Crime While Chasing Sex, Sleaze, and Celebrities* (New York: Columbia University Press 1998).
64 George Gerbner, Lawrence Gross, and others, created the cultivation hypothesis to explain how people's perceptions of reality are influenced by exposure to television. "The cultivation theory states that the more television people watch, the more likely they are to hold a view of reality that is closer to television's depiction of reality." As quoted in Thimios Zaharopoulos, *Traditional Family Relationships and Television Viewing* (Athens: TBS Archives, 2001), 6.
65 Holly Edgell, "Journalism in Belize."
66 Peter Christopher, interview by author, 12 March 2009.
67 Ken Auletta, "Citizens Jain: Why India's newspaper industry is thriving,' accessed November 14," *The New Yorker*, 8 October 2012.
68 Robert McChesney and Ben Scott, eds., *Our Unfree Press: 100 Years of Radical Media Criticism* (New York: New Press, 2004).
69 Erica Wells, interview by author, 2 July 2008.
70 Ewart Skinner, "Mass Media in Trinidad and Tobago," 33.
71 Ibid.
72 Kovach and Rosenstiel, *Elements of Journalism*, 209.
73 See literature on cultural domination, cultural imperialism, media imperialism, and electronic colonialism.
74 Rupert Missick, interview by author, 24 June 2008.
75 Hopeton Dunn, "Facing the Digital Millennium: A Comparative Analysis of Communication, Culture and Globalisation in South Africa and the Anglophone Caribbean," in *Media, Democracy and Renewal in South Africa*, Keyan Tomaselli and Hopeton Dunn, eds. (Colorado Springs: International Academic Publishers, 2002), 56–78.
76 Tia Rutherford, interview by author, 27 June 2008.
77 Jessica Robertson, interview by Quincy Parker on the "Quality of Journalism in the Bahamas," *Issues of the Day*, Love FM 97, Nassau, Bahamas 12 June 2008.
78 Nicki Kelly, interview by author, 26 June 2008.
79 Ibid.
80 Steve McKinney, interview by author, 11 June 2008.
81 Kovach and Rosenstiel, *Elements of Journalism*, 212.

5 | CARIBBEAN JOURNALISM: RELEVANT AND ENGAGING

1. This saying is a beginning and ending formulae common in Caribbean folktale storytelling, and can be traced to African storytelling. It captivates and engages the audience immediately.
2. Kovach and Rosenstiel, *Elements of Journalism*, 189.
3. Ibid., 2.
4. Ibid.
5. The *Anancy/Anansi* stories are believed to have originated in West Africa, specifically among the Ashanti people of Ghana. The tales traveled to the Caribbean via the slave trade. *Anancy/Anansi* is a cunning trickster with god-like knowledge who often takes the form of a spider with a human head. Anancy the spider is an important character in West African and Caribbean folklore.
6. Kovach and Rosenstiel, *Elements of Journalism*, 189.
7. Robert Picard "Natural Death, Euthanasia, and Suicide," 41–64; Tumber and Zelizer, "The Future of Journalism," 277–279; Örnebring and Lauk, "Does Size Matter?"
8. Gary Spaulding, "6-Y-O Dies, Sisters Injured After Freak Accident at Beach," http://jamaica-gleaner.com/gleaner/20130821/lead/lead2.html#disqus_thread (accessed 23 September 2013).
9. Ibid.
10. Annie Paul, "Demonic Jet Ski Kills 6-Year Old Girl in Jamaica August 21, 2013," http://anniepaul.net/2013/08/21/demonic-jetski-kills-6-year-old-girl-in-jamaica/ (accessed 23 September 2013).
11. Ibid.
12. Former general manager of Caribbean News Agency (CANA), interview by author, 25 May 25 2010.
13. Harold Hoyte, interview by author, 25 May 2010.
14. Ibid.
15. Ibid.
16. Ibid.
17. Ibid.
18. Ibid.
19. Reudon Eversley, interview by author, 26 May 2010.
20. Ibid.
21. Ibid.
22. Ibid.
23. Byron Buckley, interview by author, 8 June 2009.
24. Ibid.
25. Peter Ames, interview by author, 14 March 2009.
26. Rupert Missick, interview by author, 24 June 2008.
27. Ibid.
28. Byron Buckley, interview by author, 8 June 2009.
29. Oliver Boyd-Barrett, "Contra the Journalism of Complicity," *Journalism* 10, no. 3 (2009): 296–299.
30. Ibid., 297.

31 "21st-Century Censorship," http://www.cjr.org/cover_story/21st_century_censorship.php (accessed 2 August 2015).
32 "Caribbean Overview: Media Struggles with Defamation Laws, Economic Challenges," http://www.freemedia.at/home/singleview/article/caribbean-overview.html (accessed 7 May 2012).
33 "Final Report on the IPI Advocacy Mission to End Criminal Defamation in Barbados," http://www.freemedia.at/fileadmin/media/Documents/IPI_mission_reports/Barbados_Mission_Report.pdf (accessed 5 June 2013).
34 "Final Report on the 2013 IPI Advocacy Mission to the Caribbean: Focus on Criminal Defamation," http://ipi.freemedia.at/fileadmin/resources/application/Caribbean_Mission_Report_2013.pdf, 26 (accessed 3 February 2014).
35 Ibid.
36 See Hilary Beckles, *Britain's Black Debt*.
37 Byron Buckley, interview by author, 8 June 2009.
38 Ibid.
39 David Ellis, interview by author, 27 May 2010.
40 Reudon Eversley, interview by author, 26 May 2010.
41 Harold Hoyte, interview by author, 25 May 2010.
42 Ibid.
43 Reudon Eversley, interview by author, 26 May 2010.
44 Rupert Missick, interview by author, 24 June 24, 2008.
45 Harold Hoyte, interview by author, 25 May 2010.
46 David Ellis, interview by author, 27 May 2010.
47 Reudon Eversley, interview by author, 26 May 2010.
48 Karen Herig, interview by author, 30 June 2008.
49 Harold Hoyte interview by author, 25 May 2010.
50 See Herbet Gans, *Democracy and the News* (New York: Oxford University Press, 2003) and "News and the news media in the Digital Age; Implications for democracy," *Daedalus* (Spring 2010): 8–17.
51 David Ellis, interview by author, 27 May 2010.
52 Juan McCartney, interview by author, 24 June 2008.
53 Eddie Carter, interview by author, 10 June 2008.
54 "Final Report on the 2013 IPI Advocacy Mission to the Caribbean: Focus on Criminal Defamation," http://ipi.freemedia.at/fileadmin/resources/application/Caribbean_Mission_Report_2013.pdf (accessed 3 February 2014).
55 See Schiller, *Mass Communication and American Empire*; Bagdikian, *The New Media Monopoly*; and McChesney, *Rich Media, Poor Democracy*.
56 For a discussion of the impact of sensationalism, immediacy and homogenization on news content, see Edward Herman and Noam Chomsky, *Manufacturing Consent: The Political Economy of Mass Media* (New York: Pantheon Books, 1988); John McManus, "A Market-Based Model of News Production," *Communication Theory* 5 (1995): 301–338; and Ben Bagdikian, *The New Media Monopoly* (Boston: Beacon Press, 2004).
57 Charles Carter, interview by author, 13 June 2008.
58 Hopeton Dunn, interview by author, 8 June 2009.
59 Ibid.

60   Rupert Missick, interview by author, 24 June 2008.
61   Ibid.
62   John Pavlik, "The Impact of Technology on Journalism," *Journalism Studies* 1, no. 2 (2000): 229.
63   David Ellis, interview by author, 24 June 2008.
64   P. Anthony White, interview by author, 13 August 2008.
65   Nicki Kelly, interview by author, 26 June 2008.
66   Thea Rutherford, interview by author, 27 June 2008.
67   Kovach and Rosenstiel, *Elements of Journalism*, 204.
68   http://www.tribune242.com/news/2013/apr/05/rodney-moncur-charged-in-court-over-facebook/ (accessed 14 October 2013).
69   The managing editor of the *Nassau Guardian* experienced a personal attack on her character in 2015. See http://www.tribune242.com/news/2015/oct/22/defending-candia-dames/.
70   Peter Ames, interview by author, 14 March 2009.

6 | CARIBBEAN JOURNALISM: MAINTAINING INDEPENDENCE

1   Kovach and Rosenstiel, *Elements of Journalism*, 118.
2   Wesley Gibbings, "Baby Steps to Liberty," http://wesleygibbings.blogspot.com/2013_05_01_archive.html (accessed 3 November 2013).
3   Wesley Gibbings, "Media Performance and Press Freedom," http://wesleygibbings.blogspot.com/2013_05_01_archive.html (accessed 3 November 2013).
4   Kovach and Rosenstiel, *Elements of Journalism*, 118.
5   Keith Mitchell, Address to the 4th Annual Caribbean Media Conference, St. George's, Grenada, 25 May 2001, http://www.caricom.org/jsp/speeches/4mediaconf_kmitchell.jsp?null&prnf=1 (accessed 14 August 2013).
6   Ibid.
7   Nicki Kelly, interview by author, 26 June 2008.
8   Omatie Lyder, interview by author, 13 June 2009.
9   Harold Hoyte, interview by author, 25 May 2010.
10 Roxanne Gibbs, interview, 26 May 2010.
11 Juan McCartney, interview by author, 24 June, 2008.
12 Ibid.
13 Larry Smith, "Can We Change," http://www.bahamapundit.com/2008/07/can-we-change-t.html (accessed 18 October 2012).
14 http://www.caricom.org/jsp/speeches/4mediaconf_kmitchell.jsp?null&prnf=1.
15 David Ellis, interview by author, 27 May 2010.
16 Ibid.
17 Byron Buckley, interview by author, 8 June 2009.
18 See Freedom House's 2012 and 2013 reports on Caribbean freedom of the press at https://freedomhouse.org/reports. In 2013 the Bahamian government established a commission to recommend constitutional reform. One of the reforms the commission recommended was the expansion of Article 23 to "expressly include a reference to freedom of the press and the media." See "Constitutional Commission

2013 Report," http://www.bahamas.gov.bs/wps/wcm/connect/7c2fe440-cb66-4327-9bf3-432131510cc4/Constitution+Commission+Report+2013_8JULY2013.pdf?MOD=AJPERES (accessed 17 December 2013).

19. Chantal Raymond, "Free Speech Jamaica," http://freespeechjamaica.com/wp-content/uploads/2010/10/Libel-law-paper.pdf (accessed 15 April 2012).
20. Ibid.
21. Juliette Storr, "The Disintegration of the State Model in the English Speaking Caribbean: Restructuring and Redefining Public Service Broadcasting," *International Communication Gazette* 73, no. 7 (2011): 553–572.
22. Gary Allen, interview by author, 10 June 2009.
23. Hopeton Dunn, interview by author, 8 June 2009.
24. "Final Report on the 2013 IPI Mission to Guyana: Focus on Criminal Defamation," http://ipi.freemedia.at/fileadmin/resources/application/Guyana_Mission_Report_2013.pdf (accessed 3 February 2014).
25. "Freedom House 2007 Grenada Report," http://www.freedomhouse.org/report/freedom-world/2007/grenada#.U3N-aCinzjQ (accessed 19 August 2012).
26. Fay Durrant, "Openness, Access to Government Information and Caribbean Governance," *First Monday* 11, no. 7 (2006), http://firstmonday.org/htbin/cgiwrap/bin/ojs/index.php/fm/rt/printerFriendly/1369/1288 (accessed 21 March 2012).
27. "Final Report on the 2013 IPI Mission to Trinidad and Tobago: Focus on Criminal Defamation," http://ipi.freemedia.at/fileadmin/resources/application/Caribbean_Mission_Report_2013.pdf (accessed 3 February 2014).
28. Ibid.
29. 2013 Gleaner Company Annual Report, http://old.jamaica-gleaner.com/gleaner/about/pdf/GL-FIN-2013-1-99_A.pdf (accessed 7 March 2014).
30. See Venkat Iyer, "Freedom of Information: Principles for Legislation," http://www.bytesforall.org/Egovernance/html/freedom_info.htm (accessed 18 July 2012); and Toby Mendel, "Parliament and Access to Information: Working for Transparent Governance" (working paper, World Bank Institute, Washington, DC), http://siteresources.worldbank.org/WBI/Resources/Parliament_and_Access_to_Information_with_cover.pdf (accessed 18 July 2012).
31. Reudon Eversley, interview by author, 26 May 2010.
32. "Government Blamed for Newspaper Reporter's Dismissal," http://en.rsf.org/grenada-government-blamed-for-newspaper-27-03-2012,42195.html (accessed 4 January 2013).
33. Ibid.
34. Ibid.
35. Grenada journalist, interview by author 3 June, 2013. The interviewee requested anonymity for fear of repercussions.
36. See Reporters Without Borders 2012 Report, https://rsf.org/en/jamaica (accessed 5 June 2013) and Freedom House 2012 Report accessed at https://freedomhouse.org/report/freedom-press/2012/jamaica (accessed 5 June 2013).
37. Wesley Gibbings, "Free Press Challenge in the Caribbean," http://wesleygibbings.blogspot.com/2011/05/press-freedom-challenge-in-caribbean.html (accessed 15 June 2012).

38 Wesley Gibbings, "Media Performance and Press Freedom," http://wesleygibbings.blogspot.ca/2013/03/media-performance-and-press-freedom.html (accessed 15 October 2013).
39 Daniel Hallin and Stylianos Papathanassopoulos, "Political Clientelism and the Media: Southern Europe and Latin America in Comparative Perspective,' *Media, Culture & Society* 24, no. 2 (2002): 185.
40 Hallin and Papathanassopoulos, "Political Clientelism and the Media," 176.
41 Thea Rutherford, interview by author, 27 June 2008.
42 See the Code of Ethics of the Society of Professional Journalists and the Code of Conduct of the National Union of Journalists at http://www.spj.org/ethicscode.asp and http://media.gn.apc.org/nujcode.html, respectively.
43 Claude Robinson, "PSB for Education, Cultural Diversity and Social Inclusion—A Caribbean Perspective," (paper presented at the World Electronic Media Forum Workshop on Public Service Broadcasting, Geneva, Switzerland, 2003).
44 Cinzia Padovani, "Would We Create It if It Did Not Exist? The Evolution of Public Broadcasting in Jamaica," *International Journal of Media and Cultural Politics* 3 (2007): 215–234.
45 Monroe Price and Marc Raboy, eds., *Public Service Broadcasting in Transition* (Hague: Kluwer Law International, 2003).
46 Indrajit Banerjee and Kalinga Seneviratne, eds., *Public Service Broadcasting in the Age of Globalization* (Singapore: Asian Media Information and Communication Centre, 2006).
47 Price and Raboy, *Public Service Broadcasting in Transition*.
48 Hallin and Papathanassopoulos, "Political Clientelism and the Media," 176.
49 Ibid., 177.
50 Wesley Gibbings, "Media Performance and Press Freedom."
51 Hallin and Papathanassopoulos, "Political Clientelism and the Media," 182.
52 Ibid., 185.
53 "Final Report on the 2013 IPI Advocacy Mission to the Caribbean: Focus on Criminal Defamation," http://ipi.freemedia.at/fileadmin/resources/application/Caribbean_Mission_Report_2013.pdf, 26 (accessed 5 February 2014).
54 Ibid.
55 Ibid.
56 Ibid., 15.
57 Ibid.
58 Ibid., 16.
59 Anthony Forbes, interview by author, 13 June 2008.
60 Harold Hoyte, interview by author, 25 May 2010.
61 Ibid.
62 Ava Turnquest, interview by Patti Roker, *Parliament Street*, Island FM, 13 May 2013.
63 Reudon Eversley, interview by author, 26 May 2010.
64 Omatie Lyder, interview by author, 13 June 2009.
65 Reudon Eversley, interview by author, 26 May 2010.
66 Ken Gordon, interview by author, 14 June 2009.
67 Rupert Missick, interview by author, 24 June 2008.

68. Dan Gillmor, "The End of Objectivity," http://dangillmor.typepad.com/dan_gillmor_on_grassroots/2005/01/the_end_of_obje.html (accessed 10 August 2013).
69. Brent Dean, interview by author, 27 June 2008.
70. Ibid.
71. Peter Christopher, interview by author, 12 March 2009.
72. Ibid.
73. Ibid.
74. Ibid.
75. Ibid.
76. Ibid.
77. Ibid.

7 | THE FUTURE OF CARIBBEAN JOURNALISM

1. "New Media, Journalism and Democracy in the Caribbean Symposium, (Kingston, Jamaica, 18–19 July 2011)," http://www.youtube.com/watch?v=wkz4_JRur6I (accessed 15 January 2014).
2. Erica Wells, interview by author, 2 July 2008.
3. Ibid.
4. Robert Picard, "Twilight or New Dawn of Journalism? Evidence from the changing news ecosystem," *Journalism Studies* 15, no. 5 (2014): 500–510.
5. As quoted in chapter 11 of Kovach and Rosenstiel, *Elements of Journalism*, 245.
6. Ibid., 247
7. Keith Mitchell, Address to the 4th Annual Caribbean Media Conference, St. George's, Grenada, 25 May 2001, http://www.caricom.org/jsp/speeches/4mediaconf_kmitchell.jsp?null&prnf=1 (accessed 14 August 2013).
8. Ibid.
9. Harold Hoyte, interview by author, 25 May 2010.
10. Ibid.
11. Byron Buckley, interview by author, 8 June 2009.
12. Wendall Jones, interview by author, 11 June 2008.
13. Harold Hoyte, interview by author, 25 May 2010.
14. Juan McCartney, interview by author, 2 July 2013.
15. Ken Gordon, interview by author, 14 June 2009.
16. Ibid.
17. Hopeton Dunn, "The Politics of the Media in the English-Speaking Caribbean," in *Who Owns the Media? Global Trends and Local Resistance*, Pradip Thomas and Zaharom Nain, eds. (London: Zed Books, 2004), 75.
18. Keith Mitchell, Address to the 4th Annual Caribbean Media Conference, St. George's, Grenada, 25 May 2001, http://www.caricom.org/jsp/speeches/4mediaconf_kmitchell.jsp?null&prnf=1 (accessed 14 August 2013).
19. Ibid.
20. Jan Servaes, "Toward a New Perspective for Communication and Development," in *Communication in Development*, Fred Casmir, ed. (New York: Ablex, 1991); John Friedmann, *Empowerment: The Politics of Alternative Development* (Cambridge, MA:

Blackwell, 1992); Srinivas Melkote, *Development Communication in the Third World: Theory and Practice* (New Delhi: Sage Publications, 1991); Paolo Freire, *Pedagogy of the Oppressed* (New York: Continuum, 1997); Thomas Jacobson, "Modernization and Post-modernization Approaches to Participatory Development Communication," in *Participatory Communication: Working for Change and Development*, Shirley White, ed., with K. Sadanandan Nair and Joseph Ascroft (New Delhi: Sage Publications, 1994), 60–75; and Paolo Mefalopulos, *Development Communication Sourcebook: Broadening the Boundaries of Communication* (Washington, DC: World Bank, 2008).

21 Hebdige, *Cut 'n' Mix*.
22 Kraidy, *Hybridity*.
23 Jan Nederveen Pieterse, "Hybridity or the cultural logic of Globalization," www.temple.edu/tempress/titles/1770_reg.html (accessed 12 May, 2015).
24 Kraidy, *Hybridity*, xi.
25 Ibid., viii.
26 Christians et al., 179.
27 Ibid.
28 Ibid.
29 Ibid., 180.
30 Ibid., 181.
31 Ibid., 194.
32 Ibid.
33 Ibid.
34 David Loyn, "Good Journalism or Peace Journalism?" *Conflict & Communication* 6, no. 2 (2007): 1–5 and Thomas Hanitzsch, "Situation Peace Journalism Studies: A Critical Appraisal," *Conflict & Communication* 6, no. 2 (2007): 1–9.
35 David Loyn, "Good Journalism or Peace Journalism?" *Conflict & Communication* 6, no. 2 (2007): 1–5.
36 Wilhelm Kempf, "Peace Journalism: A Tightrope Walk Between Advocacy Journalism and Constructive Conflict Coverage," *Conflict & Communication* 6, no. 2 (2007): 3.
37 Ibid, 4.
38 Johan Galtung, "Peace Journalism—A Challenge," in *Journalism and the New World Order. Vol. II. Studying War and the Media*, Wilhelm Kemp and Heikki Luostarinen, eds. (Gothenburg: Nordicom, 2002).
39 Kempf, "Peace Journalism," 4–7.
40 Ibid.
41 Ibid.
42 Ibid.
43 Robert Niles, "Why We Need Advocacy Journalism," http://www.ojr.org/p2042/ (accessed 15 February 2014).
44 Ibid.
45 Ibid.
46 Ibid.
47 Ibid.
48 David Kurpius, "Community Journalism: Getting Started," https://www.rtdna.org/uploads/files/cjgs.pdf.

49 Christians et al., 193.
50 See Carpentier, Lie, and Servaes, "Making Community Media Work," 15.
51 Ibid.
52 Ibid.
53 Ibid., 10.
54 Ibid.
55 Ibid., 14.
56 Gilles Deleuze and Felix Guattari, *A Thousand Plateaus: Capitalism and Schizophrenia* (Minneapolis: University of Minnesota Press, 1987).
57 Ibid., 7
58 Ibid., 24. See also Carpentier, Lie, and Servaes, "Making Community Media Work," 24.
59 Ibid.
60 Ibid., 25.
61 Keith Mitchell, Address to the 4th Annual Caribbean Media Conference, St. George's, Grenada, 25 May 2001, http://www.caricom.org/jsp/speeches/4mediaconf_kmitchell.jsp?null&prnf=1 (accessed 14 August 2013).
62 Ibid.
63 Ibid.
64 Kempf, "Peace Journalism," 6.

Bibliography

Acemoglu, Daron and James Robinson. "Is State Capitalism Winning?" http://www.project-syndicate.org/commentary/why-china-s-growth-model-will-fail-by-daron-acemoglu-and-james-a--robinson.

Alesina, Alberto and Enrico Spolaore. *The Size of Nations*. Cambridge, MA: MIT Press, 2003.

Alesina, Alberto, Enrico Spolaore, and Romain Wacziarg. "Trade, Growth and the Size of Countries." In *Handbook of Economic Growth*, edited by Philippe Aghion and Steven Durlauf, 1500–1539. Amsterdam: Elsevier, 2004.

Alleyne, Mark. "Mass Media in Barbados." In *Mass Media in the Caribbean*, edited by Stuart Surlin and Walter Soderlund, 55–73. New York: Gordon and Breach, 1990.

Althusser, Louis. "Sur la Dialectique Matérialiste (De l'inégalité des origines)." *La Pensée* 110 (1963): 5–46.

Amsden, Alice. *The Rise of the Rest: The challenges to the West from late-industrializing economies*. Oxford: Oxford University Press, 2001.

Anderson, Benedict. *Imagined Communities: Reflections on the Origin and Spread of Nationalism*. New York: Verso Books, 1983.

Aristotle. *Politics*. Translated by Benjamin Jowett. London: Forgotten Books, 2012.

Atton, Chris. "Why Alternative Journalism Matters." *Journalism* 10, no. 3 (2009): 283–285.

Auletta, Ken. "Citizens Jain: Why India's newspaper industry is thriving." *The New Yorker*, 8 October 2012.

Bagdikian, Ben. *The New Media Monopoly*. Boston: Beacon Press, 2004.

Baker, C. Edwin. *Media, Markets and Democracy*. Cambridge: Cambridge University Press, 2002.

Bakhtin, Mikhail. *The Dialogical Imagination: Four Essays*. Austin: University of Texas Press, 1981.

Balčytienė, Aukse. "Market-led Reforms as Incentives for Media Change, Development and Diversification in the Baltic States: A Small Country Approach." *International Communication Gazette* 71 (2009): 39–49.

———. *Mass Media and Journalism in Lithuania: Changes, Development and Journalism Culture.* Berlin: Vistas, 2006.

Balčytienė, Aukse and Halliki Harro-Loit. "How to Preserve Journalism?" Paper presented at "Comparing Media Systems: West Meets East," Wroclaw, Poland, 23–25 April 2007.

Ball-Rokeach, Sandra J. and Melvin L. DeFleur. "A Dependency Model of Mass-Media Effects." *Communication Research* 3 (1976): 3–21.

Banerjee, Indrajit and Kalinga Seneviratne, eds. *Public Service Broadcasting in the Age of Globalization.* Singapore: Asian Media Information and Communication Centre, 2006.

Barber, Benjamin. "Strong democracy." In *Theories of Democracy: A Reader*, edited by Ronald Terchek and Thomas Conte, 171–180. Lanham: Rowan & Littlefield, 2001.

Beckles, Hilary. *Britain's Black Debt: Reparations for Caribbean Slavery and Native Genocide.* Kingston, Jamaica: University of the West Indies Press, 2013.

Benjamin, Lisa and Cathleen LeGrand. "Sound and Fury: Newspaper Coverage of the Marital Rape Debate in New Providence." *The International Journal of Bahamian Studies* 18 (2012): 16–35.

Bennett, Lance, Regina Lawrence, and Steven Livingston. *When the Press Fails: Political Power and the News Media from Iraq to Katrina.* Chicago: University of Chicago Press, 2007.

Best, Curwen. "Caribbean Music Videos and the Ideology of Construction." *Journal of Caribbean Studies* 16 (2001): 99–115.

Bhabha, Homi. *Location of Culture.* London: Routledge, 1994.

Bird, S. Elizabeth. "The Future of Journalism in the Digital Environment." *Journalism* 10, no. 3 (2009): 293–295.

Boyd-Barrett, Oliver. "Global News Wholesalers as Agents of Globalization." In *Media in Global Context. A Reader*, edited by Annabelle Sreberny-Mohammadi, Dwayne Winseck, Jim McKenna, and Oliver Boyd-Barrett, 131–144. London: Arnold, 1997.

———. "Contra the Journalism of Complicity." *Journalism* 10, no. 3 (2009): 296–299.

Brathwaite, Edward. "African Presence in Caribbean Literature." *Daedalus* 103 (1974): 73–109.

Bremmer, Ian. *The End of the Free Market: Who Wins the War Between States and Corporations?* New York: Portfolio/Penguin, 2010.

Brennen, Bonnie. "The Future of Journalism." *Journalism* 10, no. 3 (2009): 300–302.

Brewster, Havelock and Clive Thomas. *The Dynamics of West Indian Economic Integration.* Kingston, Jamaica: Mona Institute of Social and Economic Research, 1967.

Briguglio, Lino. "Small Island States and Their Economic Vulnerabilities." *World Development* 23 (1995): 1615–1632.

Briguglio, Lino and Eliawony Kisanga, eds. *Economic Vulnerability and Resilience of Small States.* Msida: Commonwealth Secretariat and Islands and Small States Institute of the University of Malta, 2004.

Brown, Aggrey. "The Caribbean—A Chance for Community Media to Develop." http://www.waccglobal.org/en/19981-communication-issues-in-the-caribbean/896-__The-Caribbean---a-chance-for-community-media-to-develop-.html.

———. "Caribbean Cultures and Mass Communication Technology: Re-examining the Cultural Dependency Thesis." In *Globalization, Communications, and Caribbean Identity*, edited by Hopeton Dunn, 40–54. Kingston, Jamaica: Ian Randle Publishers, 1995.

———. "A Contextual Macro-analysis of Media in the Caribbean in the 1990s." *Media Development.* http://www.wacc.org.uk/publications/md/md1998-4/brown.html.

———. "Towards Regionalization of New Communication Services in the CARICOM: A Technological Free-for-all." *Canadian Journal of Communication* 20 (1995): 301–315.

Brown, Aggrey and Roderick Sanatan. *Talking with Whom?* Mona, Jamaica: Caribbean Institute of Mass Communication, University of the West Indies, 1987.

Burgelman, Jean-Claude and Caroline Pauwels. "Audiovisual Policy and Cultural Identity in Small European States: The Challenge of a Unified Market." *Media, Culture and Society* 14 (1992): 169–183.

Busterna, John and Robert Picard. *Joint Operating Agreements: The Newspaper Preservation Act and its Application.* New Jersey: Ablex Publishing, 1993.

Carey, James. "Where Journalism Education Went Wrong." http://lindadaniele.wordpress.com/2010/08/11/carey-where-journalism-education-went-wrong/.

"Caribbean Overview: Media Struggles with Defamation Laws, Economic Challenges." http://www.freemedia.at/home/singleview/article/caribbean-overview.html.

Carlsson, Ulla. "The Rise and Fall of NWICO: From a Vision of International Regulation to a Reality of Multilevel Governance." http://www.nordicom.gu.se/sites/default/files/kapitel-pdf/32_031-068.pdf.

Carpentier, Nico, Rico Lie, and Jan Servaes. "Making Community Media Work." http://www.unesco.kz/publications/ci/hq/Approaches%20Development%20Communication/CHP15.PDF.

Christians, Christian, Theodore Glasser, Denis McQuail, Kaarle Nordenstreng, and Robert White. *Normative Theories of the Media: Journalism in Democratic Societies*. Chicago: University of Illinois Press, 2009.

Claussen, Dane. "If Even Journalism Professors Don't Know What Journalism Is, Then All Really Is Lost." *Journalism & Mass Communication Educator*, 67 (2012): 329–330.

Condé, Maryse. *Chercher nos Vérités. Penser la Créolité*. Edited by Maryse Condé and Madeleine Cottenet-Hage. Paris: Karthala, 1995.

———. *I, Tituba, Black Witch of Salem*. New York: Ballantine Books, 1994.

———. "Order, Disorder, Freedom, and the West Indian Writer." *Yale French Studies* 83, no. 2 (1993): 121–135.

Cuthbert, Marlene. "The Caribbean News Agency: Third World Model." *Journalism Monographs* 71 (1981): 1–41.

Dahl, Robert. *On Democracy*. Cambridge, MA: Harvard University Press, 2000.

Dahlgren, Peter. "The Public Sphere and the Net: Structure, Space, and Communication." In *Mediated Politics: Communication in the Future of Democracy*, edited by W. Lance Bennett and Robert M. Entman, 35–55. Cambridge: Cambridge University Press, 2001.

Dahlgren, Peter and Colin Sparks, eds. *Journalism and Popular Culture*. London: Sage, 1992.

Deleuze, Gilles and Felix Guattari. *A Thousand Plateaus. Capitalism and Schizophrenia*. Minneapolis: University of Minnesota Press, 1987.

Deuze, Mark. "The People Formerly Known as the Employers." *Journalism* 10, no. 3 (2009): 315–318.

Dunn, Hopeton. "Facing the Digital Millennium: A Comparative Analysis of Communication, Culture and Globalisation in South Africa and the Anglophone Caribbean." In *Media, Democracy and Renewal in South Africa*, edited by Keyan Tomaselli and Hopeton Dunn, 56–78. Colorado Springs: International Academic Publishers, 2002.

———, ed. *Globalization, Communications, and Caribbean Identity*. Kingston, Jamaica: Ian Randle Publishers, 1995.

———. "The Politics of the Media in the English-Speaking Caribbean." In *Who Owns the Media? Global Trends and Local Resistances*, edited by Pradip Thomas and Zaharom Nain, 69–95. London: Zed Books, 2004.

———. "Regulating the Changing Face of Electronic Media." http://www.broadcastingcommission.org/uploads/speeches_and_presentations/Regulating%20the%20Changing%20Face%20of%20Electronic%20Media%20in%20Jamaica%20-%20Background.pdf.

Durrant, Fay. "Openness, Access to Government Information and Caribbean Governance." *First Monday* 11, no. 7 (2006). http://firstmonday.org/htbin/cgiwrap/bin/ojs/index.php/fm/rt/printerFriendly/1369/1288.

Economic Commission for Latin America and the Caribbean. "Population Ageing in the Caribbean: An Inventory of Policies, Programmes and Future Challenges." http://www.cepal.org/celade/noticias/paginas/8/14928/lccarg772.pdf.

Edgell, Holly. "Journalism in Belize: It's Time to Temper Guts and Gore with Balance and Context." http://hollyedgell.wordpress.com/2012/05/09/journalism-in-belize-its-time-to-temper-guts-and-gore-with-balance-and-context/.

Edmonds Rick. "The State of the News Media 2009: An Annual Report on American Journalism." http://stateofthemedia.org/2009/.

eMarketer. "Facebook's Worldwide Ad Revenues Will Pass $5 Billion This Year." http://www.emarketer.com/Article/Facebooks-Worldwide-Ad-Revenues-Will-Pass-5-Billion-This-Year/1008858.

Enli, Gunn. "Redefining Public Service Broadcasting Multi-platform Participation." *Convergence: The International Journal of Research into New Media Technologies* 14, no. 1 (2008): 105–120.

European Publishers Council. "Global Media Trends Book 2012–2013." http://epceurope.eu/wp-content/uploads/2012/09/EPC_ExecSum_press.pdf.

Fallows, James. *Looking at the Sun: The Rise of the New East Asian Economic and Political System*. New York: Pantheon Books, 1994.

Ferré, Rosario. *Maldito Amor*. New York: Vintage Español, 1998.

———, ed. *Sobre el Amor y la Política. El Coloquio de Las Perras*. Rio Piedras: Editorial Cultural, 1990.

Ferree, Myra, William Gamson, Jürgen Gerhards, and Dieter Rucht. *Shaping Abortion Discourse: Democracy and the Public Sphere in Germany and the United States*. Cambridge: Cambridge University Press, 2002.

Foucault, Michel. *The Order of Things*. Translated by Alan Sheridan. New York: Vintage, 1966.

Franklin, Bob. "The Future of Newspapers." http://orca.cf.ac.uk/18315/1/bsc_3_-03-09_-_paper_2a_-_prof_bob_franklin_-_cardiff_university.pdf

———, ed. *The Future of Journalism*. London: Routledge, 2013.

Freedom House. "Freedom House 2007 Grenada Report." http://www.freedomhouse.org/report/freedom-world/2007/grenada#.U3N-aCinzjQ.

———. "Freedom of the Press 2013 – Belize." http://www.refworld.org/docid/51e7d0c28.html.

———. "Freedom of the Press 2013 – Guyana." http://www.refworld.org/docid/5229988514.html.

Freire, Paolo. *Pedagogy of the Oppressed*. New York: Continuum, 1970.

Friedmann, John. *Empowerment: The Politics of Alternative Development*. Cambridge, MA: Blackwell, 1992.

Galtung, Johan. "Peace Journalism—A Challenge." In *Journalism and the New World Order, Studying War and the Media*, edited by Wilhelm Kemp and Heikki Luostarinen. Gothenburg: Nordicom, 2002.

Gans, Herbert J. *Democracy and the News*. New York: Oxford University Press, 2003.

———. "News and the News Media in the Digital Age: Implications for Democracy." *Daedalus* 139, no. 2 (2010): 8–17.

Gaunt, Philip. *Choosing the News: The Profit Factor in News Selection*. New York: Greenwood Press, 1990.

Gerbner, George. "Cultivation Analysis: An Overview." *Mass Communication & Society* 1, no. 3/4 (1998): 175–194.

Gerbner, George and Lawrence Gross. "Living with Television: The Violence Profile." *Journal of Communication* 26, no. 2 (1976): 173–199.

Gibbings, Wesley. "Baby Steps to Liberty." http://wesleygibbings.blogspot.com/2013_05_01_archive.html.

———. "Free Press Challenge in Caribbean." http://wesleygibbings.blogspot.com/2011/05/press-freedom-challenge-in-caribbean.html.

———. "Media Performance and Press Freedom." http://wesleygibbings.blogspot.com/search?updated-min=2013-01-01T00:00:00-04:00&updated-max=2014-01-01T00:00:00-04:00&max-results=8.

Gillin, Paul. "Surprise! Researchers See Industry Growth." http://newspaperdeathwatch.com/surprise-researchers-see-industry-growth/.

Gillmor, Dan. "The End of Objectivity." http://dangillmor.typepad.com/dan_gillmor_on_grassroots/2005/01/the_end_of_obje.html.

Gilroy, Paul. *The Black Atlantic: Modernity and Double Consciousness*. Cambridge, MA: Harvard University Press, 1993.

Girvan, Norman. "Is ALBA a New Model of Integration? Reflections on the CARICOM Experience." http://www.normangirvan.info/wp-content/uploads/2011/09/girvan-alba-and-caricom-lmet-revised2.pdf.

———. "ALBA, PETROCARIBE and CARICOM: Issues in a New Dynamic." In *CARICOM: Policy Options for International Engagement*, edited by Kenneth Hall and Myrtle Chuck-A-Sang, 218–234. Kingston, Jamaica: Ian Randle Publishers, 2010.

———. "Notes for a Retrospective on the Theory of Plantation Economy of Lloyd Best and Kari Polanyi Levitt." In *Caribbean Economies and Global Restructuring*, edited by Marie Derne and Keith Nurse, 17–24. Kingston, Jamaica: Ian Randle Publishers, 2002.

Gramsci, Antonio. *Selections from the Prison Notebook*. Edited and translated by Quintin Hoare and Goffrey Nowell Smith. London: Lawrence and Wishart, 1971.

"Grenada Building Human Capacity Among Media Workers." http://www.unesco-ci.org/ipdcprojects/sites/default/files/ipdc-project descriptions/Grenada%20%20Building%20Human%20Capacity%20among%20Media%20Workers.pdf.

"Grenada Decriminalizes Defamation Law." http://www.freemedia.at/home/singleview/article/grenada-abolishes-criminal-libel.html.

Guenzi, Paolo and Ottavia Pelloni. "The Impact of Interpersonal Relationships on Customer Satisfaction and Loyalty to the Service Provider." *International Journal of Service Industry Management* 15, no. 4 (2004): 365–384.

Habermas, Jürgen. *The Structural Transformation of the Public Sphere*. Cambridge, MA: MIT Press, 1989.

———. *The Theory of Communicative Action*. Boston: Beacon Press, 1984.

d'Haenens, Leen, Helena Sousa, Werner Meier, and Josef Trappel. "Turmoil as Part of the Institution: Public Service Media and their Tradition." *Convergence: The International Journal of Research into New Media Technologies* 14, no. 3 (2008): 243–247.

Hall, Edward. *The Silent Language*. New York: Fawcett Publications, 1959.

Hall, Stuart. *Policing the Crisis: Mugging, the State and Law and Order*. London, MacMillan, 1978.

Hallin, Daniel. "Comment: State Size as a Variable in Comparative Analysis." *International Communication Gazette* 71, no. 1–2 (2009): 101–103.

———. *We Keep America on Top of the World*. New York: Routledge, 1994.

Hallin, Daniel and Paolo Mancini. *Comparing Media Systems*. Cambridge: Cambridge University Press, 2004.

Hallin, Daniel and Stylianos Papathanassopoulos. "Political Clientelism and the Media: Southern Europe and Latin America in Comparative Perspective." *Media, Culture & Society* 24, no. 2 (2002): 179–195.

Hanitzsch, Thomas. "Situating Peace Journalism in Jounalism Studies: A Critical Appraisal." *Conflict & Communications* 6, no. 2 (2007): 1–9. http://cco.regener-online.de/2007_2/pdf/hanitzsch.pdf.

Harro-Loit, Halliki and Kertu Saks. "The Diminishing Border between Advertising and Journalism." *Journalism Studies* 7, no. 2 (2006): 312–322.

Hayek, Friedrich. "The Political Order of a Free People." In *Theories of Democracy: A Reader*, edited by Ronald Tercheck and Thomas Conte, 92–111. Lanham: Rowan & Littlefield, 2001.

Hebdige, Dick. *Cut 'N' Mix: Culture, Identity and Caribbean Music*. London: Methuen, 1987.

Heinonen, Ari. "Reconsidering 'Journalism' for Journalism Research." Paper presented at "Journalism Research in an Era of Globalization," Erfurt, Germany 3–4 July 2004.

Herman, Edward and Noam Chomsky. *Manufacturing Consent: The Political Economy of Mass Media*. New York: Pantheon Books, 1988.

Hinds, David. "A Mailman to make Government Understand: The Calypsonian (Chalkdust) as Political Opposition in the Caribbean." http://www.music.ucsb.edu/projects/musicandpolitics/archive/2010-2/hinds.pdf.

Hjavard, Stig. "News Media and the Globalisation of the Public Sphere." In *News in a Globalized Society*, edited by Stig Hjavard, 15–54. Gothenburg: Nordicom, 2001.

Hofstede, Geert. *Culture's Consequences: International Differences in Work-Related Values*. Beverly Hills: Sage, 1980.

Hoggart, Richard. *The Uses of Literacy*, Harmondsworth: Penguin, 1958.

Humphreys, Peter. *Mass Media and Media Policy in Western Europe*. Manchester: Manchester University Press, 1996.

International Press Institute. "Final Report on the IPI Advocacy Mission to End Criminal Defamation in Barbados." http://www.freemedia.at/fileadmin/media/Documents/IPI_mission_reports/Barbados_Mission_Report.pdf.

———. "Final Report on the 2013 IPI Advocacy Mission to the Caribbean: Focus on Criminal Defamation." http://ipi.freemedia.at/fileadmin/resources/application/Caribbean_Mission_Report_2013.pdf, p. 26.

———. "Final Report on the 2013 IPI Mission to Guyana." http://ipi.freemedia.at/fileadmin/resources/application/Guyana_Mission_Report_2013.pdf

———. "Final Report on the 2013 IPI Mission to Trinidad and Tobago: Focus on Criminal Defamation." http://ipi.freemedia.at/fileadmin/resources/application/Caribbean_Mission_Report_2013.pdf.

Iyer, Venkatasubbaiyer. "Freedom of Information: Principles for Legislation." http://www.bytesforall.org/Egovernance/html/freedom_info.html.

Jacobson, Thomas. "Modernization and Post-Modernization Approaches to Participatory Development Communication." In *Participatory Communication: Working for Change and Development*, edited by Shirley White with K. Sadanandan Nair and Joseph Ascroft, 60–75. New Delhi: Sage Publications, 1994.

Jensen, Klaus Bruhn. "Why Virtuality Can Be Good for Democracy." In *News in a Globalized Society*, edited by Stig Hjavard, 93–112. Gothenburg: Nordicom, 2001.

Johnson, Lamech. "Rodney Moncur Charged in Court Over Facebook Pictures." *Nassau Tribune*, 5 April 2013. http://www.tribune242.com/news/2013/apr/05/rodney-moncur-charged-in-court-over-facebook/.

Jones, Adele D. and Ena Trotman Jemmott. "Child Sexual Abuse in the Eastern Caribbean: The report of a study carried out across the Eastern Caribbean during the period October 2008 to June 2009." Report on the UNICEF/Governments of the Eastern Caribbean Programme of Cooperation 2008–2011. http://www.unicef.org/infobycountry/files/Child_Sexual_Abuse_in_the_Eastern_Caribbean_Final_9_Nov.pdf.

Josephi, Beate. "Journalism in the Global Age." *International Communication Gazette* 67, no. 6 (2005): 575–590.

Keane, John. "Journalism and Democracy Across Borders." In *The Press, The Institutions of American Democracy*, edited by Geneva Overholser and Kathleen Hall Jamieson, 92–114. Oxford: Oxford University Press, 2005.

———. *The Life and Death of Democracy*. New York: Simon & Schuster, 2009.

———. *The Media and Democracy*. Cambridge, UK: Polity Press, 1991.

Kempf, Wilhelm. *Constructive Conflict Coverage: A Social Psychological Approach*. Edited by the Austrian Study Center for Peace and Conflict Resolution. Berlin: Regener, 2003.

———. "Peace Journalism: A Tightrope Walk Between Advocacy Journalism and Constructive Conflict Coverage." *Conflict & Communication* 6, no. 2 (2007): 1–9.

Kennedy, George and Daryl Moen. *What is Good Journalism? How Reporters and Editors Are Saving America's Way of Life*. Columbia: University of Missouri Press, 2007.

Kilman, Larry. "World Press Trends: Increasing Audience Engagement is Future for News Media." http://www.wan-ifra.org/press-releases/2013/06/02/world-press-trends-increasing-audience-engagement-is-future-for-news-media.

Kincaid, Jamaica. *A Small Place*. New York: Farrar, Straus and Giroux, 1988.

Kovach, Bill and Tom Rosenstiel. *The Elements of Journalism: What Newspeople Should Know and the Public Should Expect*. New York: Crown Publishers, 2007.

Kraidy, Marwan. *Hybridity: The Cultural Logic of Globalization*. Philadelphia: Temple University, 2005.

Krajicek, David. *Scooped! Media Miss Real Story on Crime While Chasing Sex, Sleaze, and Celebrities*. New York: Columbia University Press, 1998.

Lambert, Laurie. "The Revolution and its Discontents: Grenadian Newspapers and Attempts to Shape Public Opinion during Political Transition." *The Round Table: The Commonwealth Journal of International Affairs* 102, no. 2 (2013): 143–153.

Lashley, Lynette. "The Calypso as 'Political Football' in Trinidad and Tobago: The Status of Contemporary Political Commentary." Paper presented at 26th annual Caribbean Studies Association conference, St. Maarten, Netherlands Antilles.

———. "Television and the Americanization of the Trinibagonian Youth." In *Globalization, Communications, and Caribbean Identity*, edited by Hopeton Dunn, 83–97. Kingston, Jamaica: Ian Randle Publishing, 1995.

Lasswell, Harold. "The Structure and Function of Communication in Modern Society." In *The Communication of Ideas*, 37–51. edited by Lyman Bryson. New York: Harper & Row, 1948.

Ledgister, Fragano. "Democracy in the Caribbean: Post-Colonial Experience." http://www.academia.edu/428522/Democracy_in_the_Caribbean_Post-Colonial_Experience.

Lent, John. *Mass Communications in the Caribbean*. Iowa: Iowa State University Press, 1990.

———. *Third World Mass Media and Their Search for Modernity*. Lewisburg: Bucknell University Press, 1977.

Loyn, David. "Good Journalism or Peace Journalism?" *Conflict & Communication* 6, no. 2 (2007): 1–5. http://www.cco.regener-online.de/2007_2/pdf/loyn_reply.pdf.

Mancini, Paolo. "Political Complexity and Alternative Models of Journalism." In *De-Westernizing Media Studies*, edited by James Curran and Myung-Jin Park, 265–278. London: Routledge, 2000.

"Many Voices One World: Towards a New More Just and More Efficient Information and Communication Order." Report by the International Commission for the Study of Communication Problems. London: Kogan Page, 1980. http://unesdoc.unesco.org/images/0004/000400/040066eb.pdf.

Martin, Robert. "Broadcasting and the Struggle of Cultural Autonomy in Canada." In *Globalization, Communications, and Caribbean Identity*, edited by Hopeton Dunn, 122–134. Kingston, Jamaica: Ian Randle Publishers, 1995.

Marx, Karl. *Collected Works*. New York: International Publishers, 1975.

McChesney, Robert. *Rich Media, Poor Democracy: Communication Politics in Dubious Times*. New York: New Press, 1999.

McChesney, Robert and Ben Scott, eds. *Our Unfree Press: 100 Years of Radical Media Criticism*. New York: New Press, 2004.

McChesney, Robert and John Nichols. *The Death and Life of American Journalism: The Media Revolution That Will Begin the World Again.* Philadelphia: Nation Books, 2010.

McNair, Brain. "Journalism in the 21st Century—Evolution, Not Extinction." *Journalism* 10, no. 3 (2009): 347–349.

———. *News and Journalism in the UK.* Oxon: Routledge, 2009.

McQuail, Denis. *Mass Communication Theory.* London: Sage, 2005.

Mefalopulos, Paolo. *Development Communication Sourcebook: Broadening the Boundaries of Communication.* Washington, DC: World Bank, 2008.

Meier, Werner and Josef Trappel. "Small States in the Shadow of Giants." In *Dynamics of Media Politics: Broadcast and Electronic Media in Western Europe,* edited by Karen Siune and Wolfgang Truetzschler, 129–142, London: Sage, 1992.

Melkote, Srinivas R. *Development Communication in the Third World: Theory and Practice.* New Delhi: Sage Publications, 1991.

Mendel, Toby. "Parliament and Access to Information: Working for Transparent Governance." Washington, DC: World Bank Institute, 2004. http://siteresources.worldbank.org/WBI/Resources/Parliament_and_Access_to_Information_with_cover.pdf.

Merrill, John and Ralph Lowenstein. *Media, Messages and Men: New Perspectives in Communication.* New York: Longman, 1979.

Mitchell, Keith. Address to the 4th Annual Caribbean Media Conference, St. George's, Grenada, 25 May 2001. http://www.caricom.org/jsp/speeches/4mediaconf_kmitchell.jsp?null&prnf=1.

Moreira, Mesquita, Mauricio Mendoza, and Eduardo Mendoza. "Regional Integration: What Is in It for CARICOM?" *Economia* 8, no. 1 (2007): 97–142.

Morrison, Toni. *The Bluest Eye.* New York: Plume, 1994.

———. "Memory, Creation, and Writing." *Thought* 59, no. 235 (1984): 385–390.

———. "The Site of Memory. In *Inventing the Truth: The Art and Craft of Memoir,* edited by William Zinsser, 103–124. Boston: Houghton Mifflin, 1995.

Mosco, Vincent. "The Future of Journalism." *Journalism* 10, no. 3 (2009): 350–352.

Musacchio, Aldo and Sergio Lazzarini. "Leviathan in Business: Varieties of State Capitalism and Their Implications for Economic Performance." Working Paper 12-108, Harvard Business School, Cambridge, MA, 2012. http://www.hbs.edu/faculty/Publication%20Files/12-108.pdf.

Nerone, John. "The Death (and Rebirth?) of Working-Class Journalism." *Journalism* 10, no. 3 (2009): 353–355.

Nettleford, Rex. *Caribbean Cultural Identity: The Case of Jamaica.* Los Angeles: Center for Afro-American Studies and UCLA Latin American Center Publication, 1979.

Neumann, John von and Oskar Morgenstern. *Theory of Games and Economic Behavior.* Princeton: Princeton University Press, 1944.

"Newspaper Publishers Optimistic About Future." http://mega-conference.com/stories/RJI,21145.

Niles, Robert. "Why We Need Advocacy Journalism." *Online Journalism Review.* http://www.ojr.org/p2042/.

"Nottages Should Sue The Guardian & Tribune for Libel." *Bahamas Press*, 12 April 2008. http://www.bahamaspress.com/2008/04/12/the-nottages-should-sue-the-guardian-tribue-and-punch-for-libel/.

Nurse, Keith. "The Creative Sector in CARICOM: Economic and Trade Policy Dimensions." Working paper for "CARICOM Secretariat Regional Symposium on Services," Antigua and Barbuda, July 2009. https://www.monroecollege.edu/uploadedFiles/_Site_Assets/PDF/concept_paper_creative_sector.pdf.

Oates, Sarah. *Introduction to Media and Politics.* London: Sage, 2008.

Oliveira, Omar. "Mass Media in Belize." In *Mass Media in the Caribbean*, edited by Stuart Surlin and Walter Soderlund, 115–128. New York: Gordon and Breach, 1990.

Örnebring, Henrik and Epp Lauk. "Does Size Matter? Journalistic Values and Working Conditions in Small Countries." Paper presented at ECREA conference, Hamburg, Germany, 12–15 October 2010.

Ostini, Jennifer and Anthony Fung. "Beyond the Four Theories of the Press: A New Model of National Media Systems." *Mass Communication & Society* 5, no. 1 (2002): 41–56.

Pactor, Howard. *Colonial British Caribbean Newspapers: A Bibliography and Directory.* New York: Greenwood Press, 1990.

Padovani, Cinzia. "Would we create it if it did not exist? The evolution of public broadcasting in Jamaica." *International Journal of Media and Cultural Politics* 3, no. 3 (2007): 215–234.

Page, Benjamin. *Who Deliberates? Mass Media in Modern Democracy.* Chicago: University of Chicago Press, 1996.

Pastina, Antoinio and Joseph Straubhaar. "Multiple Proximities Between Television Genres and Audiences." *International Communication Gazette* 67, no. 3 (2005): 271–288.

Patterson, Orlando. "Rethinking Black History." *Harvard Educational Review* 41, no. 3 (1971): 297–315.

Paul, Annie. "Demonic Jetski kills 6-year old girl in Jamaica!" *Active Voice* (blog). http://anniepaul.net/2013/08/21/demonic-jetski-kills-6-year-old-girl-in-jamaica/.

Pavlik, John. "A Sea-Change in Journalism: Convergence, Journalists, Their Audiences and Sources." *Convergence: The International Journal of Research into New Media Technologies* 10 (2004): 21–29.

Pew Research Center. "Pew Project for Excellence in Journalism." http://www.stateofthenewsmedia.org/2009/narrative_newspapers_intro.php?media=4.

———. "State of the News Media 2010: Executive Summary." http://stateofthemedia.org/files/2011/05/2010_execsummary.pdf.

———. "State of the News Media 2012." http://www.pewresearch.org/2012/03/19/state-of-the-news-media-2012/.

Picard, Robert. "Natural Death, Euthanasia, and Suicide: The Demise of Joint Operating Agreements." *Journal of Media Business Studies* 4, no. 2 (2007): 41–64.

———. *The Press and the Decline of Democracy: The Democratic Socialist Response in Public Policy*. Westport, CT: Greenwood Press, 1983.

———. "Twilight or new dawn of journalism? Evidence from the changing news ecosystem." *Journalism Studies* 15, no. 5 (2014): 500–510.

Price, Monroe and Marc Raboy, eds. *Public Service Broadcasting in Transition*. The Hague: Kluwer Law International, 2003.

Puppis, Manuel. "Media Regulations in Small States." *International Communication Gazette* 71, no. 1–2 (2009): 7–17.

Puppis, Manuel, Leen d'Haenens, Thomas Steinmaurer, and Matthias Künzler. "The European and Global Dimension: Taking Small Media Systems Research to the Next Level." *International Communication Gazette* 71, no. 1–2 (2009): 105–112.

Raboy, Marc. "Dreaming in Technicolor: The Future of PSB in a World Beyond Broadcasting." *Convergence: The International Journal of Research into New media Technologies* 14, no. 3 (2008): 361–365.

———. "Public Service Broadcasting in the Context of Globalization." In *Public Service Broadcasting: The Challenge of the Twenty-First Century*, edited by Dave Atkinson and Marc Raboy, 77–90. Paris: UNESCO, 1997.

———. "The World Summit on the Information Society and Its Legacy for Global Governance." *International Communication Gazette* 66, no. 3–4 (2004): 225–232.

Raymond, Chantal. "Free Speech Jamaica." http://freespeechjamaica.com/wp-content/uploads/2010/10/Libel-law-paper.pdf.

Rawlins, Joan. "Ageing in the Caribbean: Exploring Some Major Concerns for Family and Society." Paper presented at the SALISES Conference, Port of Spain, Trinidad. http://www.accc.ca/.../440-ageing-in-the-caribbean-exploring-some-major-con.

Reddock, Rhoda, Sandra Reid, and Tisha Nickenig. "Breaking the Silence: A Multi-Sectoral Approach to Preventing and Addressing Child Sexual Abuse in Trinidad and Tobago." Report by the United Nations and University of the West Indies, St. Augustine, Trinidad and Tobago, 2011. http://uwispace.sta.uwi.edu/dspace/handle/2139/13817.

Reese, Stephen. "The Future of Journalism in Emerging Deliberative Space." *Journalism* 10, no. 3 (2009): 362–364.

Regis, Humphrey, ed. *Culture and Mass Communication in the Caribbean*. Gainesville: University Press of Florida, 2001.

Regis, Louis. *The Political Calypso: True Opposition in Trinidad and Tobago*. Gainesville: University Press of Florida, 1998.

Reporters Without Borders. "Biggest Rises and Falls in the 2014 World Press Freedom Index." https://rsf.org/index2014/en-index2014.php.

———. "Government Blamed for Newspaper Reporter's Dismissal." http://en.rsf.org/grenada-government-blamed-for-newspaper-27-03-2012,42195.html.

Riley, Ingrid. "Jamaica Gleaner Caribbean's Oldest Newspaper Profits Plummets Vows to Focus on Increased Market Share." *Silicon Caribe* 15 June 2009. http://www.siliconcaribe.com/2009/06/15/jamaica-gleanercaribbean's-oldest-newspaper-profits-plummets-vows-to-focus-on-increased-market-share-online/.

Robinson, Claude. "PSB for Education, Cultural Diversity and Social Inclusion—A Caribbean Perspective." Paper presented at the World Electronic Media Forum Workshop on Public Service Broadcasting Geneva, Switzerland, 2003.

Rohlehr, Gordon. *Calypso and Society in Pre-Independence Trinidad*. Port of Spain: G. Rohlehr, 1990.

———. "The Calypsonian as Artist: Freedom and Responsibility." *Small Axe Number 9* 5, no. 1 (2001): 1–26.

Rosen, Jay. "The People Formerly Known as the Audience." *Pressthink* (blog), 15 August 2010. http://archive.pressthink.org/2006/06/27/ppl_frmr.html.

Rousseau, Jean-Jacques. *The Government of Poland*. Translated by Willmoore Kendall. Indianapolis: Hackett Publishing, 1985.

Sachsman, David and David Bulla, eds. *Sensationalism: Murder, Mayhem, Mudsling, Scandals and Disasters in 19th-Century Reporting*. New Brunswick, NJ: Transaction Publishers, 2013.

Schiller, Herbert. *Communication and Cultural Domination*. New York: M. E. Sharpe, 1976.

———. *Culture, Inc.: The Corporate Takeover of Public Expression.* New York: Oxford University Press, 1991.

———. *Mass Communication and American Empire.* New York: Westview Press, 1992.

Schudson, Michael. "News and Democratic Society: Past, Present, and Future." *Hedgehog Review* 10, no. 2 (2008): 17–18. http://www.iasc-culture.org/eNews/2009_10/Schudson_LO.pdf.

———. *The Power of News.* Cambridge, MA: Harvard University Press, 1995.

———. "What Public Journalism Knows About Journalism But Does not Know About the Public." In *The Idea of Public Journalism*, edited by Theodore L. Glasser, 118–135. New York: Guilford, 1999.

———. *Why Democracies Need an Unlovable Press.* Cambridge, UK: Polity Press, 2008.

Schumpeter, Joseph. "Capitalism, Socialism and Democracy." In *Theories of Democracy: A Reader*, edited by Ronald Tercheck and Thomas Conte, 143–153. Lanham: Rowan & Littlefield, 2001.

Servaes, Jan. *Communication for Development. One World, Multiple Cultures.* Cresskill, New Jersey: Hampton Press, 1999.

———. "Toward a New Perspective for Communication and Development." In *Communication in Development*, edited by Fred Casmir, 51–86. Norwood, NJ: Ablex, 1991.

———. "We Are All Journalists Now!" *Journalism* 10, no. 3 (2009): 371–374.

Siebert, Fred, Theodore Peterson, and Wilbur Schramm. *Four Theories of the Press.* Chicago: University of Illinois, 1956.

Siegert, Gabriele. "The Role of Small Countries in Media Competition in Europe." In *Media Economics in Europe*, edited by Jürgen Heinrich and Gerd Kopper, 191–210. Berlin: Vistas, 2006.

Skinner, Ewart. "Mass Media in Trinidad and Tobago." In *Mass Media in the Caribbean*, edited by Stuart Surlin and Walter Soderlund, 29–54. New York: Gordon and Breach, 1990.

Solomon, Norman. "Coverage of Media Mergers: Does it Provide a Window Into the Future of Journalism?" *Neiman Reports*, 15 June 2000. http://www.nieman.harvard.edu/reports/article/101938/Coverage-of-Media-Mergers.aspx.

Spaulding, Gary. "6-Y-O Dies, Sisters Injured After Freak Accident at Beach." *Gleaner* Kingston, Jamaica), 21 August 2013. http://jamaica-gleaner.com/gleaner/20130821/lead/lead2.html#disqus_thread.

Stephens, Mitchell. "A Call for an International History of Journalism." http://www.nyu.edu/classes/stephens/International%20History%20page.htm.

———. *A History of News.* Oxford: Oxford University Press, 2007.

Steinmaurer, Thomas. "Diversity Through Delay? The Austrian Case." *International Communication Gazette* 71, no. 1–2 (2009): 77–87.

Storr, Juliette. "Changes and Challenges: A History of the Development of Broadcasting in The Commonwealth of The Bahamas, 1930–1980." PhD diss., University of Ohio, 2000.

———. "Caribbean journalism's media economy: Advancing democracy and the common good?" *International Communication Gazette* 76, no. 2 (2014): 177–196.

———. "Cultural Proximity, Asymmetrical Interdependence and a New NWICO: A Case Study of Bahamian Television 1977–1997." *International Communication Bulletin*, 43 (2008): 11–24.

———. "The disintegration of the state model in the English speaking Caribbean: Restructuring and redefining public service broadcasting." *International Communication Gazette* 73, no. 7 (2011): 553–572.

Straubhaar, Joseph. "Beyond Media Imperialism: Asymmetrical Interdependence and Cultural Proximity." *Critical Studies in Mass Communication* 8 (1991): 39–59.

Stuart, Yvette. "The Two Bahamian Dailies: A Study of International News Flow." *International Communication Bulletin* 36 (2001): 3–4.

Surlin, Stuart, and Walter Soderlund, eds. *Mass Media in the Caribbean*. New York: Gordon and Breach, 1990.

Sutherland, Anne. *The Making of Belize: Globalization in the Margins*. Westport, CT: Bergin & Garvey, 1998.

Trappel, Josef. "Born Losers or Flexible Adjustment? The Media Policy Dilemma of Small States." *European Journal of Communication* 6, no. 3 (1991): 355–71.

Tumber, Howard and Barbie Zelizer. "Editorial: Special 10th Anniversary Issue— The Future of Journalism." *Journalism* 10, no. 3 (2009): 277–279.

Turner, Graeme. *Ordinary People and the Media: The Demotic Turn*. London: Sage, 2010.

———. "Politics, radio and journalism in Australia: The influence of 'talkback.'" *Journalism* 10, no. 4 (2009): 411–430.

UNICEF Regional Office for Latin America and the Caribbean. "Violence Against Children in the Caribbean Region: Regional Assessment." Panama City: UNICEF, 2006. http://www.unicef.org/lac/Caribe_web(1).pdf.

Velasquez, Manuel, Claire Andre, Thomas Shanks, and Michael Meyer. "The Common Good." *Issues in Ethics* 5, no. 1 (1992). http://www.scu.edu/ethics/practicing/decision/commongood.html.

Waisbord, Silvio. "Democracy, Journalism, and Latin American Populism." *Journalism* 14, no. 4 (2013): 501–521.

Wallerstein, Immanuel. *The Modern World System: Capitalist Agriculture and the Origins of the European World Economy in the Sixteenth Century.* New York: Academic Press, 1974.

Weaver, David H. and Lars Willnat, eds. *The Global Journalist in the 21st Century: News People around the World.* New York: Routledge, 2012.

Weaver, Denis. "U.S. Journalism in the 21st Century—What Future?' *Journalism* 10, no. 3 (2009): 396–397.

Williams, Eric. *Capitalism and Slavery.* Raleigh: University of North Carolina Press, 1994.

World Bank. *Caribbean Youth Development, Issues and Policy Directions.* Washington, DC: The World Bank, 2003. http://info.worldbank.org/etools/docs/library/57446/15518frontmat.pdf.

World Health Organization. *World Report on Violence and Health.* Geneva: WHO, 2002. http://whqlibdoc.who.int/publications/2002/9241545615_eng.pdf.

Wright, Charles. *Mass Communication: A Sociological Perspective.* New York: Random House, 1959.

Zaharopoulos, Thimios. *Traditional Family Relationships and Television Viewing.* Athens: TBS Archives, 2001.

Index

A

Acemoglu, Daron, 4–5
ACM. *See* Association of Caribbean Media Workers
advertising
   economic censorship from, 139–41
   in the future of journalism, 187–88
   the news industry, as factor in, 113–14
advocacy journalism, 17–18, 97–98, 199–201, 204
Alesina, Alberto, 31
Alianza Bolivariana para los Pueblos de Nuestra América (ALBA), 52
Allen, Gary, 162
Alleyne, Mark, xxi, 9, 20, 35
Amazon, 61
American Hutchins Commission, 19
American Project for Excellence in Journalism, 21–22
Ames, Peter, 131, 150, 192
Amsden, Alice, 5
Anderson, Benedict, 55
Andre, Claire, 87
Antigua
   Caribarena in, 79, 172
   freedom of information laws in, 167
   Kincaid's description of, xviii, 32–34, 134
   partisanship of media in, 170
Apple, 42, 61
Aristotle, 31, 87, 193
Arthur, Owen, 189
Ashley, Paul, 44, 86

Association of Caribbean Media Workers (ACM), 133–35, 148, 183
audiovisual productions, 39–40
Auletta, Ken, 113

B

backyard journalism, 198
Bagdikian, Ben, 35, 75, 141
Bahamas, the
   advertising in newspapers, 113
   American influence, 119
   broadcast journalism, origin of, 15
   cable industry, 43
   education, institutes and professional associations, 148, 150–51
   the internet, impact of, 81–82
   journalism in, purpose of, 22
   media regulations, defamation laws, and a free press, 160–61, 165–66, 229n18
   media sources, 66
   news industry financial performance, 68–69, 77–78
   newspaper circulation, 71, 170
   newspaper operations, online media integrated into, 81
   newspapers, history of, 10, 13
   population, 37
   silence and secrecy, 95–96
   state broadcasting, 42–43
Bahamas Press Club, 37

Bakhtin, Mikhail, xvii, 32, 213n6
Balčytienė, Auksė, xx, 35
Banerjee, Indrajit, 169
Barbados
    audiovisual output, 40
    culture of silence and fear, 95
    economic crisis, 70
    education in journalism, 151
    fear as an impediment to journalists, 136, 138
    independence, challenges of maintaining, 156
    the internet, impact of, 81–82
    journalism, business model impact on, 85
    journalism in, purpose of, 23
    media regulations, defamation, and a free press, 133, 160–61, 165–66
    media sources, 66
    news industry financial performance, 69–70, 78
    newspaper circulation, 71, 170
    newspaper operations, online media integrated into, 81
    newspapers, history of, 10
    population, 37
    professional association, 148
    race relations, 174–75
    state broadcasting, 43, 162
Barbados Association of Journalists, 37
Barber, Benjamin, 35
Barbuda, 79, 167
Beckford, Mark, 44, 86
Beckles, Hilary, xxiii, 134
Belize
    attacks on journalists, 101
    cable industry, 43
    citizen journalism, 81
    education in journalism, 151
    ethnic groups, 12
    internet penetration, 81
    journalism in, purpose of, 24
    media regulations, press freedom, and freedom of information, 160–61, 164, 166–67
    media sources, 66
    news industry financial performance, 73–74, 78
    newspaper circulation, 71, 170
    newspaper operations, online media integrated into, 81
    newspapers, history of, 11–12
    partisanship of media, 169–70
    population, 37
    professional association, 148
    sensationalism of news coverage, 109
    state broadcasting, 42
Belize Press Association, 37
Bermuda, 81, 167
Bernstein, Carl, 28
Bethel, Nicolette, 95, 104–6, 117, 197
Bhabha, Homi, xvii–xviii, xxi, 32
Blair, Tosheena Robinson, 22
Boyd-Barrett, Oliver, 132
Bremmer, Ian, 4
Brennen, Bonnie, xxii
Brewster, Havelock, 52
Briguglio, Lino, 33
Britain. See United Kingdom
British Broadcasting Corporation (BBC)
    creation, 211n44
    financial infrastructure, 7
    influence, 51, 118
    public service ethos, 15, 19, 161, 211n44
Broadcasting Commission of Jamaica (BCJ), 162–63
broadcast journalism
    government influence on, 169
    history of, 14–15, 18–19
    lack of independence from elites, 157–58, 169
    radio, standards in, 111
    regulation of, 160–63 (*see also* media regulation)
    talk shows/talk radio/talkback radio, 98–103, 107–8, 176
Brown, Aggrey, xxi, 9, 20, 39, 43–44, 46
Bryan, Anthony, 10
Buckley, Byron, 25, 130–32, 135, 147, 160, 191
Burgelman, Jean-Claude, 39–40, 44
Burnham, Forbes, 14
Busterna, John, 68
Butler, Martin, xviii

C

Cahill, Thomas, 123–24
CANA. *See* Caribbean News Agency
Canclini, Néstor García, xviii
capitalism, 4–6
Carey, James, xxi, 35
Caribarena, 79, 85, 172
Caribbean
　complex problems of, xxiii
　intellectual tradition of, 207n3
　states of the, xxii–xxiii
Caribbean Broadcasting Union (CBU), 46, 50, 183
Caribbean Broadcasting Corporation (CBC), 43
Caribbean Community (CARICOM), 36, 45, 51–53
Caribbean Free Trade Association (CARIFTA), 45, 216n59
Caribbean Institute of Mass Communication (CARIMAC), xvi, 40, 46–48, 131, 147, 150
Caribbean Institute of Media and Communication, xvi–xvii
Caribbean journalism/journalists
　advocacy (*see* advocacy journalism)
　as blend of American, British, and local values, 115
　challenges/threats and questions facing, xv–xvi, 7, 33, 55–58
　commercialism and rapid changes in, 24–25, 55, 83–89 (*see also* commercialism/commercialization)
　comprehensiveness and proportionality (*see* comprehensiveness and proportionality)
　contested space occupied by, 59
　democracy and, 106–8, 158 (*see also* democracy)
　dependency thesis and, 41–45
　economic successes of, 59 (*see also* news industry)
　engagement by young journalists, lack of, 144–46
　failures of and frustrations with, 53–54, 126–31
　"foreign is better" attitude regarding, 121
　future of (*see* future of journalism)
　government and, tensions between, 6–7, 100–101, 164–67, 171–72
　Herman and Chomsky model as framework for analyzing, 132–33
　history of (*see* history of Caribbean media and journalism)
　importance of, 54
　independence, maintaining (*see* independence, maintaining)
　investigative journalism (*see* investigative journalism)
　principles of (*see* principles of journalism)
　print media and broadcasting, history of ownership of, 7
　professional associations (*see* professional associations)
　public information, difficulty of gaining access to, 105
　purposes of journalism articulated by, 22–24
　radical role of, 105–6 (*see also* radical journalism)
　regional development/integration and, 45–54
　relevance and engagement (*see* relevance and engagement)
　secrecy and silence, in a culture of, 95–106
　small states, practicing in, 33, 36–40, 100–101
　storytelling and (*see* storytelling)
　talk shows/talk radio/talkback radio, 98–103, 107–8, 176
　technological threats to, 7, 55–56 (*see also* technology)
　theories of journalism and, 20–22
　training (*see* training of journalists)
Caribbean Media Corporation (CMC), 50–51
Caribbean News Agency (CANA), 46, 49–50
Caribbean News Now, 79
Caribbean regional development and integration, 45–54
CARICOM. *See* Caribbean Community

CARICOM Single Market and Economy (CSME), 51–53, 176–77
CARIMAC. *See* Caribbean Institute of Media and Communication
Carpentier, Nico, 201–3
Carr, Nicholas, 186
Carter, Charles, 76–77, 141–42
Carter, Eddie, 102–3, 107–8, 140
Cayman Islands, 167, 170
CBU. *See* Caribbean Broadcasting Union
censorship
  economic, 139–42
  growth of litigious culture and, 121
  of investigative journalism, 108
  legal and political sources of, 133–39
  by the state in the Caribbean, 7
child abuse, 96–97
China, People's Republic of, 53
Chomsky, Noam, 85, 132–33
Christians, Clifford
  community as site for journalism, 201
  comprehensive and proportionate principle, 26
  development journalism, 17–18
  elements of normative theory of public discourse, 88
  journalism's role in the twenty-first century, 21
  journalism's tasks in a democracy, 106, 108
  radical role of journalism prescribed by, 97, 105, 196–97, 199
  as source for this book, xx
Christopher, Peter, 23–24, 83–84, 103–4, 112–13, 144, 179–81
citizen journalism
  democracy and, 82–83, 86–87
  On the Ground News Report model for, 81
  independence as principle applying to, 153
  journalist training and, 149
  London subway bombing and Boston Marathon attack, contributions during, 186
  new media and, 86–87
  role in the future of journalism, 184–87, 190, 198

as threat to journalism, 55–57, 137
Claussen, Dane, 56–57
Coke, Michael Christopher "Dudus," 158–59
collaborative journalism, 17–18
colonialism
  Antigua as a small place and, 33
  history of Caribbean journalism and, 12–16
  Leviathan institutional structures in the Caribbean and, 6
  mercantilism and, 4
  model of as factor in postcolonial Caribbean states, 34
Columbia Journalism Review, 133
commercialism/commercialization
  of broadcast journalism, 16
  in the Caribbean, 5–6
  failures of journalism due to, 35
  forms of, 4–5
  sensational coverage and, 109–15
  as threat to journalism, 3–4, 7, 55
  See also news industry
common good, 87
Commonwealth Broadcasting Association, 183, 216n60
community journalism, 193–94, 201–4
comprehensiveness and proportionality, xxiv, 25–26
  in Caribbean journalism, 93–95
  culture of secrecy and silence as difficulty for, 95–106
  economic imperatives and, 114–15
  sensational coverage and, 109–14
  tensions between British and American models and, 115–22
Condé, Maryse, xviii
cosmocracy, 35
cronyism, 4–6
CSME. *See* CARICOM Single Market and Economy
Cuba, xix, 34, 52, 74–75, 95
Cuillier, David, 58
cultivation hypothesis, 226n63
culture
  American, 43, 118
  communication style and, 93–94
  consumer, 33–35, 118

news industry success in the Caribbean and, 78–80
oral, 78 (*see also* storytelling)
of secrecy and silence, 95–108, 122
talkback radio and, 102–3
Curran, Charles, 211n44
Cuthbert, Marlene, xxi, 49

D

Dahl, Robert, 34–35
Dahlgren, Peter, 56
Davies, Nick, 28
Dean, Brent, 179
defamation laws, 6, 133–35, 148, 160–64
Deleuze, Gilles, 203
democracy
　accountability, demand for, 120
　alternative communication technologies and, 198–99
　the black press and, 13–14
　citizen journalism and, 82–83, 86–87
　the common good, concern regarding, 87
　concentration of media ownership and, 76–77, 84
　as a form of communication, 88
　the future of journalism and, 190–91 (*see also* future of journalism)
　journalism and, 3–4, 35, 64–65, 106–8, 158, 206
　market-oriented journalism and, 83–85
　media literacy programs, need for, 105
　normative theories of public discourse and, 87–89
　passivity and, 34–35
　sensationalism in the media and, 112–13
　smaller states and, 193–94
　state capitalism and, 4–5
　talk shows/talkback radio and, 101–3, 107–8
dependency, 40–45, 51, 157
Deuze, Mark, 82
developmental journalism, 16–18, 171
Dickerson Bay Agreement, 45
digital technology. *See* technology
diversity of news coverage, lack of, 116
Dominican Republic, 52, 133

Dunn, Hopeton
　American influence on Caribbean cultural production, 118
　anti-trust laws, need for, 76
　as director of CARIMAC, xvi–xvii, 47
　the *Gleaner*, history of, 10
　hybridization as the way forward, 193
　Jollywood, anticipated emergence of, 40
　local production culture, factors inhibiting, 39
　newspaper readership in Jamaica, 68
　public broadcasting, commercialization and devaluing of, 42
　regulation of private-sector ownership, need for, 142
　sexual broadcast content, public outcry against, 163
　as source for this book, xxi
　wireless phone usage in the Caribbean, 80
Dupuch, Etienne, 10
Dupuch, Leon, 10

E

Economic Partnership Agreement (EPA), 52–54, 176–77
Edgell, Holly, 24, 25, 109–10, 112
Edmonds, Rick, 60
Ellis, David
　citizen bloggers as filling a void, 83
　culture of silence as endemic, 95
　fear of victimization, reality of, 137
　freedom of information legislation, impact of, 135–36
　on journalists' self-perceptions of value, 23
　manipulation of the media and disrespect for journalists, 158–59
　new technologies, impacts of, 143
　official sources, journalists' preference for, 139
　talk radio, impact of, 99–100, 102
engagement. *See* relevance and engagement
Enli, Gunn, 82
envelope journalism, 174
EPA. *See* Economic Partnership Agreement
ethnicity. *See* race and ethnicity

European Publishers Council (EPC), 62–63
European Union (EU), 52–53
Eversley, Reudon, 83, 129–30, 136–38, 165, 173–75

F

Facebook, 42, 45, 51, 55–56, 61, 81, 86, 185
Fallows, James, 5
Ferré, Rosario, xviii
Forbes, Anthony, 172
Franklin, Bob, xxi, 63
Freedom House, 101, 108, 148, 161, 163–64, 166
freedom of information legislation
    culture of secrecy and, 104, 107, 138
    enactment of, 164–67
    lack of, press freedom and, 135
    need for effective, 148, 190
    potential benefits of, 157
freedom of the press
    concentration of private media ownership and, 76
    government intimidation as factor undermining, 100–101
    historical origins of, 8–9
    media regulation and, 160–67
Free Trade Area of the Americas (FTAA), 53
Freire, Paolo, 194
Friedmann, John, 194
Friedrich Ebert Stiftung Foundation (FES), xvi, 45–46
Fung, Anthony Y. H., xx, 20
future of journalism
    advocacy journalism, 189, 199–201
    in the Caribbean, xv, xxii, xxv, 183–88, 204–6
    citizens' role in, 184–87, 190 (*see also* citizen journalism)
    community journalism, 193–94, 201–4
    global discussion of, 183–84
    globalization and a paradigm shift, 195
    hybrid model needed for, 193–96, 201, 204
    journalists in, 184–85
    key problems for, xxi, 184
    online activity and digital technology, 185–86
    radical journalism, 189, 196–99
    role in twenty-first-century Caribbean societies, 188–94
    uncertain in the United States and Europe, xv, xxii, 3, 60–61

G

Galtung, Johan, 200
Gibbings, Wesley, 154, 166, 170
Gibbs, Roxanne, 80, 84–85, 111, 144, 156–57
Gilroy, Paul, xviii
Girvan, Norman, 35–36, 39, 51–53
Glasser, Theodore, xx, 17
Gleaner Company, 10, 68, 72–73, 114, 141, 164, 188, 192
global flow of news and information, imbalances in, 41–45
Goldson, Phillip, 11
Gollop, Fred, 10
Google, 42, 45, 51, 61
Gordon, Ken, 79–80, 83, 111, 149–50, 176, 192
green newsrooms, 84, 130
Grenada
    cable industry, 43
    education in journalism, 151
    electronic communication laws, 45
    internet penetration, 81
    media market and news industry financial performance, 74–75, 78
    media regulations, 160–66
    media sources, 66
    newspaper circulation, 71, 170
    newspapers in, history of, 10–11
    online media integrated into newspaper operations, 81
    partisanship of media, 169–70
    population, 37
    professional association, 148
    state broadcasting, 42
Guattari, Felix, 203
Guenzi, Paolo, 78
Guyana
    attacks on journalists, 101

education in journalism, 151
ethnic groups, 12
freedom of information law, 167
government advertising pressure, 141
media and politicians, hostile relations between, 171
partisanship of media, 169–70

H

Habermas, Jürgen, 34–35, 55
Hall, Edward, 93–94
Hall, Stuart, xviii
Hallin, Daniel, 55, 167, 169–71
Hanitzsch, Thomas, 199
Harro-Loit, Halliki, xx, 35
Hebdige, Dick, xviii, 194
Heinonen, Ari, 56
Herig, Karen, 22, 138
Herman, Edward S., 85, 132–33
heteroglossia, xvii, 32, 213n6
history of Caribbean media and journalism
   the black press, 13–14
   broadcast journalism, 15–16, 18–19
   colonialism and, 12–14
   development journalism, 16–18
   ethnic, racial, and class identities, 12
   global developments as precursor to, 8–9
   journalists, shifting focus of, 14–15
   printed press, origins of, 9–12
   recent changes, 19
   regional integration, efforts to promote, 45–54
Hjavard, Stig, 55
Hobbes, Thomas, 28
Hofstede, Geert, 93
Hoggart, Richard, 102
Hoyte, Harold
   fears to speak openly, concerns about, 136
   freedom of information acts, concerns regarding, 138
   independence, challenges and concerns regarding, 156, 158
   journalists and journalistic standards, low quality of contemporary, 128–29, 172
   the *Nation* co-founded by, 10

pessimistic view of the future, 190–92
relationship between government and journalists, 137, 172–73
role of the journalist, 23
Humphreys, Peter, 38
Hutnyk, John, xviii
hybridity, concept/theory of, 41
   Caribbean societies and, xix, 20, 64
   development of and literature on, xvii–xviii
   the future of journalism and, 193–96, 204
   new model for training and, 147
   reexportation framework and, 21

I

identity
   Caribbean regional, 45–54
   historical trajectory of the Caribbean and forging of, 32–33
   hybridity and, xviii, 32
incest, 96–97
independence, maintaining, xxv, 27–29
   media regulations and politics, 160–67
   mega-media mergers as threat to, 75–77
   necessity of and impediments to, 153–59
   professional associations, role of, 178–81
   in small Caribbean societies, 167–78
India, 113
International Press Institute (IPI), 6–7, 10, 133–35, 148, 163–64, 171–72
investigative journalism
   American and British tradition of, 28
   in the Caribbean, 28–29, 108, 117
   citizen bloggers and, 82–83
   constraints on, 156–57, 184
   demand for, 137, 184
   lack of in the Caribbean, reasons for, 139
IPI. *See* International Press Institute
Iyer, Venkat, 165

J

Jacobson, Thomas, 194
Jagan, Cheddi, 14
Jagdeo, Bharrat, 171
Jain, Vineet, 113

Jamaica
   audiovisual output, 40
   cable industry, 43
   debt, IMF agreement and, 220n33
   education, training and professional development, 147, 151
   extradition incident and media manipulation, 158–59
   On the Ground News Report as competitor to traditional media, 56, 79, 81
   internet and social media impact on traditional media, 82
   internet penetration, 81
   media market and news industry financial performance, 67–68, 71–73, 77–78
   media regulations, press freedom, and freedom of information, 133, 135, 160–62, 164, 166–67
   media sources, 66
   newspaper circulation, 71, 170
   newspapers in, history of, 9–10
   online media integrated into newspaper operations, 81
   oversaturation of media market, 24–25, 192
   political independence gained by, 209n7
   population and size, xxii, 24, 37
   professional associations, 22–23, 37, 161, 181
   purpose of journalism articulated by journalists, 22–23
   state broadcasting, 42–43
James, Karen Madden, 86
Janus, 11
Jensen, Klaus Bruhn, 56
Jones, Wendall, 10, 53–54, 191
Josephi, Beate, 55
journalism
   backlash against, 25
   Caribbean (*see* Caribbean journalism/journalists)
   democracy and, 3–4, 35, 64–65, 106–8, 206
   dominant media systems, 211n44
   economy of (*see* news industry)
   future of (*see* future of journalism)
   history of (*see* history of Caribbean media and journalism)
   principles of (*see* principles of journalism)
   purpose of, 19–25
   social responsibility and, 87–89
   as storytelling (*see* storytelling)
   theories of functions of, 211n45
   threats to, 3–4, 55–58

K

Keane, John, 20, 35, 85
Keen, Andrew, 186
Kelly, Nicki, 22, 54, 120–21, 145, 155–56
Kempf, Wilhelm, 200
Kennedy, George, 21
Kincaid, Jamaica
   ambivalence in description of Antigua, xviii, 32
   Antiguans as willing partners in their own subjugation, 134
   Christopher and, 103
   completeness and exactness, requirements to accomplish, 94
   oral nature of societies described by, 115
   significant matters, region's inability to attend to, 124
   small and big issues, Caribbean citizens and, xxiv–xxv, 33–34, 93, 223n2
Kisanga, Eliawony, 33
Kissoon, Freddie, 101, 171
Kovach, Bill
   cartographic function as social responsibility of journalism, 94, 116, 121
   commercialization, warnings about, 85
   engagement and relevance of journalism, 124
   ideals of journalism, 97
   independence of journalists, 153–55
   journalism and the quality of life, 123
   journalism as storytelling, 21
   principles of journalism, 22, 25–28, 121–22
   role of the journalist in the future, 188–89
   as source for this book, xx
Kraidy, Marwan, xviii, xxi, 196
Krajicek, David, 111

L

Lambert, Laurie, 74–75
Lashley, Lynette, 39
Lasswell, Harold, 15
Lauk, Epp, xxiv–xv, 36–38, 126
Lawrence, Harry, 11
Lazzarini, Sergio, 5–6
Ledgister, Fragano, 6
Lent, John, 9, 12, 20
Lie, Rico, 201–3
Liebling, A. J., 76
Locke, John, 28
Love, Krissy, 100, 102
Lowenstein, Ralph, 19–20
Loyn, David, 199–200
Lyder, Omatie, 23, 67, 70, 79–80, 156, 173–74

M

MAGNA GLOBAL, 62
Mancini, Paolo, 55
Manning, Bradley (now Chelsea), 57
Martin, Robert, 43–44
McCartney, Juan, 82, 95–96, 140, 157, 192
McChesney, Robert, xxi, 3, 35, 75, 114, 141
McKinney, Steve, 98–100, 102, 121
McNair, Brian, xxi
McQuail, Denis, xx, 17, 88
Media Association of Jamaica, 161, 181
Media Association of St. Lucia, 101
media dependency theory/thesis, 41–45, 215n40
media economy. *See* news industry
media ethics, 149
media literacy programs, 105, 120, 134, 147
media regulations
    defamation and libel laws, 6, 133–35, 148, 154, 160–65
    independence of journalists and, 160–67
Media Workers Association (Grenada), 37
Mefalopulos, Paolo, 194
Meier, Werner, 38, 42
Melkote, Srinivas, 194
Mendel, Toby, 165
Mendoza, Eduardo, 52
Mendoza, Mauricio, 52
mercantilism, 4
Merrill, John, 19–20, 186
Mesquito, Moreira, 52
methodology: interviews and data, xix–xx
Meyer, Michael J., 87
Mill, John Stuart, 28
Miller, Mark Crispin, 76
Mills, Therese, 11
Milton, John, 8, 28
Missick, Rupert, 118, 131–32, 137, 142, 176–77
Mitchell, Keith, 155, 158, 189–90, 193, 203–4
Moen, Daryl, 21
Moncur, Rodney, 149
Montserrat, xxii
Morgenstern, Oskar, 4
Morrison, Toni, xviii
Moseley, Gordon, 171
Murdoch, Rupert, 28, 75
Mussacchio, Aldo, 5–6

N

National Union of Journalists (NUJ), 168
neoliberal capitalism, 5–6
Nettleford, Rex, xviii
Neumann, John von, 4
"New Media, Journalism and Democracy in the Caribbean" symposium, 44, 81, 85–86
news industry
    advertisement model, demise of, 60–62
    advertising in Caribbean media, 113–14, 139–41
    business model of the future, 187–88 (*see also* future of journalism)
    Caribbean, impact of global trends on, 64
    Caribbean media growth, factors influencing, 77–83
    commercial success and journalistic costs in the Caribbean, 59–60, 83–89
    global trends, 60–65
    media conglomerates/oligopolies, fears regarding, 75–77, 141–42
    new media, impact of, 85–87

sensationalism and market-driven media, 111–15
survival of, concerns regarding, 60
trends in the Caribbean, 65–77
Nichols, Jon, xxi, 3, 35
Niles, Robert, 200–201
Nordenstreng, Kaarle, xx, 17, 88
normative theories of public discourse
elements of, 88–89
evolution of ideals of public communication, 87–88
market-driven model of communication vs., 89
Nottage, Kendal, 95
Nottage, Rubie, 95–96
Nunez, Paco, 77
Nurse, Keith, 36, 39, 44

O

Oates, Sarah, xxi
objectivity, 97–98
OGNR. *See* On the Ground News Report
Oliveira, Omar, 9, 20, 73
On the Ground News Report (OGNR), 56, 79, 81–82, 85
opinionation, rise of, 102
Örnebring, Henrik, xxiv–xv, 36–38, 126
Ostini, Jennifer, xx, 20

P

Pactor, Howard, 9–10, 12–14
Padovani, Cinzia, 169
Page, Benjamin, 34
Panday, Basdeo, 15
Papacharissi, Zizi, 186
Papathanasspoulos, Stylianos, 167, 169–71
Parker, Quincy, 96, 98, 107
participatory paradigm for communication and development, xvii, xix, 147, 194, 201. *See also* community journalism
Paul, Annie, 127
Pauwels, Caroline, 39–40, 44
Pavlik, John, 142–43
peace journalism, 200
Pelloni, Ottavia, 78
Persaud, Anand, 141

Peterson, Theodore, xx, 19, 211n45
Peyrègne, Vincent, 77
Picard, Robert, 20, 25, 68, 126, 186
Plato, 31, 87, 193
Polanco, Andrea, 81
political clientelism, 12, 167–72
political development
development journalism and, 16–18, 171
journalists and, 14–15
politics and political institutions
centralized, the state *vs.* liberal capitalism and, 6
hierarchy of power in, 104
influence in and over the media, 6–7, 100–101, 164–67, 171–72 (*see also* media regulations)
radical/backyard journalism and, 198–99
Prendergast, Patrick, 47–48
Press Association of Jamaica, 22–23, 37, 161, 181
Price, Monroe, 169
principles of journalism
advocacy journalism and, 97–98
comprehensiveness and proportionality, 25–26 (*see also* comprehensiveness and proportionality)
independence, maintaining, 27–29 (*see also* independence, maintaining)
for journalism in the Caribbean, 29
relevance and engagement, 26–27 (*see also* relevance and engagement)
Professional Association of Journalists, 147
professional associations
codes of ethics developed by, 160, 179
conflicts of interest as purview of, 177
new training model, role in, 147–50
potential benefits of, 170–71
professionalization, call to action regarding, 178–81
in the United States and Britain, 168
propaganda model, 132–33
proportionality. *See* comprehensiveness and proportionality
Public Media Alliance, 216n60
Puppis, Manuel, xxv, 33, 38–39, 42–43

R

Raab, Josef, xviii
Raboy, Marc, 3, 169
race and ethnicity
   in Caribbean nations, 12
   history of Caribbean journalism and, 12–15
   race relations, pressure to not cover, 174–76
radical journalism, 97, 105–6, 196–99
Raymond, Chantal, 161
Rediffusion, 7, 15–16
Regis, Humphrey, 21, 211–12n52
Reith, John, 211n44
relevance and engagement, xxiv–xxv, 26–27
   challenges to in the Caribbean, 126–32
   in journalists' output, 144–46
   the media's filtering system and, 132–43
   storytelling by journalists to provide, 123–25
Reporters Without Borders, 57–58, 108, 148, 163–64, 166
Richardson, Leigh, 11
Robertson, Jessica, 119
Robinson, Claude, 169
Robinson, James, 4–5
Rohlehr, Gordon, 224n2
Rosen, Jay, 82
Rosenstiel, Tom
   cartographic function as social responsibility of journalism, 94, 116, 121
   commercialization, warnings about, 85
   engagement and relevance of journalism, 124
   ideals of journalism, 97
   independence of journalists, 153–55
   journalism and the quality of life, 123
   journalism as storytelling, 21
   principles of journalism, 22, 25–28, 121–22
   role of the journalist in the future, 188–89
   as source for this book, xx
Rousseau, Jean-Jacques, 31, 87, 193
Rutherford, Thea, 119, 146, 168

S

Sambrook, Richard, 186
Sanatan, Roderick, xxi
Schiller, Herbert, 35, 75, 85, 141
Schramm, Wilbur, xx, 19, 211n45
Schudson, Michael, xxi, 17–18, 35, 60, 97
Scott, Ben, 114
secrecy and silence
   journalism in a culture of, 95–106, 134
   media democracy and, 107
Seneviratne, Kalinga, 169
Servaes, Jan, 194, 202–3
Shanks, Thomas, 87
Shils, Edward, 186
Siebert, Frederick, xx, 19, 211n45
Siegert, Gabriele, 38, 43
Simon, Richard, 165
Skinner, Ewart, xxi, 9, 11, 20, 43, 115
small states
   advantages and disadvantages of, 31–32
   democracy and, 193–94
   dependency and, 40–45
   foreign media threats, vulnerability to, 43
   future of journalism in, 189 (*see also* future of journalism)
   maintaining independence of the press in, 167–78
   practicing journalism in, 36–40, 100–101, 133–39
   structural peculiarities influencing small media systems, 38
   vulnerabilities of Caribbean, 32–36
Smith, Adam, 4
Smith, Eric, 23
Smith, Larry, 157–58
Snowden, Edward, 57
Society of Professional Journalists (SPJ), 168
Soderlund, Walter, xxi, 9, 20, 39, 146
Solomon, Norman, 76
Spaulding, Gary, 126
Spolaore, Enrico, 31
state capitalism, 4–6
Steinmaurer, Thomas, 42
Stephens, Mitchell, 8
Stewart, Gordon "Butch," 10, 73

St. Kitts and Nevis, xxii, 24–25
St. Lucia, 81, 101
storytelling
   backyard journalism and, 198, 203
   balanced, need for, 24, 110
   calypso music and, 223–24n2
   as element of journalism, 26–27, 87
   in the future of journalism, 195
   journalism as, 21
   legacy of, communication style and, 93
   new model for training journalists including, 147–48
   oral, 78, 183, 205
   oral tradition of, newsgathering and, 115
   relevance and engagement in, 123–25
   smallness as challenge to effective, xxiv
Stuart, Yvette, 13, 43
St. Vincent and the Grenadines, 167
Sunstein, Cass, 186
Surlin, Stuart, xxi, 9, 20, 39, 146
Sutherland, Anne, 12

T

talk shows/talk radio/talkback radio, 98–103, 107–8, 176
technology
   citizen journalism and (*see* citizen journalism)
   control of information flows transformed by, 44–45
   democracy and alternative communication, 198–99
   the future of journalism and, 185–86
   influence of digital, 142–43
   internet connectivity, 80–81
   internet penetration and newspaper readership, 78–81
   news industry trends and, 61–62
   online media integrated in newspapers, 81–82
   as threat to Caribbean journalism, 7, 55–56
   as threat to journalism, 3–4, 55
Thomas, Clive, 52
Thomas, Erwin, 9, 20
Titus, Rawle, 165–66
training of journalists
   CARIMAC as effort at, xvi–xvii, 46–48
   first academic course on journalism, xvi
   mentoring programs, 192
   need for, 129–32, 144–46
   a new model for, 146–51
transculturalism, 196
Trappel, Josef, 38, 42, 43
Trinidad and Tobago
   audiovisual output, 40
   cable industry, 43
   education, institutes, and professional associations, 148, 150–51
   ethnic groups, 12
   hybrid nature of media structure, 115
   internet penetration, 81
   intraregional trade dominated by, 52
   media owners pushing a market-driven logic, 112–13
   media regulations, defamation laws and press freedom, 133, 154, 160–62, 165–67
   media sources, 66
   news industry financial performance, 70–71, 78
   newspaper circulation, 71, 170
   newspaper-reading culture, 79–80
   newspapers in, history of, 11
   online media integrated into newspaper operations, 81
   oversaturated media marketplace, 192
   political independence gained by, 209n7
   population, 37
   professional association, 180–81
   purpose of journalism articulated by journalists, 23–24
   state broadcasting, 42
Tumber, Howard, xv, xx–xxi, 126
Turner, Graeme, 102, 225n30
Turnquest, Ava, 173
Twitter, 51, 55–56, 81, 86, 185

U

United Kingdom
   British media system, 21n44
   erosion of press freedom in, 56–57
United Nations Children's Education Fund (UNICEF), 97

United Nations Economic, Scientific and Cultural Organization (UNESCO), 46, 49, 51
United States
    American media as outsized competitor in the Caribbean, 142
    American media system, 211n44
    erosion of press freedom in, 56–57
    influence of, concerns regarding, 116–19
    state of the news industry in, 61
University of the West Indies (UWI)
    Mona campus (Jamaica), xvi, 47, 145
    St. Augustine campus (Trinidad and Tobago), xvii, 145
US Virgin Islands, 151

V

Velasquez, Manuel, 87
Venezuela, 52

W

Waisbord, Silvio, 17
Walcott, Derek, xviii
Walker, Karyl, 82
Wallerstein, Immanuel, 59
Weaver, David, xxi
Weaver, Denis, 57–58
Wells, Erica, 114, 185, 189
WhatsApp, 51, 55, 61, 82, 185
White, P. Anthony, 144
White, Robert, xx, 17, 88
Wikileaks, 44–45
Williams, Eric, xxiii, 14
Willnat, Lars, xxi
Woodward, Bob, 28
World Bank, 97
World Health Organization, 97
World News Media Network, 62
World Summit on the Information Society, 51
Worme, George, 163
Wright, Charles, 15

Y

YouTube, 40, 51, 55, 185, 199

Z

Zelizer, Barbie, xv, xxi, 126

www.ingramcontent.com/pod-product-compliance
Lightning Source LLC
Chambersburg PA
CBHW061254230426

43665CB00027B/2937